Baseball Legends & Legacies

Baseball Legends & Legacies

The Legends of the '60s & '70s Stand Up and Speak Out

By Gary Hall

©2010 by Gary Hall

Edited by Janet Telford

Book design by Dave Bonnot, Columbine Type & Design, Sonora, California

Cover by Judy Stoltenberg, Columbine Type & Design

First Printing 2010

www.BaseballLegends&Legacies.com

ISBN: 0-615-36114-7
Printed in China

Congratulations!

To Doug Harvey and Jon Miller on their selections
to baseball's greatest honor and achievement,
induction into Baseball's Hall of Fame on July 25,
2010 in Cooperstown, New York.

Going over the ground rules!

The Baseball Legends & Legacies book is a unique concept in that it represents the great players and celebrities of the 1960s & 1970s. The twenty four legends in the book boldly step forward and share their private and personal viewpoints about their peers, opponents, and others who participated while playing in arguably the greatest era of baseball history. This book is designed to capture their experiences while preserving their history for future baseball generations.

Baseball changed dramatically in several aspects during the '60s & '70s. Some of the most obvious and dramatic changes within the game, were the tremendous influx of black and Latin players on the major league level which elevated the quality of the game. Baseball during the 1960s & 1970s developed more superstars in the game, than at any other period of major league history. Just about every team during this fabulous period had multiple superstars. During the 1960s, the San Francisco Giants had five Hall of Famers on the same team! Willie Mays, Juan Marichal, Orlando Cepeda, Willie McCovey and Gaylord Perry, all played simultaneously while wearing the Giants uniform in San Francisco!

Baseball changed not only with the diversity of different ethnic groups, but, also socially and economically.

It is well documented that the early black players of the major leagues were looked upon as second class citizens, and often not very well received in several social circles. While the early black major league players received harsh and unfair treatment from the fans, teammates, and even management, it is often over looked how the Hispanic players were treated and looked upon. It is not as widely recognized or publicized, but the Latin players were viewed and treated as third class citizens. The Latin players were not only prejudged and criticized for the color of their skin, but also their language barriers. When the Latin pioneer players such as Orlando Cepeda, Juan Marichal, Luis Tiant, Tony Oliva and Tito Fuentes arrived upon the professional scene within the minor league system, they received very harsh treatment and extreme hostilities. They were not allowed into the teams' hotels, to speak their native language, or even allowed to enter the front doors of restaurants. In their native countries, they had never encountered those attitudes or behaviors. The Latin players were bewildered by the negative attitudes that they witnessed and experienced. The Latin players were in a foreign country with a challenging new language, a new culture, while adapting to a new way of life away from their families and friends, all while of entering baseball on the premier stage.

As the Dodgers courageously stepped forward and broke the color line with Jackie Robinson, the Giants boldly invested and embraced the gifted players from Latin America. In the early sixties, the Giants had numerous Latin players at the major league level when the vast majority of major league organizations had none. My friend Orlando Cepeda was one of the very first Latin players in the majors. What he and others endured is almost beyond belief!

While baseball experienced great transformations in several aspects during this tremendous period of change, the Caucasian players also were challenged within themselves as they often had no experience with others who spoke different languages, and who were from different lands, with different appearances.

The change was difficult and challenging for everyone! The major leagues experienced more change during this time, than any other period in history. However, baseball prospered more during this period than at any other time, because baseball was played at a higher caliber because of the diversity.

For example, Maury Wills truly was a pioneer while providing baseball with a new approach and concept while putting the element of speed back into the game. Soon after Maury broke Ty Cobb's stolen-base record, Lou Brock, Willie Davis, Bobby Bonds and others repeated Maury's tactics!

Baseball would never be the same. Players were more gifted and talented than at any other period in major league history.

My desire is to preserve the experiences and history of some of the games greatest talents during this wonderful era for everyone's benefit. Enjoy!

Contents

Acknowledgments

With sincere thanks to my team —

Phyllis Hall, my beautiful wife, who has always supported me in all of my endeavors and life's triumphs. Her steadfast words of encouragement have been a compass—most especially for this project!

Pat Bonds who has been like a sister for thirty nine years and has supported my desires to pay homage to her late husband Bobby Bonds.

Tito Fuentes who has been a lifetime friend and welcomed me to experience the big leagues. He has supported me with his trust and guidance for the completion of this book.

Orlando Cepeda who provided me with the necessary resources and contacts with the celebrities in order to succeed with my vision. In addition he took an interest in me as a young man and later became a dear friend. This book was made possible by his assistance and willing heart!

Jim Pagliaroni who inspired me spiritually in my personal life journey. Not only was he a valuable resource in achieving my goals, but he was a trusted friend. Pags passed away April 3, 2010 as this book was going to press.

Randy Selander who provided the inspiration and moral support throughout the entire project with his ideas for the design of the book cover and his words of encouragement.

Juan Marichal who in 1966 became my hero at twelve years old. He has supported me in accomplishing my dream of completing this book as a tribute to Bobby forty-four years after we first met. Juan has always exemplified the qualities of a gentleman.

Larry Dowds who has for fifty-six years been my mentor and coach He has helped me overcome life's obstacles and become resilient enough to achieve my dreams!

Miles McMahon and *Joe Alomia* who are my current Calvary Chapel pastors who work full time to keep me grounded.

Dave Bonnot and *Judy Stoltenberg* of *Columbine Designs*, what can I say, you are awesome fans of the game and incredible designers and advisors!

Al Lewis my former pastor who enlightened me on how to find the spiritual keys to unlock the treasure chests to God's gifts.

John Jankowski, my funny and dear friend, who always counsels me with Godly wisdom.

Dedicated to Bobby Bonds, my brother

Tribute to a True Gift – Bobby Bonds
by Gary Hall

O N JUNE 25, 1968, AS A 22-YEAR-OLD ROOKIE San Francisco Giant made confident strides to home plate, and a legend was born! This was only his third at bat in the majors, and the stage had been set with the bases loaded. That rookie was the phenomenal Bobby Bonds, and the massive grand slam he hit against the Dodgers was the second in history, and the first since 1897, to be delivered by a rookie during his major league debut! Almost immediately he was labeled the next Willie Mays. The San Francisco Giants had signed Bobby as an amateur free agent in 1964 and his 1968 major league debut was the beginning of his illustrious career.

Among Bobby's peers, he was considered to be in an elite class. Throughout this book, his peers speak from their personal and professional perspectives about how great a person and ballplayer Bobby truly was. As a man, he was second to none.

Bobby Lee Bonds was born March 15, 1946, in Riverside California. He was indeed one of the most naturally gifted athletes of the second half of the 20th century, possessing the rare blend of awesome power with the speed of a world class sprinter! While attending high school and college in Riverside, California, Bobby became a legend: in addition to playing baseball as a senior at Riverside Poly High,

1

Bobby also was the state long jump champion. He was a high school All-American in track-and-field and also was named Southern California High School Athlete-of-the-Year. At 6'1, he could slam dunk the basketball with either his left or right hand!

Throughout Bobby's entire 14-year major league career, he weighed a consistent 190 pounds. Even with his sleek powerful body, he was physically stronger than other great athletes who were much larger. Truly Bobby was one of baseball's pioneers, blending his tremendous power and world class speed in a poetic fashion on the world's stage of major league baseball.

What Bobby accomplished on the major league diamond was more than impressive! Bobby was the most dangerous leadoff hitter of his era, hitting a total of 35 home runs to lead off a game. At the time, Bobby was the second player in major league history to hit 30 home runs and steal 30 bases. The other player? The great Willie Mays! Bobby went on to accomplish that magnificent feat five more times! Bobby also became the second player in major league history to reach the coveted 300 career home runs and 300 career stolen bases! The other player? Again, the immortal Willie Mays! In addition, only two players in baseball history have accomplished the rare feat of hitting 300 career home runs with 400 career stolen bases. The first was Bobby Bonds. The second is Bobby's son, Barry Bonds!

Bobby won the Gold Glove three times—in 1971, 1973, and 1974. He was also a three-time All-Star, winning the Most Valuable Player in the 1973 All-Star game.

By the time he finished his major league career –14 seasons—he had amassed the career numbers of 332 home runs, 1024 RBIs, 461 stolen bases, 3 Gold Gloves, five 30-30 seasons, and a lifetime .268 batting average! His record is impressive by most standards and certainly Hall-of-Fame worthy when compared to others enshrined.

Bobby and his wife, Pat, had grown up living on the same street in Riverside two houses apart. As children, Pat and Bobby were sweethearts through grade school, junior high, high school and college. They married in 1964. Pat and Bobby complimented each other well. Pat always possessed an element of grace, strength, and resilience, being a perfect reflection of her soul mate. Together they had three wonderful boys, Barry, Ricky, and Bobby Jr.

What separated Bobby from most others was his huge heart. Bobby was truly one of the most likeable individuals in all of the majors. The press unfairly labeled him as temperamental and moody, but that can be attributed to Bobby's unwillingness to conform to the opinions of others or to bow to the expectations and whims of the press. Bobby was a very private man who refused to compromise or to allow others to intrude. Make no mistake; Bobby was his own man, displaying boldness and a very strong persona. But he also possessed a gentle spirit that was respectful—when he was treated with dignity and respect.

Fortunately I knew Bobby in ways very few others experienced. He adopted me as his little brother, and we were always as close as any blood brothers could have

A Tribute to Bobby Bonds

been. We went to All-Star games, World Series games, went fishing, golfing, roller skating, played pool, ping pong, basketball, and bowled. Each sport was a competition for both of us—Bobby thrived on competition and he loved to win! In thirty-two years we became brothers in every aspect.

Bobby frequently visited his mother in her home in Riverside and many times we visited her together. In March 2009, I visited Mama Bonds as she celebrated her 95th birthday. Mama Bonds often talked with me about how special Bobby was as a little boy and young man. Bobby had something rare—the heart and soul of a champion. What differentiated Bobby from most was his incredible heart!

The lessons I learned from him about life could fill volumes. I'm thankful to have had Bobby in my life as my great friend and brother! When I think of Bobby, I will always be reminded of a man who was strong, compassionate, and caring. Bobby cared for people and made time for everyone. Bobby was a great baseball player; he was an even greater person!

Bobby was a proud man of God who lived the last years of his life as a committed, born-again Christian. We often enjoyed reading the Bible together and sharing our mutual faith. His wife Pat was by his side when the Lord Jesus Christ opened His arms to welcome Bobby into his eternal home, Heaven, on August 23, 2003. I still miss him greatly!

Gary Hall

A Tribute to Bobby Bonds
by Dusty Baker

My STORY WITH THE BONDS FAMILY began before I can remember. Our families, the Bakers and the Bonds, were both from Riverside, California. Mrs. Bonds, Bobby's mother, baby sat with me so my mother could finish school.

My father, Johnny B. Baker Sr., used to pick up Bobby Bonds and take him to baseball practice, and since I was the oldest of the family, I was always included along with my dad and the other players. I went to all of Bobby's games, whether football, basketball, track meets or baseball. Bobby was the kid who could always pitch a no-hitter and hit two home runs.

Bobby was four years older than I was, and he was my prep school idol as well as every young man's hero. I wanted to emulate him! Bobby was always good to me, protecting me from the bullies. He even let me play baseball with his friends if they were short of players.

Bobby was the youngest of the great Bonds family, which included Robert, David, Rosie, and, of course, Bobby. Robert was great in football and signed with the Kansas City Chiefs, David excelled in the hurdles, and, in 1964, Rosie was an Olympic track-and-field star. Bobby took something from all three, plus he was an accomplished boxer, skills probably learned from his father, Mr. Bonds. By the time he reached high school, Bobby was a legend. And, he had the finest girl in town, Pat Howard, soon to become Mrs. Pat Bonds.

As a kid growing up I was a Dodger fan, and my favorite player and hero was #12, Tommie Davis. One day Bobby called me to shag fly balls while a Giants scout was in attendance. Bobby indeed signed with the Giants, and I became a Giants fan.

Our family moved to Sacramento, and I tried to keep up with Bobby's progress and career. During high school, I tried to attempt what Bobby had accomplished. I even went to state as a representative in the broad jump as he had, but found myself unable to duplicate his feats in football, basketball, track, baseball and the broad jump.

Shortly thereafter I signed with the Braves in August 1967. The following season, I was a September call up, and my first game appropriately was in San Francisco at Candlestick Park in front of my father, mother, family, friends, and, of course, Pat and Bobby Bonds!

In 1972 I came back to the major leagues to stay for good. I always looked forward to hanging with Bobby in my town or his. We talked, laughed, and told exaggerated stories, at least mine were. He introduced me as his home boy, and told others to keep their eyes on me, for someday I was going to be something.

A Tribute to Bobby Bonds

Finally, both of our playing careers ended, and we both became major league coaches. We would still hook up on our respective teams.

One of the greatest days of our lives was in the winter of 1992 when I was promoted to manager and Bobby became the hitting coach of the San Francisco Giants. Barry, the newborn I had held the day he was born, was united with us on the same team, the Giants.

Time passed, and one day I received the saddest news. Bobby called and told me that he had cancer. We all knew that the greatest of our time would also win this one, as he had done everything else. Then Bobby had called to tell me the excruciating pain he had was the most intense he had ever felt. The best news was that he was once again attending church regularly as we had as kids, at Park Avenue Baptist Church with Reverend Moss presiding.

There are photos of many famous people on my walls at home. My favorite, however, is of Bobby and me walking side by side to help rebuild Patterson Park, our Little League field in Riverside, California. In that photo, we were both men about the same height, but Bobby will always be the man while I am the boy.

Thank you, Bobby, for all of your inspiration, laughter, guidance, and motivation to be the best—just like you always were and always will be!

Much love,
Your little brother,
Dusty Baker

The Great Bobby Bonds—A Tribute
by Jim Davenport

BOBBY WAS ONE OF THE MOST GIFTED ATHLETES to play the game in my era of the 1960s and 1970s. As most everyone knows, Bobby could literally do it all and do it better! He was probably the fastest man in baseball at the time, and he was an exceptional fielder with an arm like a cannon. He could hit, and hit for serious power! There was no other weapon in baseball like Bobby! He was definitely a five-tool player!

But that only reveals a portion of the Bobby Bonds I knew. Bobby was more than a friend! He was a brother. Without question, he was my closest friend. We were inseparable and literally did everything together. We had a lot in common: Both of us played for the San Francisco Giants for several years and we were roommates. Both of us were avid golfers and fishermen. We spent most of our off-seasons together.

Our wives Betty and Pat were close, and still are very close. We lived in the same area of San Carlos, California, only two minutes apart.

Here are a couple stories I would like to share that were typical for us. When we went fishing, we almost always left early in the morning. One early morning we decided to fish at a lake on the east side of the bay. When we arrived at our fishing spot and had put the boat in the water, I looked at Bobby and told him to start the boat. He looked at me and told me I had to start the boat because he did not have the keys, that I had them! We had left that morning each thinking the other one had the keys to the boat!

Another time my kids had bought a brand new anchor for my boat. Bobby and I decided to go out near Third Street in San Francisco to go fishing. We arrived at our spot and launched the boat into the water. This time we definitely had the keys! However, we had wanted to try this spot to fish awhile, and I told Bobby to throw the new anchor over the side of the boat. Bobby picked up the anchor and tossed it into the water. Only one problem! He did not tie the anchor to the boat! He thought I had tied the anchor to the boat, and, of course, I thought he had tied the anchor to the boat! Like a couple of young boys we argued with each other all the way to the shore. From that point forward, we laughed like two hyenas for years about the new anchor!

The great times and memories I have of my dear brother are too numerous to mention. I can tell you for certain though, that on April 23, 2003, I lost my best friend on this earth! I loved Bobby, and I still miss him immensely!

Jim Davenport

Tribute to Bobby Bonds
by Tito Fuentes

BOBBY HAD SO MANY GOOD QUALITIES and characteristics that it would be difficult to gather enough paper for me to express my personal tribute to him. For the sake of the fans, I will attempt to be concise.

Not only were we teammates, but we were also roommates in both the minor and major leagues. When you play, travel, and share living quarters with an individual, you really learn aspects that most people would never experience or understand.

When we were on our road trips with the Giants, we enjoyed watching the same morning TV game shows. Bobby and I would watch *Let's Make a Deal*, *The Dating Game*, and *The Newlywed Game*. We would always create adventurous ways for us to pay the tip to our servers for our lunch. We would bet on the winners of each show with nickels, dimes, or quarters, and whoever would win had to leave the tip for our service. He was fun to be around and we bonded very well!

As a player he had exceptional tools and abilities for the game. Very few have ever had his talent! He had five tools in his toolbox, and believe me he could alter a game rapidly with any or all of his tools at any given moment.

Bobby played the game effortlessly with the greatest of ease. His speed in right field was a weapon within itself—he covered more territory than any other right fielder of his era.

His throws from the outfield were as strong and accurate as anyone in the game.

When he was running the bases, he was truly a picture of grace. He would run as a gazelle and would elude his predators with agility.

While batting, Bobby easily could clear any and all outfield fences; his power could not be contained by any major league park.

He could have hit for a much higher batting average had he been willing to periodically place strategic bunts down the infield chalk lines as he was almost impossible to throw out.

One of the most amazing facts I remember about Bobby took place in 1970 when he struck out 189 times. But what is so unbelievable was that he hit for a .302 batting average while clubbing 26 home runs and 48 stolen bases. Can you imagine what might have taken place had he considered bunting fifteen times that year? Although I have never said this publicly, it is my belief that Bobby did not apply himself the way he could have because of his profound respect and reverence for his childhood idol, Willie Mays. He had no desire to ever eclipse Willie in any capacity! Bobby was truly an amazing athlete!

As a person and a friend, he was loyal. Bobby had a great personality with a great sense of humor. But you better be certain to stay on his good side because if he miffed or irritated, he was more than a handful for anyone.

In conclusion, Bobby Bonds was an exceptional major league baseball player who had as much natural talent and ability that ever played the game, As a person, he was a great team mate and a trusted friend!

Tito Fuentes

A Tribute to Bobby Bonds

Raindrops and Rainbows!

It's raining outside—let's play ball!

THIS IS THE WAY I VIEW MY LIFE when reflecting on the unbelievable circumstances that I had experienced as a young boy. I present here the facts describing how baseball became more than a game to me, as it evolved into a mighty instrument that shielded me from my darkest hours.

The raindrops represent the personal challenges and experiences of my life, while rainbows illustrate my visions, desires and hope. Baseball represented the umbrellas in my life, shielding my mind from the gray elements of my life.

Raindrops—then Rainbows

My mother and father divorced when I was five years old and my mother moved to Chicago to create her new life. For the next several years I moved back and forth between the St. Louis area and Chicago like a game of ping pong. In all, I attended eighteen different schools in twelve years! The adversity I experienced in the early years developed in me a certain resiliency that gave me strength through life, a process similar to tempering steel.

In the summer of 1963 my mother and I took a memorable vacation, leaving Chicago by train for California. Our trip included a baseball game at Candlestick Park, the home of the San Francisco Giants. Legendary Giants pitcher Juan Marichal took the mound to the start the game and Orlando Cepeda played first base. In this never-to-be-forgotten game, I saw two new baseball heroes of mine–Orlando Cepeda and Juan Marichal.

Immediately I became a huge fan of Orlando Cepeda and Juan Marichal, following their careers when I returned to the Midwest. Never in my wildest imagination did I dream of becoming friends with both Orlando and Juan. Forty-four years later, I am proud to be considered their friend. This is certainly one of my earliest experiences with the rainbows of my life!

Extraordinary Experiences

Julian Javier, the terrific Cardinal second baseman from the Dominican Republic, and I became friends. In 1966 I became such a pest to Javier that he began leaving me tickets to Cardinal games when I was only twelve years old! Then one day Javier gave me a ride home after the Cardinal game so I would not have to ride the metro bus late after a night game. Soon I became acquainted with other members of the Cardinal team. At that point in my life, baseball completely consumed me and I became oblivious to the obstacles that life seemed to offer.

In 1966 I was once again moving back to Chicago with my mother. That was okay, though, because Wrigley Field had become my new refuge–my personal rainbow. I then began to hound the Chicago Cubs legend, Ernie Banks. Believe me; I was absolutely relentless with these guys. Soon, I became acquainted with Ernie to the point he acknowledged my presence.

One of the most memorable highlights was when, in 1967, Javier arranged for me to ride on the Cardinal team bus to the St. Louis airport after a night game as the Cardinals were flying out on a road trip. My aunt lived about two miles from the St. Louis airport and Javier said it would be easier for my aunt to pick me up at the airport instead of coming all the way to Busch Stadium in downtown St. Louis. There I was, riding on the bus with my heroes and future Hall-of-Famers, manager Red Schoendienst, Orlando Cepeda, Lou Brock, and Bob Gibson. I became acquainted with Brock later on who, along with my buddy Javier, were extremely kind to me. But Orlando Cepeda—the Baby Bull—was the one I truly admired.

The Cardinals visited the friendly confines of Wrigley Field to play the Cubs. While my Mother and I were sitting behind the Cardinal dugout, Cepeda hit two home runs that afternoon. After the game Orlando handed me the same bat he had previously crushed for the two home runs. There I was once again, experiencing heaven on earth at thirteen years old. Throughout the years, Orlando and I have stayed friends and I still have the picture of my mother and me posing with my prized Orlando Cepeda bat.

While living in Chicago my mother received two box seats for the 1967 World Series between the Boston Red Sox and the St. Louis Cardinals at Busch Stadium. The memories of that World Series are truly golden. My newfound friends were playing in the World Series as they defeated the mighty Red Sox from Boston for the World Championship.

In 1968, mother had experienced enough of Chicago's winters after a severe winter that unleashed forty-eight inches of snow in forty-eight hours. That was enough! We moved to Hollywood California. Within a few days I met my new friend, Harry Van Vorst.

Hollywood and Dodger Stadium

Walda Winchell, daughter of the famed columnist and radio personality Walter Winchell, lived in the same apartment complex as my friend Harry. Walda was a wonderful lady who was great to all of us kids. Realizing what a huge baseball fan I was, she invited me one evening for dinner. She was in the kitchen preparing dinner when the doorbell rang. Walda asked, "Gary, will you please answer the door for me and see who is there?" When I opened the door, to my absolute amazement stood Joe DiMaggio! I was speechless! Walda came from the kitchen with a huge grin on her face, and said, "Well, are you going to invite our guest in for dinner?" It was an amazing evening, and at sixteen-years old, it was a classic example of what a blessing baseball had become. It was obvious to me that I was experiencing more rainbows than raindrops now. My life was in the midst of great change!

Once again I discovered another refuge from my real life called Dodger Stadium! What a paradise! After visiting this baseball Mecca for three years, I became a Dodger fan. And now I was beginning to imagine heaven while dreaming of becoming a major league player.

The Chicago Cubs came to Los Angeles and I went to visit my acquaintance Ernie Banks. His mother-in-law lived in Hollywood, so he drove me from Dodger stadium after the game to my home in Hollywood. At the end of the 1970 baseball season, and at the end of Ernie's career, he introduced me to one of the Dodger coaches. Ernie told the coach that he knew me from Chicago and that I wanted to become a Dodger batboy.

In January, 1971, I went to meet Nobe Kawano, the clubhouse manager for the Dodgers. I tossed Ernie's name around in conversation as though he were my favorite uncle and Nobe hired me that day. Ernie soon retired, but we remained in contact. Several years after Ernie's retirement, he asked me to conduct his benefit auction for the Boy's & Girls Club of Pasadena, California, which I was honored to do.

The 1971 baseball season became golden! My main job with the Dodgers was to play catch and warm up each and every right fielder in the National League between each inning. Some of the right fielders in 1971 were Bobby Bonds, Pete Rose, Roberto Clemente, Downtown Ollie Brown, and Hank Aaron.

It was an exciting time as the Dodgers had an incredible pool of young players like Steve Garvey, Bill Buckner, Bill Russell, and Bobby Valentine. Walter Alston, the Hall-of-Fame Dodger manager guided the young mega-talented team, while the legendary Maury Wills and Dick Allen were the stars and veteran leaders of the Dodgers. My experiences were phenomenal. Often, after stepping off of the Sunset Boulevard bus to Dodger Stadium, Walter Alston would pick me up in his huge Buick Riviera to give me a ride up the steep Chavez Ravine hill to the Dodgers' clubhouse.

In 1971, my mother's advertising agency transferred her from Los Angeles to San Francisco. When I refused to move with her, she was furious. At the age of seventeen I would not make the move with her! Then she realized I was staying with my dream job with the Dodgers, and she finally relented and arranged for me to stay with my friend Harry and his mother at their apartment.

However, that arrangement didn't last, and later in the summer of 1971, at seventeen years of age, I became homeless. There I was, living a dream as a major league batboy and living on the streets of Hollywood. The Dodger players did not know, as I had too much pride to disclose my daily misfortunes to my heroes.

Jim Ferguson, my dear friend and spiritual mentor at Hollywood Presbyterian Church, arranged for me to stay in his office at the church building. I would shower at the church's gymnasium and leave early in the mornings before anyone from the staff realized I was spending the nights at the church building. Naturally some church staff members witnessed my leaving one morning. Ferguson then arranged for me to stay at a half-way house that the church supported financially for troubled young men. After a few fisticuffs and altercations, I once again moved. I would stash my clothes with friends and spend evenings at bus stops, along with Hollywood's finest carpeted fire escapes and hotel lobbies. Frequently I purchased late night movie tickets on Hollywood Boulevard just to sleep in their theaters until having to leave the last show around four or five in the morning. Only by God's mercy and grace did I survive this challenging ordeal! The contrast of my homeless evening and night struggles with my day job as the Dodgers' batboy provided a torrential downpour of life's raindrops in the midst of the most colorful rainbows.

One of my hero's, Dick Allen, saved my batboy's position in the middle of the 1971 season! The players used me like their personal valet which I relished, and my immediate supervisor, Nobe Kawano, the Dodger clubhouse manager disliked my popularity with the players.

Willie Crawford, one of the Dodger outfielders, was a friend, and my locker was next to his in the Dodger clubhouse. One time before a game, Crawford and I were playfully wrestling in the clubhouse. Crawford was strong as an ox and he threw me inside my locker and tore the bill of my Dodger cap completely off! The players were laughing. Kawano, however, did not think it was funny and was actually furious at me. Kawano began giving me a serious lecture in front of the players with threatening tones about how I was a Dodger employee and not a Dodger player. The very dignified and quiet Dodgers star Dick Allen slowly approached Kawano. Dick stood in front of Kawano and quietly and, in a dignified manner, told Kawano to get off of my back! Dick then nudged his glasses higher upon the bridge of his nose, like he so often did, turned and walked back to his locker.

Kawano was not pleased with me, to say the least, and he gave me a dirty look as he walked away. Dick Allen temporarily saved my pride and hide, but I knew at the seasons' end I was history with the Dodgers. So was Dick Allen for that matter, as he was traded to the Chicago White Sox in 1972 where he earned the American League MVP award. Everyone respectfully feared Dick as he was physically imposing, but was dignified and quiet. One of my favorite lines of all time from baseball players was delivered from Dick when he remarked, referring to artificial turf, "If a horse cannot eat it, I won't play on it!"

While with the Dodgers, there were some fabulous memories for me. Maury Wills had a Jaguar XKE, and a couple of times after the game he gave me the keys and asked me to bring the Jag to a closer gate. The Dodger gold glove first baseman, Wes Parker, did the same. Wes had a Maserati and I also got to drive it a couple of times. Can you imagine a high school kid driving a Jaguar and a Maserati?

I was also always impressed that after every Sunday home game when the Dodgers were not leaving for a road trip, Wes Parker would have me get two or three baseballs and one of his bats to take to the parking lot. We went to the top parking lot and Wes would hit fly balls to several kids waiting there for him. Sometimes there would be forty or fifty kids waiting. Wes Parker had a tremendous heart, and he is the only player I ever witnessed making that kind of effort with kids at the ballpark.

Some of my favorite memories as a Dodger batboy were with Pete Rose when he played with the Cincinnati Reds. Pete would summons for me to grab my glove before the games and play a game of pepper with him. Pete played pepper differently from anyone else I've ever seen. He had me toss two baseballs as he hit. When he would strike the first ball towards me, I would release the second ball towards his glove on the ground, which served as an imaginary home plate. He would keep two balls in play while simultaineously hitting perfectly placed one-hoppers back at me. He constantly worked to develop his timing and rhythm. At the end of each visit to Los Angeles, Pete would generously tip me for my efforts. Pete Rose was one-of-a-kind, and always great to me!

Another responsibility I had as a Dodger batboy was to provide the umpires with assistance before each game by shining their shoes and rubbing the special mud compound on the baseballs before each game. Doug Harvey, recently elected to Baseball's Hall of Fame, was in Los Angeles with his crew in the middle of the 1971 season. While in the umpire's dressing room, Doug asked me where I was staying on our next road trip to San Diego. I told Doug that Nobe Kawano, the Dodger clubhouse manager, told me I could make the trip and work the games, but I had to pay for my own hotel room. Doug told me, "Kid, I just happen to have a house in San Diego and you can stay as my guest with me and my family." I made the trip to San Diego, and stayed with Doug and his wife Joy at their home. Almost everyone in major league baseball was great to me! That's why baseball was more than a game—it had become an umbrella to protect me from the raindrops of life! God had allowed my love for baseball to be a safe haven.

San Francisco

Later in September of 1971, after the Nobe Kawano tirade, the San Francisco Giants came to town. Giants' right fielder Bobby Bonds and I had had become friends earlier in the year and I mentioned to him what had taken place. He encouraged me to consider moving to San Francisco at the end of the baseball season. Bobby told me that he would assist me with getting the Giants' batboy position in 1972 if I were to move to San Francisco, and that he also would assist me with getting situated in the new city. He became a big brother and did everything he promised and more!

At the end of the regular baseball season, I took Bobby's advice and moved to San Francisco. I was at the Bonds' house practically daily, much to the dismay of Pat, Bobby's wife. They had three boys—Barry, six years old, Ricky, four, and Bobby (BB) Jr., was one. Barry and Ricky and I were close and we would all go to the park just down the street from the house to play baseball. Bobby and Barry were always a team, and Ricky and I were a team. Even as a youngster Barry could easily hit the baseball two hundred fifty feet! Ricky was also a good baseball player.

Bobby soon secured the Giants' batboy position for me with the then clubhouse managers Eddie Logan and Mike Murphy. The Giants' clubhouse was like an indoor entertainment venue compared to the surreal Dodgers' clubhouse. The main entertainment attraction in the Giants' clubhouse was the fun and zany Tito Fuentes. His crazy sidekicks and cronies often were Chris Speier, and Chris Arnold! The clubhouse was fun, upbeat and lively! It was unbelievable to look around that clubhouse to see the iconic names above the lockers of Willie Mays, Juan Marichal, Willie McCovey, and, of course, my big brother Bobby Bonds!

For the next two years, Bobby, Tito Fuentes and I were inseparable. Tito would take me everywhere, especially to the Warriors' basketball games and almost always out for some fun. Later in the evening, we often went to Juan Marichal's house for late-night card games and the greatest Caribbean food this side of the Dominican Republic. Practically every day, I was either with Bobby or Tito. They me that he declared me on his income taxes. Tito did support me now that I think of it! Knowing the crazy Cuban the way I do, he probably did write me off on his income taxes, and rightfully so!

What a country! There I was, this white kid from the Midwest raised as a racist, adopted by these two black stars of major league baseball. And the great thing is that my family soon learned to appreciate and love both Bobby and Tito for their tremendous hearts. Besides, I was introduced to ways of life I could never have imagined in other cultures. That is a great example of good overcoming ignorance!

Bobby and I were very competitive in everything we did—basketball, ping pong, weights, roller skating, bowling, shooting pool, and so on. One time when Bobby's father and mother were up from Riverside visiting, Pops (Bobby's dad) decided we would play pool after dinner. This was great because Bobby and I both practically lived on the pool table! Pops told us that we could play either eight ball, or nine, whatever we preferred. But whoever loss the game would have to do ten curls each with the barbell weights for every ball that was left on the table? Bobby told me to go first. I broke the rack of billiard balls. Pops beat me quickly and handedly, and I had three billiard balls left on the table. So, I had to do thirty curls. Bobby played next, and he lost also! Bobby did his twenty curls for the two balls he had left on the table. Pops laughed at both of us, and said that we would either become better pool players, or become the strongest guys in baseball! Pops never did a single curl. Then they both howled with laughter when they revealed that Pops earlier in his day was a pool shark in Southern California! That was not so funny!

Of course, I had always dreamed of playing in the major leagues with my new family members Bobby and Tito. Because of my arrogance in showing off my gifted throwing arm, I soon developed severe elbow and shoulder problems. My arm was not yet fully developed, and I would attempt what Bobby could accomplish when throwing a baseball, and it cost me dearly. Now I realize that God had a different plan for my life.

Tryout

Tom Sheehan, a scout with the San Francisco Giants in 1974, made arrangements for me to tryout. . When I arrived (on my motorcycle) at the spring training facility in Casa Grande Arizona, I literally could not make the throws from my position at third base across the diamond to first base. My arm was shot! I went to Phoenix and told Bobby what was going on with my elbow and shoulder. Bobby arranged and paid for my cortisone shots since I was not under contract. The pain was so excruciating that I could not even comb my hair with my right hand. The doctor explained to me that I should not throw a baseball for two to three years. At twenty years old, I was in disbelief, but began to realize my baseball dreams might just be over.

The last day of spring training I left Arizona on my motorcycle for my father's house in St. Louis, completely distraught after being released. One week later, Harry called to tell me that my spiritual mentor, Ferguson, had had passed unexpectedly onto his eternal home. Two of the most meaningful purposes in my life were lost forever, baseball and Ferguson. I was over-taken with grief and distraught! The raindrops kept falling and falling!

Two months after arriving in St. Louis, my arm stopped hurting. It was my decision to go give my throwing arm a whirl. I drove to Busch Stadium and told Cardinal Manager Red Schoendiest my circumstances. Mr. Schoendienst said I could throw batting practice. The next day, Butch the Cardinal clubhouse manager, gave me a uniform. I took the mound and threw to one batter, and immediately left the mound with my arm literally dragging behind me, tears streaming down my face. It was over and I knew it! After stepping over the chalk line towards the Cardinal dugout, Lou Brock put his arm around my shoulder and walked with me to the dugout all the while imparting words of encouragement. I've always been grateful to Lou for his compassion and encouragement. When I left Busch Stadium, I drove to my dad's house to tell him I was leaving for California.

A few days later, I drained the fuel tank of my Yamaha motorcycle. The motorcycle and I flew home to San Francisco. Having lost my direction, vision, and what seemed my mind, I joined the United States Army.

The Rest of the Story

A few years later in 1982, after working in the hospitality industry, I discovered the love of my life and future wife Phyllis in Palm Springs, California. In 1984 Phyllis and I were married and we received a wonderful opportunity with the Flamingo Hotel in Las Vegas Nevada. One year later, the golden opportunity of a lifetime presented itself directly across the street at Caesars Palace in Las Vegas. For the next twelve years I worked in the famous Bacchanal and Palace Court.

In 1989 while living in Las Vegas, I asked my brother, Bobby Bonds, to assist me with producing a major baseball card show in Las Vegas. Bobby did in fact arrange for some mega-baseball stars to attend our new business venture. We had Bobby, Tito Fuentes, Orlando Cepeda, Barry Bonds, Vida Blue, Roberto Alomar, Gaylord Perry, Sandy Alomar, Greg Maddox, and Mike Maddox. The show was not successful, and both Bobby and I chuckled years later about some of the obstacles we endured. I lost a lot of money, but as usual, Bobby, Tito and I had a lot of fun!

In 1999, Phyllis and I decided to semi retire, and we made our dream a reality by moving just north of Yosemite National Park, in Sonora, California! It was great returning to northern California and being reunited within close proximity to both

Raindrops and Rainbows!

Bobby and Tito.

Bobby Bonds, in 2002, became ill for his second time and endured his final battle with cancer. This time, I was closer to him and was available to assist him with his battle. Bobby had rededicated his life to Jesus Christ, and had become spiritually strong, and this time I was there to fight on the battlefield with him side by side. Bobby and I together would read Psalms, his favorite book in the Bible.

His lifelong fishing and golfing buddy, Jimmy Davenport, was there daily for both Bobby and Pat. Every three weeks, when Bobby had to undergo his chemo treatments, I would leave Sonora at 4 a.m. and arrive at their home by 6 a.m. to drive with him to Stanford. Both Davenport and I were there with him every time. As difficult as it was, it also was a blessing for me to witness first hand his courage, tenacious attitude and his personal commitment of faith!

In August of 2003 I experienced the dark clouds once again that filled my life with the heavy raindrops. This time it was difficult to find the umbrella to shield my pain. Barry called me within moments to communicate the loss of his father, and my dear brother. That gray day a part of me left this world with him.

The last several years I have once again been allowed to make my dreams a reality while visiting the San Francisco Giants, as my dear friend Tito eloquently describes the games in Spanish. Tito and his Giants' broadcast partner, Erwin Higueros, graciously allow me to visit on occasion with their baseball broadcast. Baseball has come full circle forty-five years later.

One thing life has taught me is that we all have raindrops. Sometimes it is a mist, and at other times it pours! We have visually witnessed the beautiful and vivid colors of rainbows. For me, the answer is to discover the harmony while reaching for the umbrella to shield me from the extremes of life! Even though there may be some rain today, let's be willing to play ball! It's all about our mindset and our attitude! Our dreams are the seeds of reality!

Baseball not only shielded me from some of the darkest clouds in my life, but it became a safe and pleasant refuge. What wonderful opportunities God provided for me to experience.

George Lee "Sparky" Anderson

Born February 22, 1934, Bridgewater, South Dakota

Height 5'9" **Weight** 170 lbs.

Bats Right **Throws** Right

Debut April 10, 1959 **Final game** Sept. 27, 1959

GEORGE LEE ANDERSON, more famously referred to as Sparky, is one of the real characters of the game. The Brooklyn Dodgers signed George Lee to a contract as an amateur free agent. He made his major league debut the same year he played his last year, 1959. His major league career consisted of 477 at bats in which he collected 102 career hits, with a lifetime batting average of .218 as a second baseman. Sparky toiled for six long years in the Dodgers minor leagues system before joining the Philadelphia Phillies via trade with the Los Angeles Dodgers, fulfilling his lifelong dream of playing major league baseball

In 1964 Sparky accepted a job as the manager of a Toronto minor league team. He returned to the majors for good in 1969 as a coach with the expansion team San

Diego Padres.

In 1970 he interviewed with the Cincinnati Reds for their vacant managerial post. The Reds General Manager Bob Howsam was impressed with his confidence and played a hunch, deciding to give the young George Anderson an opportunity to influence his new and budding superstars. He hired him to direct the Reds for the 1970 season. Sparky's style of communication and special rapport was obvious and immediately there were huge dividends for the Reds. Thus, a star was born!

In his first season at the helm, Sparky, with his high level of enthusiasm, had the Reds believing, as the Reds won 70 of their first 100 games. The Reds never looked back; in Sparky's first year, they captured the National League West title, and then went on to defeat a talented Pittsburgh Pirates team. The Reds lost the World Series to the Baltimore Orioles, but the Cincinnati Reds had found the magic under the brilliant guidance of their new leader, Sparky Anderson.

Sparky's nickname, "Captain Hook," was well-deserved for his uncanny knack of making numerous pitching changes, ultimately proving his leadership. He was very authoritative and never allowed his pitchers to speak about the changes he made on the mound. The Reds respected their skipper for his confident and fireball style!

He was bold in his decisions, such as moving Pete Rose from the outfield to third base. In addition, he decided to play utility player George Foster in left field regularly. Both decisions were part of what cemented his genius as one of the greatest managers of all time!

One of baseball's most famous World Series was the fall classic of 1975 between the Boston Red Sox and Sparky's Cincinnati Reds. In game 6, the Reds fell prey to the famous Carlton Fisk home run that defeated the Reds momentarily. However, Sparky's Big Red Machine took the field for game 7 and wrestled the World Championship out of the grips of the stunned Boston Red Sox.

Sparky left Cincinnati in 1978, after refusing to bow to upper management's suggestions for coaching changes on the field. At that point he was the number one manager in career victories (863) and winning percentage for a manager.

The Detroit Tigers recognized the leadership of Sparky and seized the moment by hiring him to turn around their team. Once again, his success was immediate as Sparky led the Tigers roaring back into contention. The Tigers of Detroit under the guidance of Sparky won their first World Series in 1984 against the talented San Diego Padres. Once again, in 1987 Sparky led the Tigers to post season-play with the Tigers.

Sparky Anderson's career records speak volumes about his character and his leadership on the field. He piloted three World Championship teams to the ultimate victory, two with the Reds in the National League, and one with the Detroit Tigers in the American League. Only Connie Mack and John McGraw have more career victories. His teams won seven division titles, five pennants, and three World

Championships. He was the first manager in the history of the game to lead two different teams—Cincinnati and Detroit—to 800 career wins! In addition, Sparky Anderson is the first manager to win the Manager of the Year in both the National and American Leagues!

In 2000, Sparky was elected to Baseball's Hall of Fame by the Veterans' Committee!

In addition he is one of the most delightful and accommodating baseball legends on the planet!

In My Own Words

Here are a couple of stories and thoughts I wanted to share with baseball's fans and players.

The Men in Blue

I've always respected umpires. They have a tough job, and, for the most part, they get things right. Of course, managers and umpires will always have some disagreements. That's just part of the game!

One of umpires was Doug Harvey. He always kept things under control. There was one game though, where I had a disagreement with Doug at first base. I had been simmering in Cincinnati Reds' dugout for quite a while, and finally I had enough and had to talk about a call. When I got out to him, I looked him in the eye and said, "Doug, I just wanted you to know that when I am finished with what I have to say, you're going to run me from the game." Before I could say another word, he looked at me and said:" No, I'm not. You're out of here right now!" At the time it wasn't funny. The next day when we were exchanging lineups at home plate before the game, I asked Doug why he threw me out of the game before I had a chance to say anything. "I was going to run you out anyway, so I decided to save the time," he said. We both laughed about it and we have been friends. That's the good part of the game; I've always considered umpires to be an important part of the game.

Danger Ahead

To me, Willie McCovey was one of the most dangerous hitters. I walked Willie intentionally more times than any other player I ever faced! It seems like every time he stepped into the batter's box, I would raise four fingers indicating to our pitchers to intentionally walk Willie with four wide ones.

Late in the season the Reds were playing the Giants in San Francisco, and the division had already been settled. Before the game, Willie asked me again if I would please pitch to him. I smiled and told him since the division had already been decided, I would have our Reds pitchers pitch to him. The first time up, he hit a ball so far I thought it was going to land in Oakland. Willie is a modest man and so he tried not to look at me in the Reds' dugout as he was rounding third base. "Does that tell you why I don't pitch to you?" I yelled at him as he trotting towards home plate. Willie couldn't hold back his big smile. Every time I see him now we still laugh about that home run. And then I raise four fingers and he knows what it means.

Sparky Anderson

Tough With the Right Attitude

Pete Rose was the toughest competitor I ever saw! We were playing an exhibition game in Evansville, Indiana, one season and even though it did not matter whether we won or lost, he showed everyone again exactly how tough he was. Usually in exhibition games, starting lineups bat once and then they are replaced by the subs on the bench. Pete made an out his first time up, and I was going to take him out of the game for a little rest. When it was his turn to bat again, he grabbed his bat and asked for one more chance. Pete hit a line drive over the second baseman's head for a clean single and went barreling around first base like a locomotive out of control. I knew right away what he was doing. As he got closer to second base, he went into his head first slide and made it safely with a double. He got up and dusted off his uniform and signaled me to send in a pinch runner. When Pete reached the dugout steps, he said, "That's what people come to see!" And that's the kind of player he was! It didn't matter that the game meant nothing. That was just Pete Rose. Playing the game the right way meant everything to him. It was just an exhibition game, but it's one I'll remember for the rest of my life!

The Best of the Best

Best Fastball
Nolan Ryan & Tom Seaver

Best Curveball
Juan Marichal & Bert Blyleven

Most Intimidating Pitcher
Don Drysdale & Bob Gibson

Best Right-Handed Pitcher
Bob Gibson & Juan Marichal

Best Left-Handed Pitcher
Sandy Koufax & Steve Carlton

Best Left-Handed Reliever
Tug McGraw

Best Right-Handed Reliever
Dennis Eckersley & Rollie Fingers

Overall Most Challenging Pitcher
Bob Gibson & Sandy Koufax

Best Right-Handed Hitter
Frank Robinson

Best Left-Handed Hitter
Ted Williams & Stan Musial

Most Effective Hitter
Ted Williams

Best Catcher
Johnny Bench

Best First Baseman
Willie McCovey

Best Second Baseman
Joe Morgan

Best Shortstop
Luis Aparicio & Omar Vizquel

Best Third Baseman
Mike Schmidt

Best Left Fielder
Dave Winfield & Billy Williams

Best Center Fielder
Willie Mays

Best Right Fielder
Hank Aaron & Roberto Clemente

Fastest Base Runner
Rickey Henderson

Best Base Runner
Joe Morgan

Best Overall Opposing Player
Roberto Clemente & Frank Robinson

Most Gifted Athlete
Frank Robinson & Mike Schmidt

Strongest Outfield Arm
Cesar Geronimo

Best Team Rival
Los Angeles Dodgers & Cincinnati Reds

Best Opposing Manager
Gene Mauch

Sparky Anderson

Best Manager I Played For
George Scherger

Most Trusted Friend
Bill Consolo
(1953-1962)

My Favorite Team Mate
Bill Consolo

Funniest Player
Bill Consolo

Most Heart
Paul Molitor & Pete Rose

Most Courageous
Pete Rose

Best Work Ethics

Most Flamboyant
Rickey Henderson
& Reggie Jackson

Most Congenial
Phil Niekro & Harmon Killebrew

My Favorite Team
Cincinnati Reds & Detroit Tigers

Player I Most Admired
Willie McCovey & Ted Williams

**Player I Would Have
Liked as a Team Mate**
George Brett & Yogi Berra

My Favorite Stadium
Dodger Stadium

My Favorite City
Cincinnati & Detroit

Best Baseball Announcer
Vin Scully

**My Favorite
Baseball Announcer**
Vin Scully

The Best Umpire
Al Barlick

Umpire with The Best Attitude
Ed Vargo

Most Respected Baseball Personality
Casey Stengel

"Did You Know?"

"Why does everybody stand up and sing 'Take Me Out to the Ballgame' when they're already there?" — Larry Anderson

The highest career winning percentage for a pitcher was Whitey Ford with a .690 winning percentage.

"The secret to successful managing is to keep the five guys who hate you away from the four that have not made up their minds." — Casey Stengel

In September of 1968 the San Francisco Giants and the St. Louis Cardinals threw back-to-back no-hitters. Gaylord Perry of the Giants hurled the first no-hitter on Tuesday September 17th against Bob Gibson of the St. Louis Cardinals, while Cardinals pitcher, Ray Washburn tossed his no-hitter less than twenty four later against Bob Bolin of the San Francisco Giants.

"When they operated on my arm, I told them to put in a Koufax fastball. They did- but it was Mrs. Koufax's fastball." — Tommy John

Johnnie B. "Dusty" Baker Jr.

Born June 15, 1949, Riverside, California
Height 6'2"   **Weight** 187 lbs.
Bats Right   **Throws** Right
Debut Sept. 7, 1968   **Final game** Oct. 4, 1986

JOHNNIE B. BAKER JR. was nicknamed "Dusty" early in his career. Drafted by the Atlanta Braves in the 1967 amateur draft, Dusty Baker played major league baseball as an outstanding outfielder for the Atlanta Braves in 1968. After spending sixteen full seasons with the Braves, the Los Angeles Dodgers, the San Francisco Giants, and the Oakland Athletics, Dusty finished his illustrious career as a player with a lifetime .278 batting average, 242 career home runs, and 1,013 runs batted in.

Dusty was in the on-deck circle at the Atlanta-Fulton County Stadium when Henry Aaron hit his record breaking 715th homerun off of Dodgers southpaw, Al Downing. Dusty has vivid memories of shaking Henry's hand to congratulate him on his monumental record breaking homerun!

He was always popular as a player who was well known for his honesty and candor. He was a two-time All-Star, won three league championships and a World Series with the 1981 Los Angeles Dodgers team.

On the last day of the 1977 season while playing with the Los Angeles Dodgers, Dusty hammered his 30th home run of the season to join teammates Steve Garvey, Ron Cey, and Reggie Smith to formulate the first team to have four players with thirty home runs in the same year!

In addition to having an outstanding playing career, Dusty has had a fine managerial career as well. His very first year of managing the San Francisco Giants, 1993, he earned the National League Manager-of-the-Year award and went on to win that award two more times while leading the Giants to division titles in 1997 and 2000! In 2002, Dusty led the Giants into the World Series when the Anaheim Angels defeated them in a heart breaking and closely contended seven games.

Leaving the Giants after the 2002 season, Dusty signed as manager of the Chicago Cubs in 2003. Once again the legendary manager made an immediate impact in his first year as manager by winning the first divisional title in a decade for the Cubs. However the Cubs were eliminated in the divisional playoffs by the Florida Marlins. After the 2006 season Dusty departed the Cubs.

During the 2006 MLB post season, Dusty served as an ESPN analyst. October 13, 2007, Dusty was hired as the manager of the Cincinnati Reds, where he currently provides outstanding leadership! Dusty Baker has always been a man of integrity, courage and loyalty.

In My Own Words

First Big-League Experience

As a September call-up from Class A ball in Greenville, South Carolina, my first major league experience was at San Francisco's Candlestick Park in front of my family and friends did not start very well. Mike Murphy, the clubhouse manager for the visiting clubs, would not let me enter. Murphy thought that I was some young kid off the streets. I attempted to come in and he told me to get lost and he didn't want any trouble. I proceeded to tell him that I was a member of the Atlanta Braves. Murph said, "Me too", referring to himself. "See ya!" I was 19 years old, weighed 175 pounds, was about 6 feet tall with no facial hair—I looked about 15 or 16 years old!

I stood outside of the clubhouse entrance for about fifteen minutes looking for anyone that I might recognize. I couldn't see into the clubhouse itself from where I stood. Finally, as Jim Busby, an Atlanta coach, came out, I yelled to him and he came over. Busby said. "What are you doing standing outside?" I said, "That gentleman, Mike Murphy, who everyone calls Murph, would not let me in!" Busby then ordered me inside the Braves clubhouse. Murph was dumbfounded and could not believe this skinny and young-looking kid was actually on the team. That was an auspicious start! I started that game and collected the first big league hit of my career, an infield hit off of Juan Marichal, a friend of mine to this day!

Murph eventually ended up at the Giants' home clubhouse a few years later. In 1984 I played for the Giants and was with Murph the entire year. In 1988 through 1992 I served as the Giants hitting coach. Then from 1993 thru 2002 I was with Murph as the manager of the Giants and the boss—but Murph was really the boss!

Murph and I laughed many times about our first encounter in 1968 and how many things we have gone through since. Although my position changed numerous times over the last several years with the Giants, Murph has always been the same—"Boss of the Giants Clubhouse," and always a friend! Murph's favorite saying is. "I don't bother nobody." But he bothered me on our first introduction.

Tito Fuentes and Me!

While still playing with the Braves around 1972 or 1973, Tito Fuentes and I had quite a thing going: I was determined to get him trying to turn the double play! On many occasions I went with strawberries up and down my legs trying to nail Tito. One time, he would come across the bag. Next time he would take the throw behind second base, using the bag to shield himself from me. The next time he would be in front of the bag. Finally he told me that he would give me $5 if I touched him and

$10 if I could knock him down. Before our games would start, I would go out and watch Tito and Chris Speier turn double plays during the Giants infield practice trying to pick up something. The only thing I picked up was that they were truly amazing with a lot of mustard on the top! I never did collect from Tito! He was like a ghost, having fun disappearing from the base runners.

About twenty-five years later I was over at Tito's one day having a nice Sunday meal and on the wall by the dinner table was a photo of Tito with his hand extended trying to assist me up off the ground after he had turned another successful double play! That's Tito, though, always extending a hand after the base runner failed to upend him.

Hall-of-Fame Eye Openers

My first year in the major leagues, 1972, I was in awe during spring training with the Atlanta Braves! We arrived in St. Petersburg, Florida, around 5 p.m. The Mets and Cardinals shared the stadium across from the hotel where the Braves were staying. Hank Aaron asked me to go to the game with him that started at 7 p.m. between the Cardinals and Mets with Bob Gibson pitching. Naturally, yes was my immediate answer! My good friend on the Mets, John "The Hammer" Milner. (named after Hank "The Hammer" Aaron) was playing. Milner and I had been on opposing teams all the way through the minor leagues and now we were both in the major leagues. Bob Gibson hit Milner with the first pitch, dead center in the back. After the game, Hank Aaron invited me for dinner and a drink with Bob "Hoot" Gibson, as Hank called him. Hank asked Hoot why he had hit the young John Milner. Gibson replied, "I heard he could hit pretty good and I wanted to get into him right away." I never said a word all night, wondering what Hoot had heard about me, and if I would receive the same fate as John "The Hammer" Milner. One thing about Gibson, he was as fierce a competitor as ever walked onto a major league field.

Dusty Baker

The Best of the Best

In most instances I have selected two people instead of one! Some places I
would have liked to have written three or four names!

Best Fastball
Tom Seaver, J. R. Richards

Best Curveball
Bert Blyleven, Clay Kirby,
Don Sutton

Most Intimidating Pitcher
Bob Gibson, Don Drysdale

Best Right-Handed Pitcher
Bob Gibson, Tom Seaver

Best Left-Handed Pitcher
Sandy Koufax, Steve Carlton

Best Left-Handed Reliever
Sparky Lyle, Ron Perranoski

Best Right-Handed Reliever
Rollie Fingers, Goose Gossage

**Overall Most Challenging
Pitcher**
Bob Gibson, J.R. Richards

Best Right-Handed Hitter
Willie Mays, Hank Aaron

Best Left-Handed Hitter
Tony Oliva, Rod Carew

Overall Best Clutch Hitter
Tony Perez, Orlando Cepeda

Best Catcher
Johnny Bench, Earl Battey

Best First Baseman
Bill White, Wes Parker

Best Second Baseman
Bill Mazeroski, Tito Fuentes

Best Shortstop
Mark Belanger, Dal Maxvill

Best Third Baseman
Brooks Robinson, Clete Boyer

Best Left Fielder
Cleon Jones, Billy Williams

Best Center Fielder
Willie Mays, Paul Blair

Best Right Fielder
Roberto Clemente, Al Kaline

Fastest Base Runner
Lou Brock, Bobby Bonds

Best Base Runner
Lou Brock, Willie Mays

Best Overall Player
Willie Mays, Roberto Clemente

**Player Who Didn't Reach
Maximum Potential**
Adolfo Phillips, Ivan Murrell

Strongest Outfield Arm
Ollie Brown, Reggie Smith

33

Best Team Rival
Cincinnati Reds &
Pittsburgh Pirates

Best Opposing Manager
Sparky Anderson, Walter Alston

Best Manager I Played For
Tom Lasorda, Clyde King

Most Trusted Friend
Gary Matthews Sr., Ralph Garr

My Favorite Team Mate
Ralph Garr, Reggie Smith

Funniest Player
Ralph Garr, Tito Fuentes

Most Heart
Pete Rose, Jimmy Wynn

Most Courageous
Joe Morgan, Frank Robinson

Best Work Ethics
Hank Aaron, Tommy John

Most Flamboyant
Tito Fuentes, Vic Power

Most Congenial
Brooks Robinson, Willie Stargell

My Favorite Team
L.A. Dodgers, S.F. Giants

Player I Most Admired
Hank Aaron, Roberto Clemente

Player I Would Have Liked as a Team Mate
Curt Flood, Al Kaline

My Favorite Stadium
Dodger Stadium, Old Veterans
(Phil.)

My Favorite City
Montreal, San Diego

Best Baseball Announcer
Vin Scully, Jack Buck

My Favorite Baseball Announcer
Vin Scully, Jack Buck

The Best Umpire
Al Barlick, Tom Crawford

Umpire with The Best Attitude
Frank Pulli, Lee Weyer

Most Respected Baseball Personality
Hank Aaron, Ralph Kiner

Johnnie "Dusty" Baker
Lifetime Statistics

Year	Age	Tm	Lg	G	PA	AB	R	H	2B	3B	HR	RBI	SB	CS	BB	SO	BA	OBP	SLG
1968	19	ATL	NL	6	5	5	0	2	0	0	0	0	0	0	0	1	.400	.400	.400
1969	20	ATL	NL	3	7	7	0	0	0	0	0	0	0	0	0	3	.000	.000	.000
1970	21	ATL	NL	13	27	24	3	7	0	0	0	4	0	0	2	4	.292	.333	.292
1971	22	ATL	NL	29	64	62	2	14	2	0	0	4	0	1	1	14	.226	.238	.258
1972	23	ATL	NL	127	503	446	62	143	27	2	17	76	4	7	45	68	.321	.383	.504
1973	24	ATL	NL	159	686	604	101	174	29	4	21	99	24	3	67	72	.288	.359	.454
1974	25	ATL	NL	149	656	574	80	147	35	0	20	69	18	7	71	87	.256	.335	.422
1975	26	ATL	NL	142	567	494	63	129	18	2	19	72	12	7	67	57	.261	.346	.421
1976	27	LAD	NL	112	421	384	36	93	13	0	4	39	2	4	31	54	.242	.298	.307
1977	28	LAD	NL	153	604	533	86	155	26	1	30	86	2	6	58	89	.291	.364	.512
1978	29	LAD	NL	149	579	522	62	137	24	1	11	66	12	3	47	66	.262	.325	.375
1979	30	LAD	NL	151	616	554	86	152	29	1	23	88	11	4	56	70	.274	.340	.455
1980	31	LAD	NL	153	638	579	80	170	26	4	29	97	12	10	43	66	.294	.339	.503
1981	32	LAD	NL	103	438	400	48	128	17	3	9	49	10	7	29	43	.320	.363	.445
1982	33	LAD	NL	147	640	570	80	171	19	1	23	88	17	10	56	62	.300	.361	.458
1983	34	LAD	NL	149	616	531	71	138	25	1	15	73	7	1	72	59	.260	.346	.395
1984	35	SFG	NL	100	287	243	31	71	7	2	3	32	4	1	40	27	.292	.387	.374
1985	36	OAK	AL	111	396	343	48	92	15	1	14	52	2	1	50	47	.268	.359	.440
1986	37	OAK	AL	83	271	242	25	58	8	0	4	19	0	1	27	37	.240	.314	.322

19-Year Totals

G	PA	AB	R	H	2B	3B	HR	RBI	SB	CS	BB	SO	BA	OBP	SLG
2039	8021	7117	964	1981	320	23	242	1013	137	73	762	926	.278	.347	.432

"Did You Know?"

How did home plate derive its name? Before 1869 the players would use a circular object for home. Often the circular object used as a base was an actual oval dinner plate, thus came the name, home plate.

Balancing the books: The very last batter that faced Bob Gibson in a major league game was Pete Lacock of the Chicago Cubs. Lacock hit a grand slam off Gibson. Ten years later in an old timers game when Lacock came to bat against Gibson, and Lacock accidently got hit in the rib cage?

How many baseballs can be made from one cow hide? One Cow hide on an average can make between 90 and 120 baseballs

When accused of using foreign substances, Don Sutton retorted emphatically that it was not true. Sutton stated that Vaseline is manufactured right here in the United States.

Nolan Ryan is tied for the most career grand slams allowed with 10.

Vida Blue

Born July 28, 1949, Mansfield, Louisiana
Height 6'0"   **Weight** 189 lbs.
Bats Both   **Throws** Left
Debut July 20, 1969   **Final game** Oct. 2, 1986

IN SEPTEMBER 1970, VIDA BLUE was promoted to the major leagues with the Oakland Athletics. The Athletics caught of glimpse of their bright future with the fireballing left hander who quickly became the talk of the entire major leagues. Vida had arguably one of the most phenomenal entrances into the major leagues ever!

On Friday September 11, 1970, Vida went out to perform an outstanding one-hitter against the Kansas City Royals at Municipal Stadium in Kansas City. Pat Kelly of the Royals got the first and only hit in the bottom of the 8th inning. In addition, Vida collected two hits that day, one which was a double to right field. Ten days later the poised lefthander from Louisiana pitched a masterpiece! Vida simply went out and pitched a no-hitter against the mighty Minnesota Twins no less! The Twins were 92 and 61 when Vida threw his no-hitter against them. The lineup included Tony Oliva and Harmon Killebrew, some of the American Leagues most proficient and feared hitters! In the 4th inning, Vida walked Killebrew for their only base runner of the game.

Vida had a blazing fastball that frequently was dialed in at 100 mph! Pete Rose once stated that Vida threw harder than anyone he had ever faced.

1971 was Vida's first full season in the big leagues and that season he went out and won both the American League Cy Young Award, and the American League Most Valuable Player Award, becoming the youngest American League player to win the Most Valuable Player Award in the 20th century. He was also the starting pitcher for the American League All-Star game in 1971.

In 1978, Vida's first year with the San Francisco Giants, he had another remarkable year. He pitched 258 innings while winning 18 games and losing 10 games with a team that was 89-73. Vida's ERA for that year was 2.79. Once again Vida was the starting pitcher in the All-Star game, this time in the National League representing the San Francisco Giants. That year, Vida finished third in the National Cy Young Award.

He made six All-Star appearances—1971, 1975, 1977, 1978, 1980 and 1981!

Vida Blue is one of those immensely gifted athletes who appear on the horizon rarely. He was truly one the game's premier pitchers of his era. Most of his peers would agree he dominated the game when considering his records and accomplishments, When his peers were anticipating that exploding 100 mph fastball approaching them in the batter's box, they realized he was one the games very best! Indeed, he had Hall-of-Fame credentials in his illustrious career, but more significantly, he is a Hall-of-Fame person!

Vida blue

In My Own Words

S A YOUNG MAN growing up in my home state of Louisiana, I was first scouted by Buck O'Neil, the very first black scout for a major league team. I always had a special appreciation for being scouted first by Buck because, not only was he a fine gentleman, he also was one of the truly great players in the old Negro Leagues.

One day in September 1970, while I was in Omaha playing for the A's Triple A ball club, I received word that the A's had promoted me to the majors. I had a very auspicious start! Gene Tenace, Rene Lachman, Jim Driscol and I had all received calls promoting us to the major leagues, and we decided to go celebrate. We were walking in downtown Omaha looking for a nice steakhouse. Honest to goodness, we got picked up and arrested for jaywalking! Can you believe it? Not for excessive drinking, rowdy or being disorderly, but for jaywalking! Unbelievable!

Welcome, now leave!

Then I finally got to start in my very first game in the big leagues. The home plate umpire that day was Bill Kunkel. Believe it or not, I got tossed in that game for arguing strikes. Not as a pitcher arguing strikes, rather as the batter against the then Anaheim Angels, one of our fiercest competitors. If there had been the designated hitter's rule in place, I would have been able to at least go further in my first start!

Respect for Mr. Flood

This is a good opportunity for me to share some of my personal views and thoughts that I believe are important. Curt Flood was a fantastic baseball player! More importantly he was an incredible man of courage who was intelligent and ahead of his generation! This man made unbelievable sacrifices for every single major league player! The major league owners would never admit they were wrong in their attitudes and treatment of players; owners treated players as property with virtually no rights! Curt Flood believed otherwise, and took his beliefs, convictions, and vision to the highest court in the land, the United States Supreme Court.

Some of the older players said to me that they were warned not to testify on Curt Flood's behalf. Unfortunately for Curt, the baseball players' union was not as strong or as powerful then as it is today. Now that court case would have been overwhelmingly won by Curt and his attorneys, exposing the questionable practices by the owners in baseball! All the players of Curt's era were in the same or similar situations as Curt, but he lost his career for everyone's benefit! Believe me, Curt Flood paid the ultimate price with his career for every single player who played in his era and thereafter!

The players' union today is stronger because of the heroic efforts of Curt Flood. Now, today's players have the luxury of stating in their contracts specific requests regarding who or when they can be traded to and more, all because of Mr. Curt Flood! A great debt of gratitude is owed to Curt for his courage and personal sacrifices! I really believe that every current and future major leaguer player who attains the $1 million plateau as his financial compensation should donate money into a Curt Flood Fund for Curt's widow, siblings, and direct descendents.

Curt Flood, the bell hop?

One time, when Curt and I were in Reno to assist in conducting a baseball clinic, we were staying at the same hotel. We were sitting around and chatting about humorous stories and Curt told a story about when the St. Louis Cardinals were on a road trip and staying at their hotel. Curt was standing in the hotel lobby and two people who had just checked in at the front desk walked up to him and told him what room they were staying in and handed him their baggage. Curt took the bags, and delivered them to their room and came back down to the lobby with his five dollar tip and went on with his business! For some reason these hotel guests seemed somewhat certain Curt was a bellboy! Now that is funny! We both chuckled at what we are all sometimes guilty of—assuming! Instead of being offended, he simply made lemonade from the lemons. Curt Flood was a great guy!

Applause for these three

When I agreed to participate in this book, Gary Hall, the author, asked me about today's players and today's game. When I think about baseball strictly from a fan's perspective, there are some great young players in the game today. Three players that come to mind that I would be willing to pay watch play are Jimmy Rollins, Derek Jeter, and Pablo "The Panda" Sandoval! Of course there are others, but I enjoy these three immensely!

The operation of baseball has changed. It has become too corporate. Baseball is still a game and should be played as such!

The Best of the Best

Best Fastball
Nolan Ryan

Best Curveball
Rudy May, Bert Blyleven

Most Intimidating Pitcher
J.R. Richard

Best Right-Handed Pitcher
Bob Gibson, Tom Seaver
(Positive role model - Bob
Gibson was my favorite)

Best Left-Handed Pitcher
Sandy Koufax

Best Left-Handed Reliever
Sparky Lyle

Best Right-Handed Reliever
Dennis Eckersley

Overall Most Challenging Pitcher
Bob Gibson

Best Right-Handed Hitter
Dick Allen

Best Left-Handed Hitter
George Brett

Overall Best Clutch Hitter
Pete Rose

Best Catcher
Johnny Bench

Best First Baseman
Keith Hernandez

Best Second Baseman
Joe Morgan

Best Shortstop
Ozzie Smith

Best Third Baseman
Brooks Robinson

Best Left Fielder
Carl Yastrzemski

Best Center Fielder
Willie Mays

Best Right Fielder
Dave Parker

Fastest Base Runner
Willie Wilson

Best Base Runner
Willie Mays

Best Overall Opposing Player
Frank Howard, Willie Horton

Most Gifted Athlete
Reggie Jackson

Strongest Outfield Arm
Reggie Jackson

Best Team Rival
Athletics vs. Royals
Athletics vs. Angels

Best Opposing Manager
Sparkey Anderson

Best Manager I Played For
Dick Williams

Most Trusted Friend
Bill North

My Favorite Team Mate
Mike Norris

Funniest Player
Gene Tenace

Most Heart
Joe Rudi

Most Courageous
Dick Green

Best Work Ethics
Joe Rudi

Most Flamboyant
Willie Montanez

Most Congenial
Catfish Hunter

My Favorite Team
New York Yankees

Player I Most Admired
Dick Allen

Player I Would Have Liked as a Team Mate
Brooks Robinson

My Favorite Stadium
Old Yankee Stadium

My Favorite City
San Diego

Best Baseball Announcer
Harry Carey

My Favorite Baseball Announcer
Harry Carey

The Best Umpire
Doug Harvey

Umpire with The Best Attitude
Doug Harvey

Most Respected Baseball Personality
Jackie Robinson

Vida Blue
Lifetime Statistics

Year	Age	Tm	Lg	W	L	W-L%	ERA	G	GS	GF	CG	SHO	SV	IP	H	R	ER	HR	BB	SO
1969	19	OAK	AL	1	1	.500	6.64	12	4	1	0	0	1	42.0	49	34	31	13	18	24
1970	20	OAK	AL	2	0	1.000	2.09	6	6	0	2	2	0	38.2	20	12	9	0	12	35
1971	21	OAK	AL	24	8	.750	1.82	39	39	0	24	8	0	312.0	209	73	63	19	88	301
1972	22	OAK	AL	6	10	.375	2.80	25	23	0	5	4	0	151.0	117	55	47	11	48	111
1973	23	OAK	AL	20	9	.690	3.28	37	37	0	13	4	0	263.2	214	108	96	26	105	158
1974	24	OAK	AL	17	15	.531	3.25	40	40	0	12	1	0	282.1	246	118	102	17	98	174
1975	25	OAK	AL	22	11	.667	3.01	39	38	1	13	2	1	278.0	243	103	93	21	99	189
1976	26	OAK	AL	18	13	.581	2.35	37	37	0	20	6	0	298.1	268	90	78	9	63	166
1977	27	OAK	AL	14	19	.424	3.83	38	38	0	16	1	0	279.2	284	138	119	23	86	157
1978	28	SFG	NL	18	10	.643	2.79	35	35	0	9	4	0	258.0	233	87	80	12	70	171
1979	29	SFG	NL	14	14	.500	5.01	34	34	0	10	0	0	237.0	246	143	132	23	111	138
1980	30	SFG	NL	14	10	.583	2.97	31	31	0	10	3	0	224.0	202	79	74	14	61	129
1981	31	SFG	NL	8	6	.571	2.45	18	18	0	1	0	0	124.2	97	40	34	7	54	63
1982	32	KCR	AL	13	12	.520	3.78	31	31	0	6	2	0	181.0	163	80	76	20	80	103
1983	33	KCR	AL	0	5	.000	6.01	19	14	4	1	0	0	85.1	96	62	57	12	35	53
1985	35	SFG	NL	8	8	.500	4.47	33	20	5	1	0	0	131.0	115	70	65	17	80	103
1986	36	SFG	NL	10	10	.500	3.27	28	28	0	0	0	0	156.2	137	65	57	19	77	100

17-Year Totals

W	L	W-L%	ERA	G	GS	GF	CG	SHO	SV	IP	H	R	ER	HR	BB	SO
209	161	.565	3.27	502	473	11	143	37	2	3343.1	2939	1357	1213	263	1185	2175

"Did You Know?"

"I hate all hitters. I start a game mad, and I stay that way until it is over." — Don Drysdale

The first post-1900 switch hitter to win the National League batting title was Pete Rose.

"They said I was such a great prospect they were going to send me to winter ball to sharpen me up. When I stepped off of the plane, I was in Greenland." — Bob Uecker

Roberto Clemente was the only player in the 1960s to lead the major leagues in batting average three times.

"When a pitcher throws a spitball, don't worry and don't complain. Just hit the dry side like I do." — Stan "The Man" Musial

William "Billy Buck" Joseph Buckner

Born December 14, 1949, Vallejo, California
Height 6'0   **Weight** 185 lbs.
Bats Left   **Throws** Left
Debut Sept. 21, 1969   **Final game** May 30, 1990

BILL BUCKNER was born in Vallejo, California, December 14, 1949. Bill was the second player chosen by the Los Angeles Dodgers in the 1968 draft. He was mostly an outfielder playing for the Dodgers through the 1976 season.

Bill played in his first major league game with the Los Angeles Dodgers in 1969 at the age of 19. The following year he had a total of 68 at bats with a .191 batting average. But it was obvious to Dodgers General Manager Al Campanis and Dodgers Manager Walter Alston that the Dodgers organization had a very special young player. Bill was a tough, blue-collar type player who quickly earned the respect of his peers and L.A. fans.

Bill Buckner became more than accomplished as a major league player. As an outstanding athlete, he was better than average as a defensive player and had very good speed as a base runner. In 1974 he stole 31 bases for the Dodgers. In 1985 at age 35, with bad knees and a bad ankle, he stole 18 bases for the Boston Red Sox. At the end of his career, Buckner had accumulated a total of 183 career stolen bases.

Twice he led the league in doubles. Early in the 1970s Bill had a severe ankle injury which hobbled him, and he had to receive extensive treatment for his ankle the rest of his big league career. Buckner was a gritty player who came every day to the ball park to play the game with intensity.

After the 1976 season, the Los Angeles Dodgers traded Bill Buckner to the Chicago Cubs, and there he thrived primarily as a first baseman. In that position; he played in 1555 games, and, in 13,901 opportunities at first base, he made only 128 errors!

However, it was as a hitter that Buckner excelled. He won the National League batting title with the Chicago Cubs while batting a robust .324 with 41 doubles in 1980. Contact was Billy's game—he almost always made contact and, as a hitter, was accomplished in every area. In his 22-year career, he only struck out three times more than he walked. On 10 different occasions Bill had more walks than strikeouts for an entire season.

After 22 outstanding major league seasons, he amassed 2715 hits! Bill had more career hits than several Hall-of-Famers including Ted Williams, Billy Williams, Jimmy Fox, Ernie Banks, Mickey Mantle, Reggie Jackson, Jim Rice, Ozzie Smith, Luis Aparicio, plus over 70 more Hall-of-Famers! He batted over .300 in eight different seasons. By the time his career ended, Bill had accomplished a .289 lifetime batting average.

Bill hit 498 doubles! There are over 90 Hall-of-Famers Bill surpassed with lifetime doubles, including Mickey Mantle, Joe DiMaggio, Joe Morgan, Roberto Clemente, Rod Carew, Lou Brock, and at least 84 others!

Bill Buckner was an outstanding major league baseball player who deserves the respect of baseball fans and his peers—as he was truly one of the game's best hitters in his era!

In My Own Words

THERE IS NO QUESTION THAT, as a baseball player, you need to know where the ball is at all times. There can be a lot of confusion and even embarrassment when you do not know where the ball is at all times. This happened while playing against the Pittsburgh Pirates in the late '70s when I played for the Chicago Cubs. Rennie Stennett of the Pirates hit a sinking line drive to the Cubs right fielder Larry Biittner, and Biittner made a diving attempt to catch the ball. As Biittner hit the ground, both his glove and his hat came off, and he quickly jumped up to retrieve the ball from his glove. The only problem was that the ball was not in his glove. Stennett was heading like a locomotive towards second base. Biittner was confused, and he began to spin in circles looking desperately for the ball. Meanwhile, Stennett was racing for third base. Biittner saw his hat lying on the ground 10 feet away and he frantically ran towards his hat as Stennett approached third base. Biittner picked up his hat. There was the ball as Stennett rounded third! Biittner grabbed the ball and fired a perfect strike to the Cubs catcher just in time to nail Stennett at the plate for the out! This was an unintentional hidden ball trick that just so happened to work in the Cubs' favor!

Embarrassing with intent

Then there was the intentional hidden ball trick during a 1986 Boston Red Sox and California Angels game! Gene Mauch, the Angels manager, believed that no opposing team could ever pull off such a trick against a team that he managed.

My good friend and team-mate Marty Barrett had pulled off several hidden ball tricks in the minor leagues and one previous time in the major leagues. In this game, he was playing second base, and I was playing first base. Marty gave me the heads up to be ready, as he thought we could pull off the hidden ball trick against Mauch's Angels. There are several ways to pull off a hidden ball trick but usually it followed some kind of dish action: Marty would get the ball at second base, and he and I were the only ones in the park to know exactly where the ball was. This time, Bobby Grich of the Angels was on first base. Doug DeCinces of the Angels hit a grounder on the infield, and the ball was thrown to me playing first base for the out. There was a brief argument, and Marty, who was standing next to me, told me to give him the ball—and no one saw the transfer! Marty then took his position at second base, and Grich, the runner for the Angels, took his normal lead off of second. Marty went towards Grich as if to bluff him back to second, and simply tagged him out!

Mauch, the fiery manager for the Angels, was absolutely furious! After the game, Mauch stated for the record that that was the first time anyone had ever pulled a hidden ball trick on one of his teams, and went on to say that it would never happen again to one of his teams that he managed! Later on, we found out that Doug DeCinces of the Angels got on Bobby Grich pretty good for letting a team pull the hidden ball trick on him.

Well, guess what happened a few day's later while the Red Sox were playing the Angels? Marty Barrett pulled the hidden ball trick again against the Angels, only this time against Doug DeCinces! Can you imagine how Angels Manager Gene Mauch reacted this time? Probably to this day, Bobby Grich is still giving Doug DeCinces a hard time. I guess whoever came up with the phrase, "You better keep your eye on the ball!" knew what he was talking about!

The Best of the Best
Bill Buckner

Best Fastball
Nolan Ryan

Best Curveball
Bert Blyleven

Most Intimidating Pitcher
Bob Gibson

Best Right-Handed Pitcher
Tom Seaver

Best Left-Handed Pitcher
Steve Carlton

Best Left-Handed Reliever
Tug McGraw

Best Right-Handed Reliever
Bruce Sutter, Goose Gossage

**Overall Most
Challenging Pitcher**
Jerry Koosman

Best Right-Handed Hitter
Hank Aaron

Best Left-Handed Hitter
George Brett

Overall Best Clutch Hitter
George Brett

Best Catcher
Johnny Bench

Best Second Baseman
Joe Morgan

Best Shortstop
Ozzie Smith

Best Third Baseman
George Brett

Best Left Fielder
Lou Brock

Best Center Fielder
Willie Mays

Best Right Fielder
Roberto Clemente

Fastest Base Runner
Willie Wilson

Best Base Runner
Lou Brock

Best Overall Player
Willie Mays, Hank Aaron

**Player Who Didn't Reach
Maximum Potential**
Bobby Bonds

Strongest Outfield Arm
Ollie "Downtown" Brown,
Roberto Clemente

Best Team Rival
L. A. Dodgers & S. F. Giants

Best Opposing Manager
Joe Torre

Best Manager I Played For
John McNamara, Tommy Lasorda

Most Trusted Friend
Marty Barrett, Mike Krukow

My Favorite Team Mate
George Brett, Marty Barrett

Funniest Player
Tug McGraw

Most Heart
Pete Rose

Most Courageous
Danny Thompson

Best Work Ethics
Maury Wills

Most Flamboyant
Tito Fuentes

Most Congenial
Brooks Robinson

Most Zany
Richie Hebner

My Favorite Team
L.A. Dodgers & Chicago Cubs

Player I Most Admired
Paul Molitor

Player I Would Have Liked as a Team Mate
Robin Yount

My Favorite Stadium
Dodger Stadium,
Original Yankee Stadium

My Favorite City
Kansas City

Best Baseball Announcer
Vin Scully

My Favorite Baseball Announcer
Vin Scully

The Best Umpire
Doug Harvey, Steve Palermo

Umpire with The Best Attitude
Dutch Rennert

Most Respected Baseball Personality
Stan Musial

Bill "Billy Buck" Buckner
Lifetime Statistics

Year	Age	Tm	Lg	G	PA	AB	R	H	2B	3B	HR	RBI	SB	CS	BB	SO	BA	OBP	SLG
1969	19	LAD	NL	1	1	1	0	0	0	1	0	0	0	1	0	0	.000	.000	.000
1970	20	LAD	NL	28	71	68	6	13	3	1	0	4	0	1	3	7	.191	.225	.265
1971	21	LAD	NL	108	383	358	37	99	15	1	5	41	4	1	11	18	.277	.306	.366
1972	22	LAD	NL	105	405	383	47	122	14	3	5	37	10	3	17	13	.319	.348	.410
1973	23	LAD	NL	140	606	575	68	158	20	0	8	46	12	2	17	34	.275	.297	.351
1974	24	LAD	NL	145	620	580	83	182	30	3	7	58	31	13	30	24	.314	.351	.412
1975	25	LAD	NL	92	315	288	30	70	11	2	6	31	8	3	17	15	.243	.286	.358
1976	26	LAD	NL	154	680	642	76	193	28	4	7	60	28	9	26	26	.301	.326	.389
1977	27	CHC	NL	122	457	426	40	121	27	0	11	60	7	5	21	23	.284	.314	.425
1978	28	CHC	NL	117	470	446	47	144	26	1	5	74	7	5	18	17	.323	.345	.419
1979	29	CHC	NL	149	628	591	72	168	34	7	14	66	9	4	30	28	.284	.319	.437
1980	30	CHC	NL	145	614	578	69	187	41	3	10	68	1	2	30	18	.324	.353	.457
1981	31	CHC	NL	106	453	421	45	131	35	3	10	75	5	2	26	16	.311	.349	.480
1982	32	CHC	NL	161	709	657	93	201	34	5	15	105	15	5	36	26	.306	.342	.441
1983	33	CHC	NL	153	665	626	79	175	38	6	16	66	12	4	25	30	.280	.310	.436
1984	34	TOT	MLB	135	517	482	54	131	21	2	11	69	2	2	25	39	.272	.313	.392
1984	34	CHC	NL	21	46	43	3	9	0	0	0	2	0	0	1	1	.209	.239	.209
1984	34	BOS	AL	114	471	439	51	122	21	2	11	67	2	2	24	38	.278	.321	.410
1985	35	BOS	AL	162	718	673	89	201	46	3	16	110	18	4	30	36	.299	.325	.447
1986	36	BOS	AL	153	681	629	73	168	39	2	18	102	6	4	40	25	.267	.311	.421
1987	37	TOT	AL	132	498	469	39	134	18	2	5	74	2	3	22	26	.286	.314	.365
1987	37	BOS	AL	75	304	286	23	78	6	1	2	42	1	3	13	19	.273	.299	.322
1987	37	CAL	AL	57	194	183	16	56	12	1	3	32	1	0	9	7	.306	.337	.432
1988	38	TOT	AL	108	311	285	19	71	14	0	3	43	5	1	17	19	.249	.287	.330
1988	38	CAL	AL	19	48	43	1	9	0	0	0	9	2	0	4	0	.209	.271	.209
1988	38	KCR	AL	89	263	242	18	62	14	0	3	34	3	1	13	19	.256	.290	.351
1989	39	KCR	AL	79	183	176	7	38	4	1	1	16	1	0	6	11	.216	.240	.267
1990	40	BOS	AL	22	48	43	4	8	0	0	1	3	0	0	3	2	.186	.234	.256

22-Year Totals

G	PA	AB	R	H	2B	3B	HR	RBI	SB	CS	BB	SO	BA	OBP	SLG
2517	####	9397	1077	2715	498	49	174	1208	183	73	450	453	.289	.321	.408

"Did You Know?"

"It's no fun throwing fastballs to guys who can't hit them. The real challenge is getting them out on stuff they can hit." — Sudden Sam McDowell

Mickey Mantle was the first switch hitter to ever win the American League Batting title, and he had a .353 batting average.

"You have two hemispheres in your brain – a left and a right side. The left side controls the right side of your body and right controls the left half. It's a fact. Therefore, left-handers are the only people in their right minds." — Bill " Spaceman" Lee

Reggie Jackson is the only American League player in history to hit over 100 homeruns for three different teams?

"Of course I would like to have a guy on the team that can hit a home run every time he steps up to the plate, and strike out every single batter he faces. The only problem is to get that fella to put his cup of beer down, and climb over the railing from the stands and onto the field." — Danny Murtaugh

Orlando "Baby Bull" Cepeda

Born September 17, 1937, Ponce, P.R.
Height 6' 2"   **Weight** 210 lbs.
Bats Right   **Throws** Right
Debut April 15, 1958   **Final game** September 19, 1974

ORLANDO CEPEDA was born in Ponce, Puerto Rico. His father was the famous Pedro "The Bull" Cepeda, the best player in Puerto Rico of his generation. Hence Orlando became known as the Baby Bull! Orlando became a huge fan of the game watching his father in his beautiful native country and, early on in the Cuban League, he eagerly watched the career of the mega-talented Minnie Minoso.

While playing in Santurce, Puerto Rico, in 1957 he was scouted by Horace Stoneham, owner, Bill Rigney, manager, and Tom Sheehan, advanced scout of the San Francisco Giants. Along with Felipe Alou, Orlando was invited to the Giants' spring training facility.

Orlando signed his first professional contract with the New York Giants as an amateur in 1955. He was not fluent in English, and he was often ostracized. In addition, he encountered racial segregation while playing in Salem, Virginia, as well as other locations in the south. Orlando's character and inner strength eventually overcame the many cultural obstacles.

He was called up to the big leagues by the San Francisco Giants in 1958, and that season he batted .312 with 25 home runs and 96 RBIs, and led the National League with 38 doubles. He was selected as the National League Rookie of the Year! Orlando and Willie Mays were the only two National League players who finished the 1958 season ranked as leaders in every major offensive category—hits, home runs, runs batted in, batting average, runs scored, and stolen bases! Orlando won the San Francisco Examiner's poll as the "Most Valuable Giant" amongst fans! Orlando Cepeda brought great success and fanfare the very first year the Giants moved from New York.

The 1959 season began where the 1958 season ended. Orlando led the Giants with a .317 batting average and had 105 runs batted in. In 1960 he hit a robust .297 with 24 home runs and 96 run batted in and 15 stolen bases.

However, 1961 was arguably the Baby Bull's finest season. Orlando went out and stroked a .311 batting average along with the eye popping figures of 46 home runs with 142 runs batted in. By all accounts this was a monster year for anyone, but most especially for Orlando as this was accomplished in only his third season! The National League chose Frank Robinson as the league's Most Valuable Player, however, Orlando's numbers were better. The Baby Bull deserved, and should have won, his first Most Valuable Player Award from the National League in 1961!

The Baby Bull was quickly developing into one of baseball's most feared sluggers who could also hit for average. There was no easy way to get him out, and others in the league learned that lesson well during Orlando's first three years of playing in the National League.

One major hurdle existed for Orlando as well as for the rest of the Latinos on the Giants team. Under the leadership of Alvin Dark, who managed the San Francisco Giants from 1961—1964, serious controversies grew and tension quickly manifested itself. Dark mandated that there was to be no Spanish spoken in the Giants clubhouse. Most of the Latin players often felt inadequate speaking English, but, more importantly, they felt like second-class citizens . But they felt accepted and privileged to be able to speak to fellow country men their first language. Orlando took exception to the rule! After Dark started excluding Hispanic players from team meetings, Orlando confronted him about these issues.

While training in the winter of 1963, Orlando developed a serious knee disorder and was in extreme pain. He began to create extremely strenuous workout regiments that no other major league player at the time even attempted. Not only did his condition improve, but he influenced other players to increase their training. Juan Marichal once told me that because of Orlando's workout routine, he became stronger and in better condition! Orlando was a pioneer and visionary with both his workout regiments and nutrition. It can't be denied, however, that throughout his career Orlando played on bad legs that created excruciating pain for the big fella.

In 1966, the San Francisco Giants traded Orlando to the St. Louis Cardinals. He went on to assist in leading the newly nicknamed "El Birdos" in to the National League Championship in 1967, and then onto a monumental World Series victory against the mighty Red Sox of Boston. The Baby Bull was also the 1967 unanimous choice for the National League's Most Valuable Player of the Year with a .325 batting average, 25 home runs, and 111 runs batted in for the season!

The St. Louis Cardinals 1968 season was also a tremendous year for the team as they went on to win 97 games and were clearly at the top of the class in the National League. However, even though they were the favorites to win the World Series against the Tigers of Detroit, they lost in seven games.

The Cardinals traded Orlando to the Atlanta Braves in 1969. Once again Orlando was surprised, but he adjusted well to his new surroundings in Atlanta. This move gave him the opportunity to play with one the game's truly great heroes, Mr. Hank Aaron, which he enjoyed immensely!

The Braves won the newly constructed National League West Title with 93 wins, only to lose in the playoffs to the eventual World Champions New York Mets. Orlando hit 22 home runs with 88 runs batted in and a .258 batting average for his new team in 1969. He played almost four years with the Braves and had some solid seasons.

In 1973 Orlando was signed to a contract with the Boston Red Sox as the first player to be exclusively used as a designated hitter. He simply went out to collect 20 home runs, 86 runs batted in and a .289 batting average at the age of 36. Overall, Orlando's knees most definitely took a major toll on his illustrious career. But, as with everything else, the Baby Bull persevered and took his rightful place within the hallowed Halls of Cooperstown in Baseball's Hall of Fame!

Orlando Cepeda was arguably the best clutch hitter of his era, and, in addition, was one of the greatest clutch hitters of all time! Orlando has always been one of the most congenial and giving people in the major leagues and continues to be with his huge heart to this very day!

Orlando, The Baby Bull, is a man of courage who endured great adversity as one of the earliest Hispanic pioneers. Even though there were numerous barriers regarding languages, jealousies and strife, when Orlando picked up his lumber from the bat rack, his message was crystal clear.

In My Own Words

The Beginning Was a Challenge

In 1955 I was signed to my first professional contract while playing in my native country of Puerto Rico. The San Francisco Giants had signed me when I was seventeen years old. The gentleman who scouted me was Pete Zorrilla who also owned the team I played for in Puerto Rico. Pete was a wonderful person who I greatly respected and admired. I received five hundred dollars as a signing bonus, which was pretty good for a Latin ball player back then.

After I signed my contract, I was travelling to a foreign country with a foreign language. On that same plane ride from Puerto Rico to the United States was Jose Pagan, Roberto Clemente and myself. This was a new beginning not only for us, but for major league baseball, as Latin players now were presented with new opportunities. However, with those opportunities came challenging obstacles. Some of those obstacles were the language barrier which was a tremendous hindrance for me personally. In addition, the color of my skin was different as I was obviously not black or white so I experienced racism first hand.

Our plane landed in Florida and I headed for Melbourne Florida for my first spring training assignment. It was exciting, but it was also very frightening as I was extremely close to my parents and I had never been to the United States, and I spoke no English. So the land, language, and customs were very different than what I had experienced in Puerto Rico.

Soon, I was released by the Giants out of spring training and was sent to the Giants class D baseball team in Salem, Virginia. Two weeks later, I received the worse possible news, my father had died unexpectedly back home in Puerto Rico. To say that I was devastated would be an understatement. I took the five hundred dollar signing bonus I had received from the Giants and flew to Puerto Rico to bury my father.

After the funeral, I did not want to return to the United States. Even though baseball was my life, the loss of my father paralyzed me mentally and emotionally. Finally my mother insisted that I return as she needed for me to assist her financially as we were very poor and she understood my passion for baseball. I returned to Salem, Virginia where the team released me as I was completely distraught and unresponsive because of the loss of my father.

My mother encouraged Pete Zorrilla to try and speak some sense to me, and insist that I stay in the states to play ball as we needed the financial income and she wanted me to succeed.

Pete found a one hundred dollar contract for me to play with the Kokomo Giants for a ten day contract, as their third baseman had gotten hurt, Walt Dixon, the manager of the Kokomo team liked me and was kind and compassionate, as he and his wife assisted me greatly with my new life.

One time while playing with the Kokomo Giants, the team was travelling in the Midwest and I saw the first cross I had ever seen on a blaze of fire. Later I was told that it was the KU Klux Klan. I had no idea of what that meant, but shortly after that I witnessed several firsthand accounts of discrimination which I did not understand.

Even though life was a real challenge for me at the beginning, I have to share with you how grateful and absolutely blessed I have been with the opportunities that were available to me in this wonderful country. The San Francisco Giants provided so many of my favorite and most vivid memories! I was tremendously blessed to have the career that I did with the Giants, but also to have the opportunity to play with some of the most incredible people who played the game in my era!

1958, the year when I was called up by the San Francisco Giants as their first baseman, was a phenomenal year. That year the National League recognized me as the Rookie of the Year, a huge honor and distinction! It was obvious to me I was with a great organization. I was proud to be a Giant with their legendary history!

The San Francisco Giants was the first organization to seek and sign Latin ballplayers, and for several years the Giants had several Latino ballplayers on their major league roster when other major league teams had none. My respect for the Giants in this particular area is enormous as the Giants were the team that took a leadership role in providing golden opportunities for Hispanics. In the early 1960s, the Giants were pioneers in providing other talented players from around the world an opportunity to play major league baseball.

In 1958, my first year with Giants, we had Felipe Alou, Ruben Gomez, and me. In 1959 the Giants added Jose Pagan. Great strides were made in 1960 when we added my good friends Juan Marichal and Matty Alou. Within a couple years, the Giants included Manny Mota, Jose Cardenal and Jesus Alou. The Alou brothers were the only trio of brothers at the same time on a major league roster! In 1965, the Giants added the fleet-footed and multi-talented second baseman, Tito Fuentes out of Cuba. Learning a new culture along with a new language was made somewhat easier with other Latino ball players who were experiencing the same obstacles. The Giants were most definitely a family. To this very day, some of the individuals I mentioned are my closest friends.

Those early years were challenging and very difficult at times as most people in the United States had no experience with Latinos. I remember one time in Houston when I decided to go see a movie at the theater. Much to my amazement I was not allowed to enter—a shock to say the least! That mindset was common in certain parts of the country at that time.

Good Natured Ribbing

One funny story comes to mind when a couple of my Giants teammates and

Masanori Murakami had some good-natured fun. Murakami, the Giants' pitcher, was the first player from Japan in the major leagues. Murakami was proficient only in Japanese, and Jack Hiatt and a couple others taught him some English words. Herman Franks, the manager of the Giants, was a little roly poly to say the least. One day, Herman came to the pitchers' mound to remove Murakami from the game. When Herman was within a few feet, beginning to reach to take the ball, Murakami tried out his new English words. "Go back to the dugout, fatso!" Herman was not amused; however, he realized Murakami was simply the messenger.

Devastation

In 1966, after playing only 19 games for the Giants, I was traded to the St. Louis Cardinals. What was really strange was that I had just gone 11 for 15 with the Giants against the Cardinals in that series in St. Louis.

More than anything, the real hurt was the manner in which the trade was made and then revealed to me. It truly was heartbreaking for me as the Giants were my family. The Giants were playing the Cardinals in St. Louis. After the last game of the series, Giants Manager Herman Franks came to me in the dugout and literally said, "You're staying here!" My English at that time was still not very good. I looked and asked what he meant. Once again Herman said, "You've been traded to the Cardinals, so you are staying!" I felt as though a ton of bricks had just been dropped upon my head. Most players understand that trades are part of the game, but this particular experience was more than unpleasant, and it was not communicated in a cordial or respectful manner. I sat down and wept.

The trade was confusing to me for a number of reasons, but it became much clearer when San Francisco Giants' owner Horace Stoneham took the time to explain to me later in explicit detail the determining factors. Mr. Stoneham was extremely respectful and gracious, saying that my trade to the Cardinals was against his personal wishes and that the trade was not made strictly from a baseball perspective. Herman Franks was one of the central forces behind the trade to ship me off to St. Louis, and there were others behind the scenes who participated out of jealousies and were influential, according to Mr. Stoneham.

I took my baseball gear and walked across to the other clubhouse at Busch Memorial Stadium to join my new team. Tim McCarver, the fiery Cardinal catcher, was one of the first to welcome me, saying, "Orlando, you are now a Cardinal. Forget the Giants. We're glad you are with us!" McCarver was great to me as were all of the Cardinals. It was not long before I felt as though I belonged, and my heart became one with the Cardinal organization.

My new team flew immediately to Chicago to play the Cardinals' number one rival, the Cubs. In the very first game I played for them, I connected pretty well, driving a pitch deep over the outfield ivy for my new team. I have to admit I felt much better. Besides, the Cardinals were in the midst of building a championship team and I would have a major role in their future success.

Better Days

Later in 1966, when the Giants returned to St. Louis for a four-game series, I was in a 0 for 20 slump. However, seeing some of my good friends obviously perked me right up, and I delivered a double in the ninth inning to win the game and beat my former teammates. I was happy! Herman Franks, however, was not!

When the Cardinals made a west coast visit to play the Giants in San Francisco, I thought I had the Giants in an embarrassing moment. There was a controversial play with me being on first after delivering a single. The Giants were arguing with the umpire crew, and I realized time had not been called. That meant that the ball was still in play and therefore live! I moseyed off of first base and slowly walked towards second base without being noticed in with what I thought was an easy steal. There stood my good friend, Tito Fuentes. Tito looked at me and said, "Where do you think you are going?" He showed me his glove with the ball that he had cleverly hidden from me and tagged me out! I was screaming to no avail for timeout! It was embarrassing at the time, but it sure is funny now. My friend set me up and suckered me!

In 1967 the Cardinals were a great team. We had everything—speed, power, defense, and great pitching! Roger Maris had joined the Cardinals from the New York Yankees, and he once told me how amazed he was that I was able to almost single handedly defeat the San Francisco Giants that magical season each time the two teams met. I have to admit, I had some pretty good success against my former teammates.

Five times in 1967 I beat Gaylord Perry, one of the star pitchers with San Francisco. It seemed almost as though Gaylord was tipping his pitches, but I just was fortunate and had some success. Each time, though, I would look over into the Giants' dugout and scream loudly at Manager Herman Franks, "How's that trade working out for you, Herman?" Maris was a good guy and we had become good friends, and he would just shake his head at how many times I had been able to deliver the timely and game-ending defeats for Mr. Herman Franks.

The city of St. Louis is a great baseball city. The fans got behind the team early in that season as we were romping through the National League, nicknaming the Cardinals the "El Birdos!" Every time I came to bat, they would yell, "Come on, Cha Cha!" My nickname Cha Cha became known all over St. Louis. In 1967 in St. Louis, there was a love affair going on that included the Cardinal team, the city and all of the fans.

The Cardinals had a tremendous year in 1967 as we won 101 and lost 60. In addition I was voted the National League Most Valuable Player! Finally, one of my greatest dreams became a reality, when we won the World Series, defeating the talented Red Sox of Boston.

After all of these years though, I have returned to my first love, the Giants. I've been back with the Giants after my playing career ended, and I have been reunited with the organization that gave me my golden opportunities, my beloved Giants!

The Best of the Best

Orlando Cepeda

Best Fastball Juan Pizzaro	**Best Curveball** Sandy Koufax
Most Intimidating Pitcher Bob Gibson	**Best Right-Handed Pitcher** Juan Marichal
Best Left-Handed Pitcher Sandy Koufax	**Best Left-Handed-Reliever** Sparky Lyle
Best Right Handed-Reliever Goose Gossage	**Overall Most Challenging Pitcher** Bob Gibson
Best Right-Handed Hitter Rico Carty	**Best Left-Handed Hitter** Tony Oliva
Overall Best Clutch Hitter Hank Aaron	**Best Catcher** Johnny Bench
Best First Baseman Vic Power	**Best Second Baseman** Julian Javier
Best Shortstop Luis Aparicio	**Best Third Baseman** Brooks Robinson
Best Left Fielder Lou Brock	**Best Center Fielder** Willie Mays
Best Right Fielder Roberto Clemente	**Fastest Base Runner** Willie Davis
Best Base Runner Maury Wills	**Best Overall Opposing Player** Frank Robinson
Strongest Outfield Arm Ollie "Downtown" Brown	**Best Team Rival** Los Angeles Dodgers
Best Manager I Played For Red Schoendienst	**Most Trusted Friend** Tito Fuentes

My Favorite Team Mates
Hank Aaron, Bob Gibson, Lou Brock, Tim McCarver, Willie Mc-Covey, Curt Flood, Jose Pagan, Tito Fuentes

Funniest Player
Luis Tiant,
Bob Gibson,
Tim McCarver

Most Heart
Luis Tiant,
Juan Marichal,
Bob Gibson

Most Courageous
Willie McCovey
(Played even when he was in a unbelievable amount of pain!)

Best Work Ethics
Bob Gibson

Most Flamboyant
Tito Fuentes
(Made it look very easy, and was an excellent second baseman!)

Most Zany
Tito Fuentes

Most Congenial
Roger Maris, Tim McCarver,
Hank Aaron, Bob Gibson

My Favorite Team
St. Louis Cardinals Teams
1967 & 1968

Player I Most Admired
Hank Aaron

Player I Would Have Liked as a Team Mate
Tony Oliva

My Favorite Stadium
Wrigley Field

My Favorite City
New York

Best Baseball Announcer
Harry Carey

My Favorite Baseball Announcer
Harry Carey

The Best Umpire
Doug Harvey

Umpire with The Best Attitude
Doug Harvey,
Al Barlick

Most Respected Baseball Personality
Mike Murphy (S .F. Giants clubhouse manager for several decades)

Orlando Cepeda
Lifetime Statistics

Year	Age	Tm	Lg	G	PA	AB	R	H	2B	3B	HR	RBI	SB	CS	BB	SO	BA	OBP	SLG
1958	20	SFG	NL	148	644	603	88	188	38	4	25	96	15	11	29	84	.312	.342	.512
1959	21	SFG	NL	151	647	605	92	192		4	27	105	23	9	33	100	.317	.355	.522
1960	22	SFG	NL	151	615	569	81	169	36	3	24	96	15	6	34	91	.297	.343	.497
1961	23	SFG	NL	152	636	585	105	182	28	4	46	142	12	8	39	91	.311	.362	.609
1962	24	SFG	NL	162	676	625	105	191	26	1	35	114	10	4	37	97	.306	.347	.518
1963	25	SFG	NL	156	629	579	100	183	33	4	34	97	8	3	37	70	.316	.366	.563
1964	26	SFG	NL	142	587	529	75	161	27	2	31	97	9	4	43	83	.304	.361	.539
1965	27	SFG	NL	33	40	34	1	6	1	0	1	5	0	0	3	9	.176	.225	.294
1966	28	TOT	NL	142	563	501	70	151	26	0	20	73	9	9	38	79	.301	.361	.473
1966	28	SFG	NL	19	54	49	5	14	2	0	3	15	0	1	4	11	.286	.352	.510
1966	28	STL	NL	123	509	452	65	137	24	0	17	58	9	8	34	68	.303	.362	.469
1967	29	STL	NL	151	644	563	91	183	37	0	25	111	11	2	62	75	.325	.399	.524
1968	30	STL	NL	157	656	600	71	149	26	2	16	73	8	6	43	96	.248	.306	.378
1969	31	ATL	NL	154	636	573	74	147	28	2	22	88	12	5	55	76	.257	.325	.428
1970	32	ATL	NL	148	627	567	87	173	33	0	34	111	6	5	47	75	.305	.365	.543
1971	33	ATL	NL	71	276	250	31	69	10	1	14	44	3	6	22	29	.276	.330	.492
1972	34	TOT	MLB	31	94	87	6	25	3	0	4	9	0	0	7	17	.287	.340	.460
1972	34	ATL	NL	28	91	84	6	25	3	0	4	9	0	0	7	17	.298	.352	.476
1972	34	OAK	AL	3	3	3	0	0	0	0	0	0	0	0	0	0	.000	.000	.000
1973	35	BOS	AL	142	608	550	51	159	25	0	20	86	0	2	50	81	.289	.350	.444
1974	36	KCR	AL	33	117	107	3	23	5	0	1	18	1	0	9	16	.215	.282	.290

17-Year Totals

G	PA	AB	R	H	2B	3B	HR	RBI	SB	CS	BB	SO	BA	OBP	SLG
2124	8695	7927	1131	2351	417	27	379	1365	142	80	588	1169	.297	.350	.499

"Did You Know?"

The most career hits by a National League player who never lead the league in hits was Lou Brock with 3,023?

"Umpiring is best described as a profession of an individual standing between two seven year olds with only one ice cream cone." — Ron "Umpire" Luciano

The most career home runs by an American League player that never led the league in homers was Al Kaline with 399?

"So many ideas come to mind when you are in a hitting slump, that you want try them all. It is like being a mosquito at a nudist camp. You don't know where to start." — Reggie Jackson

HOF pitcher who had the most wins in the 1970s was Jim Palmer with 186.

Jim Davenport

Born August 17, 1933, Siluria, Alabama

Height 5'11'   **Weight** 170 lbs.

Bats Right   **Throws** Right

Debut April 15, 1958   **Final game** June 23, 1970

JIMMY DAVENPORT, an exceptional gentleman from Alabama, attended the University of Mississippi and was signed by the New York Giants as an amateur free agent in 1955. Jim made his major league debut on April 15, 1958, and played his last major league game for the San Francisco Giants on June 23, 1970.

Jimmy was put on the major league roster with the Giants in San Francisco primarily as a third baseman and had the good fortune to play his entire major league career for the Giants.

He played in one World Series with the Giants in 1962, the same year they defeated the Los Angeles Dodgers in a playoff game, thereby earning the right to play the New York Yankees for the World Championship. Entering the World Series, the Giants had a season team ERA similar to the Yankees, but had the edge on the

Yankees in every major offensive category including home runs, RBIs, and batting average. However, the Yankees defeated the Giants in the seventh game of a closely played series. It was a heartbreaking loss for the entire Giants team who had experienced a memorable summer. Jimmy won his Gold Glove in 1962 and in that same year he made an All-Star appearance. He hit a robust .297 for the season.

Davenport was well known and respected for being a slick fielding third baseman and one of the best glove men in baseball.

He finished his professional career with a lifetime batting average of .258, and 77 timely home runs in 13 major league seasons.

For several seasons he successfully served as a coach, and he had a brief stint as the Giants manager replacing Danny Ozark in 1985.

In 2006 Davenport was recognized by his home state, receiving the honor of being inducted into the Sports Hall of Fame in Alabama!

Currently Jimmy serves in a capacity of a roving coach within the minor league system enriching the future stars for the San Francisco Giants.

He and Betty, his wife of 47 years, reside in their home of San Carlos in Northern California.

Jimmy has had several triumphs in his baseball career, but none can compare to the fact that Jimmy Davenport is a fabulous and genuine ambassador for the great game of baseball. He is one of the true gentlemen of the game, and has always been an absolute delight for fans, players and management alike!

Jim Davenport

In My Own Words

Crazy Jesus!

Jesus Alou was a great teammate and a great guy who was well liked by just about everyone. He had an infectious smile and personality that was fun to be around. One time when the Giants were playing the St. Louis Cardinals, Jesus Alou was batting leadoff for us, and I was in the on deck circle, batting second. Bob Gibson, the great pitcher for the Cardinals, was on the mound that day for St. Louis. Jesus went to the batter's box to lead off, and Gibson threw three quick strikes consecutively to Jesus to strike him out. As Jesus came back towards the Giants bench, I asked him, "What's Gibson got today?" Jesus looked at me with that quirky smile of his, shook his head no, and said "Gibson ain't got crap. We will definitely light him up today!" Gibson struck out about sixteen Giants that day to beat us. Later on during the game, I was talking with Felipe Alou about what his brother had said to lead off the game, and we both laughed hysterically!

Jesus was just naturally funny. We use to laugh and tease Jesus by saying that he batted as if there were no catcher, and he was going to have to chase or retrieve the baseball himself if he missed the pitch. The reason we joked about that was because Jesus would swing at anything and everything! I even saw him get a base hit after the pitcher threw the ball to the plate in the dirt in front of the plate. Jesus golfed the baseball into the outfield for a hit! Jesus Alou was one of those great characters of the game.

Casey the Comedian

The only experiences I had with Casey Stengel were when he came over to the National League to manage the Mets. I heard stories from the Mets that every year at the beginning of spring training Casey would start the season by taking the entire team out to the infield. Casey would say, "Okay, boys. Follow me." He would then walk the team from home plate to first base. Casey would say, "Boys, this here is first base. It is very important you come here first when you get a hit or walk!" Then he would walk to second base and say, "Boys, this here is second base, and you run directly here right after first base." Then he would take the team to third base as he would say, "Boys, this here is third base and you run here directly from second base. Got it? Now we are almost complete with possibly scoring a run!" Then Casey would walk back to home plate as he would say, "Boys, if you make it this far, be sure to step directly on the plate, and believe it or not, we will have scored a run!" The players were cracking up as Ol' Casey made this a yearly event.

You're Out Of Here, Davenport!

Only twice in my career was I tossed out of games by umpires, the first time was by Chris Pelekoudas. I said to Pelekoudas, "Chris, you know that pitch was not a strike, and if you would get that big nose of yours out of the way, you would have seen much more clearly that pitch was not a strike." Pelekoudas did not think my comment was funny—and he tossed me out of the game!

Not Once, But Twice!

The Giants were in Phoenix for spring training, and our catcher and my room-mate, Jack Hiatt, loaned me his car, a brand new Cougar, as I wanted to go out to the dog track for some amusement. We agreed that I would drop by a nightclub later in the evening to see if he needed a ride back to the hotel. When I headed to the dog track, it was raining. I was coming down a side street to enter the parking lot at the dog track and I stopped at a red light. A car came through the red light, slammed his brakes on, and slid into the passenger's side of Hiatt's new car, damaging the fender. Fortunately, the Cougar was still drivable! I saw Ray Sadecki out at the dog track, offered him a ride, and he and I started to drive to the nightclub. As I came down a lane, I just barely eased the nose of the Cougar out to see if it was clear and wham-my! A police car with a mammoth push-bumper creamed the front end of Hiatt's new Cougar! The cop gave me a handful of tickets for entering from an illegal street and so forth. By now, the Cougar was demolished, and I go and find Hiatt. I said. "Jack, I got some bad news." He said, "You didn't have an accident, did you?" I said, "No, not one, but two!" Hiatt said, "Oh, no!" I was the one who had to go to court. When I got in front of the judge with the handful of tickets, the judge said, "Well, Mr. Davenport, this looks like a pretty good night for you!" He wasn't funny either.

Gaylord Perry, the Cheater

For years Gaylord was accused of cheating! Well, I've got proof that Gaylord did, in fact, cheat! Towards the end of the season we decided to create a little game: when we would return from a road trip, we would bet one dollar each on whose bags would be the first to come down the conveyer belt at the baggage claim at the airport. Gaylord won about five times in a row. A bunch of us would make re-marks, chuckling how Gaylord must have been cheating as he had that reputation. Anyway, it didn't matter, because he consistently collected our money. For the last road trip of the season, Gaylord's bags again were the first off the plane. I got to talking to Mike Murphy, our clubhouse manager, about Gaylord being so lucky. Murph laughed, explaining that earlier in the year Gaylord had made a deal with him to make sure his bags were first off each plane as long as we had that game go-ing. Gaylord told Murph that he would split his winnings. So the National League was correct—Gaylord Perry was a cheater! What we now understand was that he was willing to take our money by being in cahoots with Murph.

The Best of the Best

Best Fastball
Jim Maloney

Best Curveball
Sandy Koufax

Most Intimidating Pitcher
Don Drysdale & Bob Gibson

Best Right-Handed Pitcher
Juan Marichal & Bob Gibson

Best Left-Handed Pitcher
Sandy Koufax

Best Left-Handed Reliever
Ron Perranoski

Best Right-Handed Reliever
Elroy Face

Overall Most Challenging Pitcher
Juan Marichal

Best Right-Handed Hitter
Willie Mays

Best Left-Handed Hitter
Willie McCovey

Overall Best Clutch Hitter
Pete Rose & Tommy Davis

Best Catcher
Johnny Bench

Best First Baseman
Willie McCovey All Around
Wes Parker Defensively

Best Second Baseman
Joe Morgan

Best Shortstop
Ozzie Smith All Around
Ernie Banks Offensively

Best Third Baseman
Ron Santo
(I never played against Brooks Robinson)

Best Left Fielder
Billy Williams

Best Center Fielder
Willie Mays

Best Right Fielder
Roberto Clemente

Fastest Base Runner
Bobby Bonds
(Willie Davis would have been a close second)

Best Base Runner
Maury Wills

Best Overall Player
Pete Rose
(He became an All-Star at multiple positions)

Jim Davenport

Player Who Didn't Reach Maximum Potential
Ollie "Downtown" Brown

Best Team Rival
Los Angeles Dodgers
& San Francisco Giants
(No matter the standings or circumstances, there was excitement!)

Best Manager I Played For
Alvin Dark & Bill Rigney

My Favorite Team Mate
Harvey Kuehn & Bobby Bonds

Most Heart
Pete Rose
(He always played with intensity and had the heart of a champion!)

Best Work Ethics
Pete Rose
(Once again he played several positions & he worked constantly to make himself exceptional!)

Most Congenial
Ernie Banks (One of the nicest people anyone could ever meet anywhere!)

My Favorite Team
1962 San Francisco Giants
(This was a great group of guys who came together and won 103 games).

Strongest Outfield Arm
Roberto Clemente
(Bobby Bonds also had a great arm!)

Best Opposing Manager
Walter Alston & Sparky Anderson

Most Trusted Friend
Bobby Bonds

Funniest Player
Tito Fuentes & Ray Sadecki

Most Courageous
Frank Robinson

Most Flamboyant
Tito Fuentes
(No doubt about it. This guy was fun & entertaining for the fans & players!)

Most Zany
Jesus Alou
(Always fun loving and had something up always!)

Player I Most Admired
Ted Williams
(When I was growing up!)
Juan Marichal, Orlando Cepeda, Willie McCovey & Willie Mays
(Guys I played with)

Player I Would Have Liked as a Team Mate
Al Kaline
(Not only was he an exceptional all around great player, but a great gentleman!)

My Favorite City
Pittsburgh
(I always enjoyed the fans & I had great friends there!)

My Favorite Baseball Announcer
Lon Simmons

Umpire with The Best Attitude
Jocko Conlan

My Favorite Stadium
Dodger Stadium
(It was always jam packed with fans when the Giants played there!)

Best Baseball Announcer
Vin Scully

The Best Umpire
Doug Harvey
(When he was voted in the Hall Of Fame this year, I thought, "Boy, did he deserve it!)

Most Respected Baseball Personality
Alvin Dark
(Not only was he a good manager, but he is an extraordinary man!)

Jimmy Davenport
Lifetime Statistics

Year	Age	Tm	Lg	G	PA	AB	R	H	2B	3B	HR	RBI	SB	CS	BB	SO	BA	OBP	SLG
1958	24	SFG	NL	134	493	434	70	111	22	3	12	41	1	3	33	64	.256	.317	.403
1959	25	SFG	NL	123	510	469	65	121	16	3	6	38	0	1	28	65	.258	.301	.343
1960	26	SFG	NL	112	404	363	43	91	15	3	6	38	0	2	26	58	.251	.306	.358
1961	27	SFG	NL	137	503	436	64	121	28	4	12	65	4	3	45	65	.278	.342	.443
1962	28	SFG	NL	144	543	485	83	144	25	5	14	58	2	5	45	76	.297	.357	.456
1963	29	SFG	NL	147	509	460	40	116	19	3	4	36	5	2	32	87	.252	.297	.333
1964	30	SFG	NL	116	342	297	24	70	10	6	2	26	2	0	29	46	.236	.299	.330
1965	31	SFG	NL	106	302	271	29	68	14	3	4	31	0	0	21	47	.251	.304	.369
1966	32	SFG	NL	111	336	305	42	76	6	2	9	30	1	1	22	40	.249	.300	.370
1967	33	SFG	NL	124	347	295	42	81	10	3	5	30	1	4	39	50	.275	.366	.380
1968	34	SFG	NL	113	307	272	27	61	1	1	1	17	0	3	26	32	.224	.292	.246
1969	35	SFG	NL	112	339	303	20	73	10	1	2	42	0	1	29	37	.241	.304	.300
1970	36	SFG	NL	22	46	37	3	9	1	0	0	4	0	0	7	6	.243	.356	.270

13-Year Totals

G	PA	AB	R	H	2B	3B	HR	RBI	SB	CS	BB	SO	BA	OBP	SLG
1501	4981	4427	552	1142	177	37	77	456	16	25	382	673	.258	.318	.367

"Did You Know?"

Juan Marichal won 25 games three times and never received a single vote for the Cy Young Award.

" I can see how Sandy Koufax won twenty five games. What I don't understand is how did he lose five?"
— Yogi Berra

"It took me seventeen years to reach three thousand hits in baseball. I did it in one afternoon playing golf."
— Henry Aaron

Jim Maloney holds the record for the most walks (10) given up while pitching a no-hitter.

"Candlestick Park in San Francisco was built on the water, it should have been built under the water."
— Roger Maris

Tito 23 Fuentes

Born January 4, 1944, Havana, Cuba

Height 5'11"   **Weight** 175 lbs.

Bats Both   **Throws** Right

Debut August 18, 1965   **Final game** July 9, 1978

Tito Fuentes was born in Havana on the island of Cuba. As a teenager, he lived through the tumultuous period of the Cuban revolution in the 1950s. He was a bona fide star infielder for the Cuban National team in 1958, 1959 and 1960 and became one of Cuba's favorite stars. In Cuba, Tito played with other Cuban players—Jose Cardenal and Luis Tiant, for example—before they all made it to the major leagues. He was signed as an amateur free agent at eighteen years of age in 1962 by the San Francisco Giants. He was the last baseball player signed out of Cuba before the United States initiated the embargo against the Cuban nation.

Tito originally was signed as a shortstop, but a serious fracture of his right leg jeopardized his future. The prognosis of his medical specialist was that his career was over, but his love for the game and tenacious work ethics overcame all obstacles. Tito simply moved from shortstop to second base and continued on with his sterling career!

In the 1970s, the nimble second baseman was a regular starter for the San Francisco Giants. He was exceptional on defense and had more range than any other national league second baseman of his era. Tito's lightening quickness and ability to elude base runners allowed him to play his entire 13-year career without ever being spiked, up-ended or even touched by opponents. Opposing players and even managers often placed a bounty on taking him out at second base. Of course Tito would incite his opponents by offering them a hand up, facetiously attempting to assist them. Frequently he would tell them if they were to touch him with their slides, he would give them $5, and if they could knock him down during the play, he would give them $10. It was all good-natured ribbing and fun from Tito's perspective, but he drove opposing base runners bananas with his aloof and comical antics. On defense, he presented a flashy persona in the field.

He set a national league record when, in 1973 with the Giants, he committed only six errors with a .993 fielding percentage while playing an incredible 160 games.

He was the ideal second hitter—he was a switch hitter who rarely struck out. He had the ability to accurately place the ball in the field where he wanted to advance his team's runners. In 1973 he drove in 78 runs while hitting second in the lineup. In 1977, playing for the Detroit Tigers, he drove in 83 runners and hit a robust .309 batting average for the season with 190 hits.

One dubious honor that the flashy Cuban still holds is being struck by three pitches in one game by the same pitcher, still a major league record.

In addition he had major league service with the San Diego Padres, Detroit Tigers and the Oakland A's.

Tito was one of the most unique, entertaining and colorful stars of the entire era of the 1960s and '70s! Each time he would approach the batter's box, he would flip his bat in the air and catch it with precision as if he were a magician. He is still a favorite of the San Francisco fans—they especially like the way he makes himself available and his fun-loving attitude. Today when he is announced on the field at AT&T Park for special presentations and ceremonies, he is given an incredible ovation with the fans exuberantly demonstrating their approval of him. They respond to him in a very appreciative and loving way! Walking through the streets or the stadium, he is accessible to almost everyone and wears his celebrity status in the most accommodating manner.

In 2002, Tito officially changed his name by adding his famed number 23, thereby becoming Tito 23 Fuentes!

A career .268 hitter barely tells the story of his terrific 13-year career: he was a multi talented individual who created ways to manufacture and produce runs for his teams.

He was voted by the San Francisco fans as the starting second baseman for the 25th anniversary Giants dream team.

Tito was inducted into the Cuban Baseball Hall of Fame in 1997. In 2002, he was inducted into the Hispanic Heritage Baseball Museum.

Tito currently is entering his seventh season as the Hispanic analyst with the San Francisco Giants along with his play-by-play announcer, Erwin Higueros. Together they form an outstanding team as they clearly and poetically describe the game highlights for their loyal listening audience.

Prior to entering his contract with the Giants, Tito served as a member of Spanish broadcast team with Fox Sports International 1981–1992 and 1996–2004.

Today's players could do well in emulating the gregarious Tito 23 in his endeavors and in recognizing his gratitude, and respect for, not only the fans, but people all over the world!

In My Own Words

WHEN I WAS FIRST ASKED to share some of my stories, I thought to myself, what stories? But, after thinking about some of the great people and the era when I was fortunate enough to play, I am pleased to share the memories that have been in the back of my mind for several years.

First of all, baseball today is so different than when we played in my era of the 1960s and 1970s. To me, baseball was more of a game back then. Today, it is still the same rules and overall goals of playing for championships, but the fun aspects of the game and the great camaraderie we experienced appear to have been greatly diminished because of the business aspects of today's game. It is too bad that the players today view baseball more as a business than a game. During my era, the enjoyment we experienced was immense, and truly, baseball was played at the major league level as a game. After all, it is suppose to be a fun! But make no mistake, the players today are delightful people and are mere tools of today's business climate created by the owners and business agents. Also, I wish that the teams today would make more effort and focus towards the fundamentals of the game. It is amazing to me that teams are willing to forego and ignore the significance of daily infield practice before each game.

Now here are some of my fond stories and memories. Yesterday's players and games were light hearted and almost every day there were lots of fun times. I'll give you a few examples.

Cepeda Was "Confused"

In my rookie year, the Giants went to Cincinnati to play the Reds at Crosley Field. Orlando Cepeda and I were roommates, and after one of the games Orlando and I went back to our hotel room. The phone rang and Orlando answered the phone, and the person on the other end of the phone asked for Tito. Orlando told the person they had the wrong number. Then the caller said they wanted to speak with Tito Fuentes. Orlando told the caller to ask for the person by the last name and handed me the phone. After the call, I walked over to the window and pulled the curtains back looking into the night's sky. After a couple of minutes, Orlando asked me what I was staring at. I told him that the caller told me that there was a lunar eclipse. Orlando then looked at me and said, "Do you realize Jim Maloney is pitch ing tomorrow?" I looked at him and shrugged my shoulders. I was just brought up into the big leagues and I had no idea about Jim Maloney. Orlando could not believe that here I was, this young big leaguer about to face one of the toughest pitchers on the planet and I was gazing at the sky. I became educated the next day regarding Jim Maloney!

The Hero

The Giants were playing the Dodgers at Candlestick Park in 1972 and Bobby Bonds was batting leadoff; I always batted second, right behind him. As usual, the Dodgers and the Giants were playing a tight game, and it went into extra innings. In the eleventh inning, Walter Alston, the manager of the Dodgers, brought in Jim Brewer, their great left-handed reliever, to take the mound. Brewer was tough as he had an excellent screwball that sharply broke away from the right-handed hitters. Bobby went to bat against Brewer in the eleventh and struck out on three pitches. The people closest to the pitching mound are the hitter, of course, the catcher, the umpire, and then the next batter who is standing at the on-deck circle. The hitters in the on-deck circle are always watching closely for the velocity of the pitch as well as the movement and there I was watching. When Bobby was on his way to return to our dugout after striking out, he passed by me, and I simply asked him, "What is he throwing today?" He looked at me as he growled, "What game are you watching, chump?" Weren't you paying attention when he threw the pitches? He threw strikes!"

I proceeded towards home plate where I did not want to be—I was uncomfortable with the idea of facing Brewer as I had not had very much success against him. During my at-bat against Brewer he got ahead of me in the count as he threw two strikes and one ball. His next pitch he threw was a screwball which did not break sharply—in fact he hung it! I hit a fly ball to left field and for some strange reason the wind was blowing towards Candlesticks' left field fence. To my surprise, the ball proceeded in flight over the left field wall for a game-winning home run—the Giants defeated the Dodgers in eleven innings. Of course Bobby was one of the first to greet me at home plate with that big infectious grin he had. But, believe me, Jim Brewer was a tough lefty, and he practically owned me!

Where Is Our Second Baseman?

Early on in my first year in the big leagues, Herman Franks was the manager of the Giants. We were playing the Cubs in Wrigley Field when there was some disruption on the field—a controversy and argument which did not include me. After a minute or so, I ran to the Giants' dugout where Lon Simmons, the Giants broadcaster, placed the microphone to conduct the post game show with the star of the game. For some reason I decided to pick up the headset and was surprised— I was listening to Lon Simmons broadcast the game live on the field. I was intrigued as he was explaining in detail of what was taking place with the disruption between the two teams and the umpire crew. Well, our manager Herman Franks returned to the Giants' dugout after making his point with the umpires, and the game was ready to proceed, except one minor detail. The Giants second baseman was nowhere to be found on the playing field! I was so mesmerized by the announcer Lon Simmons! This was the first time I had heard him and I was enjoying his broadcast. Then all of a sudden, I heard Lon Simmons say over the radio airwaves, "Where is Tito? The Giants cannot find their second baseman!" Then I finally woke up from my short daydream. Herman Franks saw me on the bench with the headphones on my head and started yelling at me to get my butt out to my position at second! I have to admit, it was a brief embarrassment! But I was fully informed of what had just taken place. I also realized firsthand what an awesome announcer Lon was!

My Buddy, Gaylord!

The year was 1969 and Gaylord was having a great year—he won 19 games and had a 2.49 era for the year. Clyde King was the so-called manager. He and I did not get along, and, because of that, he did not want to play me. Gaylord and I would play an infield routine before the game where someone would hit grounders to us with a fungo bat. Our game was this: whoever missed the most grounders had to be the other one's personal butler until game time, retrieving cokes, sunflower seeds, etc. Gaylord was excellent and would often win. But he also knew I was the more proficient second baseman. Finally he went to Clyde King and told him that when he pitched, he wanted Tito 23 Fuentes at second base on defense to increase his odds of winning. Then Juan Marichal did the same, and pretty soon the other starting pitchers insisted that I play second base when they were pitching. If it were not for Gaylord Perry having the guts to step forward on behalf of the team, I would have perhaps been ostracized even longer because of personal issues and vendettas. Instead, this was the best decision for the overall benefit of the team. I always respected Gaylord for having the guts to face the so-called manager with the facts!

Bench – the Comedian

I always had the same routine of twirling the bat which became pretty well known around the league; and it was entertaining for the fans. Just before I was ready to hit, I would throw my bat on the rubber plate at home to flip it spinning up into my hands all the while looking at the third base coach, and not at my bat. One time when the Giants were playing the Reds in Cincinnati, I threw my bat at the rubber home plate, looked at my third base coach and was waiting for the bat to enter my hands like always. Only the bat never came back to me. After a second or two, I glanced to locate my bat. Johnny Bench had reached out and grabbed my bat. Since I never looked at my bat, I looked like a clown with my hands out waiting for my bat to return to my hands. I turned around after what seemed like forever, and there was Bench laughing hysterically, rolling on the ground looking up at me. He handed my bat back to me, and as I looked around the infield, I saw Pete Rose,

Davy Conception, Joe Morgan and Tony Perez with their hands over their mouths trying not to let me see them laughing. The umpire also must have been in on the prank as he did not issue any warnings and in fact allowed the incident. It was humorous to everyone except me. Even though it was at my expense and initially an embarrassing moment for me, it was also very funny and eventually I had to laugh also! Now that I look back on the incident, it is even funnier! It illustrates once again how baseball was fun and the players realized it was still a game that we were playing! We looked for ways to have fun and enjoy our moments in the limelight.

Jesus Versus Willie

In the early sixties, Jesus was one of the three Alou brothers who played together on the Giants team. The team went to Cincinnati to play the Reds. The Reds had a young phenom pitcher who was called up to the big leagues in September—late in the season. He was pitching aspirin tablets! Jesus Alou went to the plate four times and collected four hits. Willie Mays came to the plate and struck out four times. The next day Jesus showed me the local newspaper, and Willie was the big story because he had struck out four times. Jesus looked me with a funny grin and shaking his head. He said, "Can you believe it? I have the game of the season for me and do not make an out, and Willie has a terrible time at the plate and he still captures the headlines?" We both chuckled as Jesus was just being funny, but Willie was almost always the main story.

Doug Harvey

It is great that Doug made it to the Hall of Fame because he was the best umpire in our era and is a fine gentleman. He was not always easy, but he was always fair and a true professional who was as consistent as an umpire could ever possibly be.

One time the Giants were playing in San Diego, and it was early in the game, maybe the second or third inning. I was playing third base that day, and for some reason I wanted to leave the game early. So I attempted to pick an argument with Doug who was the third base umpire that day. Doug was almost always in control and kept his cool. He looked at me, smirking as he said, "Kid, I know what you are trying to pull, and it is not going to work. It's a nice day to play a game, I have to stay for nine innings, and you might as well also! I would like for you stay with me out here today. So, forget about your shenanigans and enjoy the game and the day."

Today's Players

The players today are extremely talented. They are stronger! They have the opportunities to work out and train all year round with access to videos, personal trainers, in home gymnasiums, etc. Some of the people who are exciting that I would be willing to pay or watch play are Tim Lincecum, Pablo "Panda" Sandoval, CC Sabathia, Matt Kemp, Ichiro Suzuki, and Ryan Howard! There are several other young players who are extremely talented and exciting, but these I believe are worth the price of admission alone and would enjoy immensely watching them play. One player who was tremendous was Roberto Alomar. In my opinion the best two players I saw play were Roberto Clemente and Roberto Alomar.

In closing

Baseball is the same game, but the attitudes and the approach to the game is much different than from my era. It seems to me that players would be more fundamentally sound if the infielders would take grounders before each game as we did. The same with the outfielders. Coaches used to hit fly balls with fungo bats for the outfielders to reinforce their routes or patterns to fly balls. All players would benefit if they would make themselves more accessible at the ball parks for the fans! Some of my fondest memories are with fans at the ball parks before and after the games.

The Best of the Best

Best Fastball
J.R. Richard
(J.R.'s fastball was truly explosive.)

Best Curveball
Sandy Koufax
(I never faced a better curveball, and it was a real challenge, not only for me but several within the league.)

Most Intimidating Pitcher
Bob Gibson & Goose Gossage
(I faced Gibson a lot, and from my personal experience, you had better be ready at all times when you were standing in that batters box!)

Best Right-Handed Pitcher
Juan Marichal
(With the Giants for years I witnessed firsthand the leagues extreme difficult task in facing Juan's multiple pitches and deliveries.)

Best Left-Handed Pitcher
Sandy Koufax
(Without question in my mind. He could make hitters wake up in the middle of the night thinking about facing him the next day.)

Best Left-Handed Reliever
Ron Perranoski
(Steady and consistent!)

Best Right-Handed Reliever
Mike Marshall

Overall Most Challenging Pitcher
Juan Marichal
(Juan had several pitches and release points and could be intimidating also!)

Best Right-Handed Hitter
Roberto Clemente & Hank Aaron
(With the game on the line, these two were both like money in the bank.)

Overall Best Clutch Hitter
Orlando Cepeda & Billy Williams
(Orlando was unbelievable with his courage at the plate. He never gave an inch and seemed to always drive the ball in clutch situations!)

Best Catcher
Johnny Bench

Best First Baseman
Orlando Cepeda
(Every baseball fan from the era realizes Orlando was an exceptional hitter, but he also was a very good first baseman!)

Best Second Baseman
Joe Morgan & Julian Javier

Best Shortstop
Zoilo Versalles
(Often over looked, and perhaps under rated but was outstanding!)

Best Third Baseman
Mike Schmidt

Best Left Fielder
Billy Williams

Best Center Fielder
Willie Mays & Curt Flood
(Curt Flood I believe is often over looked for his all around talent and ability. Of course everyone knows of Willie, but Curt also was exceptional as a centerfielder!)

Best Right Fielder
Roberto Clemente
(Clemente was simply the best!)

Fastest Base Runner
Willie Davis
(From first to third and from first to home, no one was faster. Bobby Bonds is an honorable mention.)

Best Base Runner
Maury Wills
(Maury was not only exceptionally quick, but was a very intelligent base runner!)

Best Overall Opposing Player
Roberto Clemente
(It was a delight to play against such a fabulous all around talent!)

Player Who Didn't Reach Maximum Potential
Cesar Cedeno & Dick Allen

Strongest Outfield Arm
Downtown Ollie Brown & Roberto Clemente

(Ollie often gets over looked, but for those who played with him, or against him know firsthand he had a cannon!)

Best Team Rival
Los Angeles Dodgers & San Francisco Giants
(Way too many personal encounters for anything else!)

Best Opposing Manager
No such thing in my mind

Best Manager I Played For
John McNamara
(John always had the door to communication wide open, and he was fair.)

Funniest Player
Doc Ellis

Most Heart
Everyone
(To face a 95 mph plus fastball, or to stand on the pitchers mound within sixty feet six inches of fearsome hitters took heart!)

Most Flamboyant
Willie Montanez

Most Zany
Joe Pepitone

My Favorite Team
Brooklyn Dodgers
(Because Jackie Robinson broke the color line and he played second base, and besides he was a true hero of mine!)

Player I Most Admired
Roberto Clemente

Player I Would Have Liked as a Team Mate
Babe Ruth, Jackie Robinson & Maury Wills!
(Jackie Robinson was my favorite player, and Maury Wills is my favorite person. Babe Ruth was an icon!)

My Favorite Stadium
Dodger Stadium
(It was always packed when the Giants played with a lot of anticipation!)

My Favorite City
Los Angeles, Chicago & New York
(Each city has its own great assets, but these three I most looked forward to visiting because of the cultures, language and restaurants; they have the largest Latin population.)

Best Baseball Announcer
Vin Scully
(Vin is the most recognized, but I never had the opportunity to listen to him. Everyone who knows baseball realizes Vin Scully is great! But, I also have to mention Lon Simmons who in his own right was absolutely incredible with his stories and his rich baritone voice.)

My Favorite Baseball Announcer

Lon Simmons
(Once again, I have to say the voice of the Giants, our very own Lon Simmons was my favorite! Bob Prince, Pittsburgh Pirates, I wanted to mention also as a favorite.)

Umpire with The Most Charisma

Ron Luciano
(I only played briefly in the American League, but Luciano was a character and I looked forward to the times he was part of the umpire crew, as he was always enjoyable.)

The Best Umpire

Doug Harvey
(Too many stories to remember with this gentleman, and he was always fair and accurate!)

Most Meaningless Record

Most consecutives games played!
(It is unbelievable that so much attention is given to a record that does not matter. This record does not help a team win games, in fact it is a selfish record.)

Tito Fuentes

Tito 23 Fuentes
Lifetime Statistics

Year	Age	Tm	Lg	G	PA	AB	R	H	2B	3B	HR	RBI	SB	CS	BB	SO	BA	OBP	SLG
1965	21	SFG	NL	26	78	72	12	15	1	0	0	1	0	1	5	14	.208	.269	.222
1966	22	SFG	NL	133	564	541	63	141	21	3	9	40	6	3	9	57	.261	.276	.360
1967	23	SFG	NL	133	383	344	27	72	12	1	5	29	4	3	27	61	.209	.266	.294
1969	25	SFG	NL	67	203	183	28	54	4	3	1	14	2	4	15	25	.295	.350	.366
1970	26	SFG	NL	123	490	435	49	116	13	7	2	32	4	5	36	52	.267	.323	.343
1971	27	SFG	NL	152	672	630	63	172	28	6	4	52	12	2	18	46	.273	.299	.356
1972	28	SFG	NL	152	634	572	64	151	33	6	7	53	16	5	39	56	.264	.310	.379
1973	29	SFG	NL	160	731	656	78	182	25	5	6	63	12	6	45	62	.277	.328	.358
1974	30	SFG	NL	108	428	390	33	97	15	2	0	22	7	3	22	32	.249	.293	.297
1975	31	SDP	NL	146	613	565	57	158	21	3	4	43	8	8	25	51	.280	.309	.349
1976	32	SDP	NL	135	559	520	48	137	18	0	2	36	5	3	18	38	.263	.287	.310
1977	33	DET	AL	151	673	615	83	190	19	10	5	51	4	4	38	61	.309	.348	.397
1978	34	OAK	AL	13	45	43	5	6	1	0	0	2	0	0	1	6	.140	.159	.163

13-Year Totals

G	PA	AB	R	H	2B	3B	HR	RBI	SB	CS	BB	SO	BA	OBP	SLG
1499	6073	5566	610	1491	211	46	45	438	80	47	298	561	.268	.307	.347

"Did You Know?"

Rick Monday while playing in the outfield for the Chicago Cubs sprinted to confiscate an American flag that two protesters were preparing to burn on the field during the game at Dodger stadium in 1976.

"The kid doesn't drink, curse, chew tobacco, or chase broads, I do not see any way that he can make it!" — Richie Ashburn

In 1971 the Baltimore Orioles had four 20 game winners. Jim Palmer, Mike Cuellar, Pat Dobson and Dave McNally.

"In the olden days a umpire didnt have to take courses in psychology, the pitcher would tell you he was going to throw at you!" — Leo Durocher

"A baseball game is simply a nervous breakdown divided into nine innings." — Earl Wilson

Harold Douglas Harvey

Born March 13, 1930, South Gate, California
Height 6'2 **Weight** 195 lbs.
Debut April 10, 1962 **Final Game** Oct. 4, 1992

Harold Douglas Harvey was born in South Gate, California, on March 13, 1930. Doug was the finest major league umpire of his era, and arguably of all time. Doug had the respect of the National League players for his knowledge of the rules and consistency. There is no doubt that Doug Harvey is one of baseball's most respected and famous umpires!

His reputation among his peers and within the professional baseball circles was that of an extremely dedicated professional umpire who had an authoritative command of the game and the rules. When he retired in 1992, Doug ranked third with 4,670 games umpired at the major league level. Doug was often revered, and some the players would respectfully refer to him as "god." He did not necessarily embrace the tongue-in-cheek moniker, but realized that the nickname was strictly one of humor and great respect. The players knew and acknowledged that he wanted to get the calls right and to be objective, and fair to everyone!

At 16 years old Harvey began his career by officiating at high school basketball, softball, and baseball games. Later at San Diego State College in 1955 and 1956, he played both baseball and football. Doug had no hero as a young man, but as a player he attempted to emulate Stan Musial's quirky batting stance. After his collegiate experiences, Doug officiated at college basketball and football games.

From 1958—1960 he umpired in the California League and in 1961 umpired in the Pacific Coast League.

On September 24, 1960, Doug married his sweetheart, Joy Ann Glascock. Joy and Doug had two sons, Scott and Todd. The Harveys are currently residing in their central California home and enjoying his new Hall-of-Fame Baseball selection, honoring what he has deserved and achieved!

Doug recognizes three umpires—Shag Crawford, Al Barlick, and Jocko Conlan—who mentored him and were positive influences early in his career on the major league scene in 1962.

Al Barlick was Doug's first crew chief when he first arrived in the big leagues. He became great friends with Shag, as Crawford later became the crew chief after Barlick retired. Some of the most admirable traits Doug respected in Shag were his honor, his unwavering courage, and his steadfast attitude no matter what the obstacles or circumstances were.

Doug first umpired in the majors at the grand opening of the new Dodger Stadium in 1962. Dodger Stadium naturally was packed with 52,564 enthusiastic fans. Al Barlick was behind the dish at home plate. Shag Crawford was at first base. Ed Vargo was at second base, and Doug took his first position in Dodger Stadium at third base. Before the game, Barlick, the crew chief, walked over to Doug and asked him, "Well, what do you think of this joint, kid?" Being a farm boy, Doug said, "I can tell you one thing. I sure could stack a lot of hay in this place!"

Doug went on to a sterling career, umpiring five World Series in 1968, 1974, 1981, 1984, and 1988. In addition, he worked All-Star games in 1963, 1964, 1971, 1977, 1982 and 1992. Doug also set a record for umpiring nine National League Championship Series, a record which has since been broken by Bruce Froemming.

Later in his career, he became known and recognizable during the weekly Game-of-the-Week segments named, "You Make the Call!"

In 1990, Sport Magazine named Doug the best umpire in the game, based on his ethics, his relentless application of the rules, and his steadfastness in enforcing the balk move!

Some notable games he umpired were August 22, 1965, Roseboro and Marichal incident; Roberto Clemente, 3,000th hit; the three Alou brothers' game at Candlestick, and many more!

Some of Doug's greatest achievements were his introduction to the timing of his calls. For decades umpires had anticipated calls on instinct instead of waiting to see the play, resulting in incorrect or questionable calls. In Doug's early days in the big leagues, it was common for the umpires to make calls quickly. He even has a photograph of Jocko Conlan making a call while the ball was still in flight and the runner was still short of the bag—he remembers it well! He valued getting the call accurate over making a speedy call. Doug was persistent in his encouragement of other umpires and made a positive impact by delaying calls for the sake of accuracy and proficiency.

We are fortunate to preserve the historical perspectives of perhaps the greatest umpire in major league history.

My Own Words

San Diego Chicken

THE SAN DIEGO CHICKEN MASCOT was at the height of his popularity when my umpire crew was in Jack Murphy stadium in my hometown, San Diego. This time I was behind home plate and I looked down the third base line just in time to witness the Chicken take a towel and put it around the neck of one of my fellow umpires. I immediately walked down to third base to put an end to the nonsense, and the Chicken placed his knee in the middle of the third base umpires back. Believe me, I was not pleased! When I was close to them, I picked up the Chicken, costume and all, and threw him into the first row of the stands! The crowd absolutely roared. Although I always liked the San Diego Chicken, that day I felt he crossed the line of prudence and respect in his behavior towards one of my fellow umpires.

Frank Robinson

One day, as Frank Robinson came towards home plate to bat, he was mumbling and grumbling and growling under his breath. Approaching, he was even more deliberate getting into the batter's box. I asked Frank, "What's the matter, Frank?" Frank continued his grumbling and was reluctant to get ready to hit. I told Frank to get into the batter's box. Frank refused! I signaled for the pitcher to throw the ball. "Strike one!" Frank mumbled and growled some more. I told Frank once again to get in the batter's box. Frank said, "I'll get into the batter's box when I am good and ready!" He refused again. I motioned for the pitcher to continue. "Strike two!" Frank growled some more. Shag Crawford, first base umpire and the crew chief, trotted towards us at home plate and asked me what the heck was going on. I explained. Shag told Frank that he was going to trot back to his first base umpiring position, and if Frank was not standing in position when he reached the halfway point toward first base, he would eject him! When Shag got halfway, he turned and looked. Frank was still not in the batter's box! Shag tossed Frank! The Cincinnati Reds manager, Dick Sisler, came charging out of the Reds' dugout to protest his superstar's ejection. Shag and Sisler got into a very heated argument, and then Sisler challenged Shag to fisticuffs. Shag told Sisler he would meet him after the game. Shag was a man's man and he wouldn't back down ever! Even though Shag was the crew chief, I later told Shag in our umpires' dressing room I would have handled the circumstances with Frank Robinson differently!

The Nickname

The New York Mets were playing the Padres in San Diego and San Diego

Padres were leading their division. It was late in the season and every game was, of course, significant for them. Padres' player Steve Garvey had slipped out-fielding a ball, and the next inning I called a rain delay. My umpire partner Joe West went into the Padres' dugout. Garvey asked West if anyone had checked the field conditions. West said, "Yes, the Chief always checks the field conditions!" referring to me. Terry Kennedy, the Padres catcher sitting in the dugout close to Garvey and West said, "That doesn't count, because that SOB walks on water." Soon after that, other guys around the league started calling me "god." A few games later, my crew went to Chicago to umpire a Cubs series. Jerry Holtzman, the famed Chicago sportswriter, asked one of the umpires what I was doing out on the field before the game. My crew told Holtzman the story about the rain delay in San Diego and Terry Kennedy's comment about me. The next day in the Chicago newspaper, Holtzman wrote in his newspaper column, "god visits Chicago!" That was my nickname from then on!

Pete Rose

Pete had an exceptional eye and was a magician with the bat. One time when I was behind the plate calling balls and strikes, I called a strike when Pete was at bat. Pete jumped up in the batter's box and said "Harv, you know darn well that pitch was not a strike!" I waited to respond until the pitcher was completing his windup and then released the next pitch. I replied, "Pete, you may be right. That pitch could have been a quarter of an inch outside. Then again, at fifty-eight years old my eyes aren't what they use to be." Pete got on base, and after reaching first, he pointed at me jawing to the first base umpire! I just looked towards first base at Pete, and he realized he better stop jawing at me.

Humorous

When umpiring any game, I always believed that players and managers ejected themselves from games, as I always warned them what the boundaries were. This one particular time, however, was a little different. Sparky Anderson, the Hall-of-Fame Manager for the Cincinnati Reds, came running out on the field to protest a call I had made. He said, "Doug, you are probably going to run me out of the game when I am finished with you!" I looked at Sparkey and said, "No, I am not, Sparkey! You're out of here right now! There is no use wasting any more of your time or mine."

The Best of the Best

Best Fastball
Jim Maloney, Bob Gibson, Juan Marichal, Sandy Koufax

Best Curveball
Sandy Koufax
(Fell off the table, no one close)

Most Intimidating Pitcher
Bob Gibson

Best Right-Handed Pitcher
Bob Gibson
(If I could select a pitcher against the devil for all of the souls, I would choose Bob Gibson! He would complain about everything!)

Best Left-Handed Pitcher
Sandy Koufax

Overall Most Challenging Pitcher
Don Drysdale
(Absolute control and unbelievable movement!)

Best Right-Handed Hitter
Willie Mays
(If Willie had played anywhere other than Candlestick, he would be the all-time home run king!)

Best Left-Handed Hitter
Stan Musial
(After Stan would get two strikes, he would swing at anything within four inches)

Overall Best Clutch Hitter
Pete Rose
(He could hit a line drive on his deathbed!)

Best Catcher
Johnny Bench

Best First Baseman
Willie McCovey

Best Second Baseman
Joe Morgan -all around;
Bill Mazeroski - defensively only

Best Third Baseman
Mike Schmidt

Best Shortstop
Ozzie Smith

Best Left Fielder
Stan Musial

Best Center Fielder
Willie Mays

Best Right Fielder
Roberto Clemente

Fastest Base Runner
Willie Davis

Best Base Runner
Willie Davis
(He took 9 steps from first base to
second base!)

Strongest Outfield Arm
Roberto Clemente

Best Manager
Walter Alston, Sparky Anderson,
Gil Hodges

My Favorite Team Mate
Shag Crawford
(Best guy I ever umpired with!!)

Most Heart
Pete Rose (He accomplished the
absolute most with what he had!)

Most Flamboyant
Every one of them!

Most Zany
Jimmy Piersall

Player I Most Admired
Sandy Koufax and Stan Musial

**Player Who Didn't Reach
Maximum Potential**
Steve Dolkowski

Best Team Rival
L.A. Dodgers & S.F. Giants

Most Trusted Friend
Every umpire on God's Green
Earth

Funniest Player
None of them were funny. It was a
serious job to me and I took it
seriously

Most Courageous
Don Drysdale (He played with the
painful shingles.)

Most Congenial
Bill Mazeroski and Stan Musial

My Favorite Team
Does not exist. The ones that kept
their mouths shut!

**Player I Would Have Liked
as a Team Mate**
Don Drysdale (Absolutely no fear!)

My Favorite Stadium
Dodger Stadium

Best Baseball Announcer
Vin Scully

The Best Umpire
Shag Crawford

My Favorite City
Chicago

**My Favorite Baseball
Announcer**
Vin Scully

**Most Respected Baseball
Personality**
Vin Scully

"Did You Know?"

George Foster hit the most home runs (52) in a season during the 1970s.

"Baseball is the only sport I know that when you are on offense, the other team controls the ball." — Ken Harrelson

Stan Musial was the only player to lead the major leagues in extra base hits seven times.

"If a horse can't eat it, I don't want to play on it!" — Dick Allen on artificial turf

"What does a mama bear on the pill have in common with the World Series? No Cubs." — Harry Carey

Willie Horton

Born October 18, 1942, Arno, Virginia

Height 5' 11"   **Weight** 209 lbs.

Bats Right   **Throws** Right

Debut Sept. 10, 1963   **Final game** Oct. 5, 1980

WILLIAM HORTON, born in Arno, Virginia, was the youngest of 21 children. Early in Willie's life, his family moved to Detroit. As a young man, Willie overcame great obstacles learning to live in the projects of Detroit. Soon he became a local hometown favorite to the fans of Detroit, displaying his athletic prowess on the baseball diamonds of Detroit.

Willie's major league baseball career spanned 18 years, 14 of which were spent with the local team, his beloved Tigers.

The most memorable baseball season for Willie and the Detroit Tigers was the phenomenal year 1968. The Detroit Tigers went on to defeat the former World Champion St. Louis Cardinals in seven games. He, along with his mega-talented close-knit teammates, faced the incomparable pitcher, Bob Gibson. Gibson of the Cardinals had just completed his sterling year, dominating the National League with his unbelievable 1.12 ERA! Willie played a huge role in defeating the mighty Cardinal team batting .304 for the 1968 World Champions! He hit a home run and had 3 RBIs in assisting with the stunning victory for his city of Detroit! In addition, Willie threw out the fleet-footed and surprised Lou Brock trying to score at home plate in game 5. This game was one of the most memorable defensive gems in the history of the World Series!

At the end of his impressive career, his statistics consisted of a lifetime batting average of .273, 325 career home runs, 1163 RBIs, and 1,993 career hits! He was more than an accomplished power hitter. He also was an effective defensive player patrolling left field.

In both 1975 and 1979 he won the American League Designated Hitter award. In addition, two times he won the American League Come-Back Player of the Year.

Willie was selected seven times to play in the All-Star game representing the American League!

On July 15th, 2000, Willie received the highest honor bestowed by the Detroit Tigers when he was chosen to be inducted into the Tigers Hall of Fame. In addition, they retired his famous #23 jersey, and unveiled the "Willie Horton" bronze statue to grace the new Tigers' home, Comerica Park!

The Michigan State Legislature passed a bill designating October 18 to be recognized state-wide as "Willie Horton Day"!

Willie never took his high level of success for granted, but always graciously thanked the Detroit Tigers for providing the opportunities for him to display his passion of his first love, baseball.

He exhibits his heart while providing ways to give back to the community in numerous manners and on several levels. He is just as humble off the field as he was in a Tigers uniform! Willie Horton's vision has been to assist communities by using his talents, championing others who are less fortunate. He believes that people working together can make great strides to improve the lives of those in need. Willie is a visionary who produces positive results for the benefit of others while he leads with his example!

Willie is married to Gloria Horton and presently has seven children, eighteen grandchildren, and seven great grandchildren. They reside happily in the Detroit, Michigan area!

In My Own Words

Doggin' It Twice!

ONE OF THE BEST STORIES involves my great baseball friend, Gates Brown, affectionately known as Gator! Gator was one of the best pinch hitters in baseball. As a pinch hitter Gator knew he usually wouldn't be called on until late in the game, so he would hang out in the bullpen. At Tiger Stadium, the relief pitchers always had food spread out in the bullpen—a smorgasbord with hot dogs, pretzels, peanuts, and so on. One night in the fifth inning, Tigers manager Mayo Smith called down to the bullpen for Gator to pinch hit. The guys in the bullpen told me that Gator had just dressed up a couple of hotdogs and had only eaten one of them when he received that call from Mayo to get ready to hit. "If I leave this dog, one of you guys will eat it!" Gator said to the guys in the bullpen as he wrapped the ketchup-slathered dog and slid it in his jersey. This was 1968 and Gator was stroking the baseball like Ted Williams. Not surprisingly, Gator ripped a line drive down the right field line and made a head first slide into second base with a double. Gator rolled over to get up, and the second base umpire looked at him with panic in his eyes, "Don't move, Gator!" he yelled! "You're hurt." There were ketchup stains streaking down Gator's jersey, and it looked like he was bleeding profusely! Gator told the concerned umpire it was an exploded hot dog and to please keep quiet because he didn't want manager Mayo Smith knowing he was eating every night in the all-you-could eat bullpen buffet. Then Mayo inserted a pinch runner for Gator, who came out holding his side—he didn't want Mayo to spot the ketchup stain. All the players were really chuckling over the Gator!

Apparently he didn't learn his lesson, because another time Gator hit a home run off of Boston pitcher Lee Stange, and a hotdog fell out of his uniform as he was rounding the bases!

The New York Moon

Once when I was playing with the Texas Rangers in 1977, we had a terrible loss to the New York Yankees. The next day as we were leaving the hotel for the ballpark, Bert Blyleven mooned Yankee Stadium fans and continued to do so for the entire bus ride!

Keep Away

Teammate Wayne Comer always liked to go out and have a good time, but, in spite of what he thought, he could not drink! After a few drinks, he would start a conversation by asking someone where they were from. When they told him, he would say, "That's a screwed up place." Most people didn't find his humor funny! One night in Minnesota after a game, Jim Northup, Don Wert, Wayne, and I went out for drinks. Soon Wayne was at it again, but this time the bar was filled with soldiers in uniform from a local base. After rubbing a couple of the soldiers the wrong way, Wayne got under the skin of one soldier, and the whole bar erupted into a fight! The four of us had to fight our way out of the bar, with Jim and me taking on the most of them. Wayne, of course, ducked out as soon as the punches started flying. The next day I had multiple knots on my head, and Tigers manager Mayo Smith was furious with Wayne and ordered him to stay permanently at least 60 feet away from me at all times. Wayne, being Wayne, asked Mayo how he could accomplish this. Our dugout bench was only 60 feet long, the locker room was small, the team bus was only 60 feet long, and—on top of all of that—we were roommates! That was just Wayne being Wayne!

No Gator Tonight

One night while the Tigers were on the west coast, Gator Brown and I were invited to a party hosted by the Four Tops at the Copacabana in Hollywood. They sent a limo to pick us up at our hotel, but Gator was scared to get in the limo, saying they might not bring us back. So I went alone. The place was packed with Hollywood-type people—executives and movie stars   —and I stayed way past the closing hours! I stayed up all night, and I called Gator to let him know that I was going straight to the ballpark. I felt terrible and just knew that there was no way I could play. Mayo Smith told me that I was playing anyway! I went out and hit three home runs. On the last one I threw up as I was rounding the bases. Boy, did I miss Gator, but I had a blast!

Breaking the Streak!

There were nightly poker games on the road, but only once did I ever win. The games usually included Gator, who organized the games, Jim Northup, Norm Cash, John Hiller, Jon Warden, Tom Matchick, Denny McLain and me. The regulars always liked it when Denny McLain played because he wasn't very smart when he played, but he always wanted to be the shooter in the game. On this occasion, Jim Northup caught Denny McLain going in light on the pot and confronted him. The yelling started and quickly turned into pushing and shoving with the table turning over and money flying everywhere. Gator and I broke up the fight before it got too far out of control. As they continued to argue, I picked up as much money as I could off the floor and headed for my room. The money I took with me was the only money I ever "won" at the poker games!

Life Changing

One moment that changed my life happened on May 30, 1970! Al Kaline and Jim Northup collided as they were chasing a line drive hit by Roberto Pena of the Brewers. Upon impact, Al swallowed his tongue and began to turn blue. From my days as a boxer I knew I had to get his jaw open and pull his tongue out! In this type of situation the jaw was just about locked, so I used all of my strength to pry his jaw open and pull his tongue back. I ended up with the best Al Kaline autograph—I will forever have his bite marks on my hand where his jaw clamped down! The Heart Association honored me for saving Al's life!

The Best of the Best

Willie Horton

Best Fastball
J. R. Richard & Nolan Ryan

Best Curveball
Camilo Pascual & Luis Tiant
(These guys also had three or four
different fastballs!)

Most Intimidating Pitcher
Bob Gibson
(This guy would come after you
with everything!)

Best Right-Handed Pitcher
Jim Palmer Luis Tiant

Best Left-Handed Pitcher
Dave McNally

Best Left-Handed Reliever
Sparky Lyle

Best Right-Handed Reliever
Stan Williams

**Overall Most
Challenging Pitcher**
Denny McLain &
Jim "Catfish" Hunter

Best Right-Handed Hitter
Willie Mays & Roberto Clemente

Best Left-Handed Hitter
Tony Oliva & Carl Yastrzemski

Overall Best Clutch Hitter
Tony Perez

Best Catcher
Thurman Munson &
Manny Sanguillen
(This was very tough to call!)

Best First Baseman
George Scott & Boog Powell

Best Second Baseman
Rod Carew & Bob Grich

Best Shortstop
Luis Aparicio

Best Third Baseman
Brooks Robinson

Best Left Fielder
Carl Yastrzemski & Willie Horton

Best Center Fielder
Paul Blair & Mickey Stanley

Best Right Fielder
Al Kaline & Frank Robinson

Fastest Base Runner
Rod Carew & Cesar Tovar

Willie Horton

Best Base Runner
Cesar Tovar

Best Overall Opposing Player
Frank Robinson

Player Who Didn't Reach Maximum Potential
George Scott

Strongest Outfield Arm
Rocky Colavito

Best Team Rival
New York Yankees & Baltimore Orioles

Best Opposing Manager
Earl Weaver & Dick Williams

Best Manager I Played For
Charlie Dressen & Billy Martin

Most Trusted Friend
Gates Brown & Ben Oglivie

My Favorite Team Mate
Gates Brown & Mickey Stanley

Funniest Player
Bert Blyleven & John Hiller

Most Heart
Dick McAuliffe

Most Courageous
Mickey Stanley & Ken Berry

Best Work Ethics
Don Baylor & Willie Horton

Most Flamboyant
Dave "Soup" Campbell

Most Congenial
Toby Harrah & Tommy Davis

Most Zany
Wayne Comer & Doc Ellis

My Favorite Team
Detroit Tigers & Baltimore Orioles

Player I Most Admired
Rod Carew

Player I Would Have Liked as a Team Mate
Tommy Davis

My Favorite Stadium
Memorial Stadium, Baltimore

My Favorite City
Minneapolis

Best Baseball Announcer
Ernie Harwell

My Favorite Baseball Announcer
Ernie Harwell & Joe Buck

The Best Umpire
Nester Chylak

Umpire with The Best Attitude
Bill Haller

Most Respected Baseball Personality
Jim Campbell & Charles O. Finley

Willie Horton
Lifetime Statistics

Year	Age	Tm	Lg	G	PA	AB	R	H	2B	3B	HR	RBI	SB	CS	BB	SO	BA	OBP	SLG
1963	20	DET	AL	15	43	43	6	14	2	1	1	4	2	0	0	8	.326	.326	.488
1964	21	DET	AL	25	92	80	6	13	1	3	1	10	0	0	11	20	.163	.272	.288
1965	22	DET	AL	143	572	512	69	140	20	2	29	104	5	9	48	101	.273	.340	.490
1966	23	DET	AL	146	578	526	72	138	22	6	27	100	1	1	44	103	.262	.321	.481
1967	24	DET	AL	122	445	401	47	110	20	3	19	67	0	0	36	80	.274	.338	.481
1968	25	DET	AL	143	578	512	68	146	20	2	36	85	0	3	49	110	.285	.352	.543
1969	26	DET	AL	141	568	508	66	133	17	1	28	91	3	3	52	93	.262	.332	.465
1970	27	DET	AL	96	404	371	53	113	18	2	17	69	0	1	28	43	.305	.354	.501
1971	28	DET	AL	119	498	450	64	130	25	1	22	72	1	5	37	75	.289	.349	.496
1972	29	DET	AL	108	367	333	44	77	9	5	11	36	0	0	27	47	.231	.293	.387
1973	30	DET	AL	111	443	411	42	130	19	3	17	53	1	4	23	57	.316	.362	.501
1974	31	DET	AL	72	263	238	32	71	8	1	15	47	0	1	21	36	.298	.361	.529
1975	32	DET	AL	159	667	615	62	169	13	1	25	92	1	2	44	109	.275	.319	.421
1976	33	DET	AL	114	456	401	40	105	17	0	14	56	0	0	49	63	.262	.342	.409
1977	34	TOT	AL	140	573	523	55	151	23	3	15	75	2	3	42	117	.289	.337	.430
1977	34	DET	AL	1	4	4	0	1	0	0	0	0	0	0	0	0	.250	.250	.250
1977	34	TEX	AL	139	569	519	55	150	23	3	15	75	2	3	42	117	.289	.337	.432
1978	35	TOT	AL	115	425	393	38	99	21	0	11	60	3	1	28	69	.252	.303	.389
1978	35	CLE	AL	50	186	169	15	42	7	0	5	22	3	0	15	25	.249	.314	.379
1978	35	OAK	AL	32	112	102	11	32	8	0	3	19	0	1	9	15	.314	.369	.480
1978	35	TOR	AL	33	127	122	12	25	6	0	3	19	0	0	4	29	.205	.228	.328
1979	36	SEA	AL	162	696	646	77	180	19	5	29	106	1	1	42	112	.279	.326	.458
1980	37	SEA	AL	97	384	335	32	74	10	1	8	36	0	4	39	70	.221	.306	.328

18-Year Totals

G	PA	AB	R	H	2B	3B	HR	RBI	SB	CS	BB	SO	BA	OBP	SLG
2028	8052	7298	873	1993	284	40	325	1163	20	38	620	1313	.273	.332	.457

"Did You Know?"

In 1977 while stealing his 893rd career stolen base, Lou Brock passed the legendary Ty Cobb's stolen base record.

"Bob Gibson is the luckiest pitcher I ever saw. He always pitches when the other team doesn't score any runs." — Tim McCarver

Rollie Fingers pitched in 640 games for the most games pitched in the 1970s.

In 1968 the first black umpire, Emmet Ashford takes the major league field.

"When Steve and I die, we are going to be buried in the same cemetery, 60-feet 6-inches apart." — Tim McCarver, who caught all of Steve Carlton's games, 1977

Jaime Jarrin
HOF Spanish Broadcaster
Los Angeles Dodgers

JAIME JARRIN is the most popular Hispanic announcer in the world for major league baseball. Jaime is very popular with major leaguers past and present, representing the Los Angeles Dodgers with grace and dignity. He is one of baseball's true gentlemen.

The Quito, Ecuador, native was born December 10, 1935. When he was 16, Jaime started his broadcast career in sports in Ecuador. He went on to study philosophy, letters, journalism and broadcasting at Central University of Ecuador in Quito.

In 1973, fourteen years after he joined the Dodgers family, the Los Angeles Dodgers made Jaime their number one Spanish Broadcaster. He has now been with the Dodgers for over fifty years, and, along with Vin Scully, is one of only two broadcasters inducted into the Baseball Hall of Fame!

In 1981 Jaime became a household name while representing and serving as a language interpreter for the Los Angeles Dodgers young pitching phenom, Fernando Valenzuela. Together Jaime and Fernando Valenzuela were the main topic and most popular baseball duo in the major leagues during the 1980s!

He received baseball's highest honor as a broadcaster when he was inducted into National Baseball Hall of Fame in Cooperstown, New York, on July 26th, 1998, the recipient of the Ford C. Frick Award.

September 1998 he received a star on the Hollywood Walk of Fame. In June the same year he earned the highest award bestowed by the National Association of Hispanic Journalist. He was also inducted into the Hispanic Heritage Baseball Museum during pre-game ceremonies at Dodger Stadium by president and founder, Gabriel "Tito" Avila.

In the 2005 book, *Voices of Summer*, he was named as baseball's all-time best Spanish language broadcaster. The California Sports Broadcasters honored him in 2004 with the 2003 Foreign Language Sports Broadcasters award, and he was inducted into Southern California Sports Broadcasters' Hall of Fame.

In March 2006 Jaime served as play-by-play announcer for the inaugural World Baseball Classic.

More importantly, Jaime Jarrin is respected and revered by everyone who is fortunate enough to know him. Even those who just hear his eloquent Los Angeles Dodgers broadcasts have come to love him. Jaime Jarrin is a friend to baseball, and a man of humility and grace!

Jaime Jarrin

In My Own Words

I HAVE BEEN FORTUNATE to make a couple of visits to the White House in my long career. However, the most memorable was the visit I made with Fernando Valenzuela. It was a very special visit for me! We were invited to the White House for lunch hosted by President of Mexico Jose Lopez Portillo along with President of the United States Ronald Reagan. There were about fifty guests in attendance, most of whom held prominent government roles. The first thing that impressed me was the music I heard as we made our way to the reception. The United States Marine Corps Band was playing a beautiful medley of classic Mexican music. The luncheon followed.

Next, was the memory that really evokes emotion in me. Fernando was just nineteen years old, and, with his long hair and youth, he had an innocence about him—and he could not speak a word of English. In spite of this, he captured the attention of the entire room, most of who were easily twice his age. I stood in awe as a long list of very powerful people who controlled the country and represented the United States in international affairs—including President Reagan, Vice President George Bush, the Attorney General, and Chief of Staff—stood in line to get an autograph from Valenzuela, this young kid from Mexico. That is ingrained in my memory, and I remember thinking, "Look at this! Some of the most powerful people in the world are waiting in line to get an autograph from this young man." It's something that could only happen in this country! It was such a testament to Valenzuela's achieving the American Dream, and I was able to witness this grand moment. It is one the most memorable and impressive experiences I have had in my fifty years of baseball.

Trip to Bethlehem

In 2002, a group of friends and I traveled to Bethlehem, Israel. One of my favorite memories occurred while we were there on Christmas Day. This was the precise day Bethlehem was given back to the Palestinians and there was much resulting commotion in the city. Vehicles with soldiers made their way through the streets. Palestinian leader Yasser Arafat was present throughout the city as well. We attended midnight mass there. After the mass, we walked to the main square in Bethlehem where about 50,000 people were making their way around the main square and throughout the city. This area, typical of a center city area, was filled with night clubs, cafes, restaurants, and other businesses with thousands of people milling about. Suddenly I heard someone yell my name, coming from a crowd of people about fifty meters away. "Jaime Jarrin! Jaime!" I turned around and listened, as the individual continued, "Yes, I know you because of the Dodgers! That's my team! I've seen you so many times and I'm glad to see you here!" I was amazed that among so many people thousands of miles away from home, there was a Dodger fan in the crowd and he recognized me!

Incidentally a similar incident occurred while I was traveling with friends in Shanghai, China. A group of people made their way alongside our group. "Jaime Jarrin! You're Jaime Jarrin!" said a tourist, "What are you doing here?" I replied, "The same as you!" I also was a tourist. The tourist then proceeded to tell me that he recognized me from seeing me at Dodger Stadium, and also mentioned that he had grown up listening to my broadcasts. He said his mother, father, and even his grandfather listened to my broadcasts. Then he hugged me and said that it was great to see me so far from home. Both these incidents are very special as they remind me how much of a memory I am for fans, and how much I represent the Dodger organization for them. And these impressive encounters happened so far from home!

World Series

I have called 25 World Series and 20 All-Star games. One of the most memorable was the 1997 World Series. For this particular series, Major League Baseball formed the extensive radio network with more than 680 stations worldwide. As a part of that network, the well known Columbian radio network Caracol had the rights to Spanish-language broadcasts. In Columbia alone, the broadcast was run on 300 to 400 stations. Caracol is so extensive that they even had a radio affiliate in Paris, France—a station of Columbian music with French announcers—which they used at this time for game broadcasts. This deal was predominantly done because of Marlins shortstop Edgar Renteria, a Columbian native. The extent of the broadcast for this series was impressive, and the series itself was exciting. The Marlins won the first game, then the Indians won game 2, then the Marlins came back to win game 3 and so on! Finally in game 7, the Marlins won the series.

After the win, I proceeded to the field to be present for the trophy presentation and celebration. Marlins owner Huizenga was very excited for this victory. I remember thinking that, in spite of how much money and all the luxuries Huizenga had, there was nothing that brought him more pleasure than this particular moment. At the time, there were ample rumors that he planned to sell the team. I was convinced there was no truth to this as I saw firsthand how thrilled he was to achieve this world championship. Huizenga did in fact go on to sell the team, however that did not take away from his sincere excitement I witnessed as I stood on the field. It was a very special experience, and the wide extent of the broadcast made it one of my favorite memories. Baseball has truly evolved into a magnificent international game!

Jaime Jarrin

The Best of the Best

Best Fastball
Nolan Ryan & J.R. Richard

Best Curveball
Sandy Koufax & Bert Blyleven

Most Intimidating Pitcher
Bob Gibson & Don Drysdale

Best Right-Handed Pitcher
Juan Marichal & Bob Gibson

Best Left-Handed Pitcher
Sandy Koufax & Steve Carlton

Best Left-Handed Reliever
Ron Perranoski

Best Right-Handed Reliever
Mike Marshall & Goose Gossage

**Overall Most
Challenging Pitcher**
Don Drysdale & Bob Gibson

Best Right-Handed Hitter
Henry Aaron & Willie Mays

Best Left-Handed Hitter
Stan Musial & Rod Carew

Overall Best Clutch Hitter
Pete Rose & Tony Perez

Best Catcher
Johnny Bench & Carlton Fisk

Best First Baseman
Willie McCovey & Wes Parker

Best Second Baseman
Joe Morgan & Cookie Rojas

Best Shortstop
Ernie Banks & Dave Conception

Best Third Baseman
Brooks Robinson & Mike Schmidt

Best Left Fielder
Billy Williams & Carl Yastrzemski

Best Center Fielder
Willie Mays & Mickey Mantle

Best Right Fielder
Roberto Clemente & Tony Oliva

Fastest Base Runner
Willie Davis & Bert Campaneris

Best Base Runner
Maury Wills & Lou Brock

Strongest Outfield Arm
Roberto Clemente & Ellis Valentine

**My Favorite
Broadcast Colleague**
Jack Buck

Most Trusted Friend
Vin Scully

Most Heart
Pete Rose

Most Courageous
Tommy John

Best Work Ethics
Steve Garvey

Most Flamboyant
Willie Mays & Roberto Clemente

My Favorite Team
L.A. Dodgers & Cincinnati Reds

Player I Most Admired
Roberto Clemente & Henry Aaron

My Favorite Stadium
Fenway Park & Dodger Stadium

My Favorite City
Chicago & Montreal

Best Baseball Announcer
Vin Scully

My Favorite Baseball Announcer
Vin Scully & Jack Buck

The Best Umpire
Doug Harvey

Umpire with The Best Attitude
Jocko Conlan

The Umpire I Most Respected Doug Harvey

The Most Controversial Umpire Joe West

Most Respected Baseball Personality
Peter O'Malley

Most Positive & Consistent Player
Stan Musial & Gil Hodges

Three Best Representatives of the Game
Henry Aaron, Sandy Koufax, & Roberto Clemente

Three Most Enjoyable Interviews
Don Drysdale, Felipe Alou, & Orlando Cepeda

Player Who Most Exemplified Dignity & Respect
Stan Musial & Gil Hodges

Most Challenging To Interview Sandy Koufax
(He was a very reserved person and did not enjoy giving interviews. The media was always after him!)

The Player Who was the Most Articulate
Steve Garvey

The Most Challenging Interview
Mickey Mantle

The Player I Would Have Enjoyed Interviewing Me
Sandy Koufax & Don Drysdale

Jaime Jarrin

"Did You Know?"

"What are we at the park for except to win? I'd trip my mother. I'd help her up, brush her off, tell her I'm sorry. But trust me, mother doesn't make it to third." — Leo Durocher

In 1963, Elston Howard becomes the first black MVP winner in American League history.

"I only had a high school education and believe me, I had to cheat to get that." — Sparky Anderson

Jim Palmer HOF won the most games (186) in the 1970s.

"I knew when my career was over. In 1965, my baseball card came out with no picture." — Bob Uecker

Ferguson "Fergie" Jenkins

Born December 13, 1942, Chatham, Ontario, Canada

Height 6'5"   **Weight** 210 lbs.

Bats Right   **Throws** Right

Debut September 10, 1965   **Final game** September 26, 1983

FERGUSON JENKINS was born in Chatham, Canada, on December 13th, 1943. He was more than a baseball player. As a young man he chopped wood to strengthen his upper body even though his parents had no wood-burning fireplace. He also developed his arm strength by standing 100 feet from the railroad tracks and tossing coal into the empty speeding box cars. He was an exceptional athlete who excelled at playing soccer, basketball, track, and hockey in Canada's harsh winters.

Ferguson was drafted by the Philadelphia Phillies as a relief pitcher in 1962 after being scouted by Tony Lucadello. He made his major league debut with the Phillies in 1965 as a young and impressive 22-year-old. In 1966 his baseball career was dramatically changed: he was traded to the Chicago Cubs.

Leo Durocher, the fireball Manager of the Chicago Cubs, decided to make Ferguson a starter and he would become one of the very elite pitchers in the game. Quickly Chicago embraced the enigmatic pitcher, referring to him by his nickname, Fergie. He became a beloved celebrity in Chicago, and they adopted him as one of their superstars. Fergie went on to become the ace of the staff and spent ten glorious and memorable years in Chi town!

Pitching for the Cubbies, he had 6 consecutive 20-game seasons and won 25 games with the Texas Rangers in 1974. In his career, he had 7 seasons in which he won 20 games.

In 1971, he walked only 37 batters while striking out 263, one of the best strike-to-walk ratios in the history of the game. Without question, Ferguson was one of the great control pitchers of all time, all the while intimidating his opponents in the batter's box! Hall-of-Fame Manager Leo Durocher once said, "Ferguson Jenkins was one of the best pitchers ever in the history of the game!"

He also starred with the Texas Rangers and Boston Red Sox, both on two separate occasions. In addition, Fergie pitched exclusively in two of baseball's most hitter-friendly parks, Wrigley Field and Fenway Park! His 3192 career strikeouts and 997 walks illustrate the pinpoint accuracy that he displayed to his opponents when he was standing on the hill.

On three occasions he led the National League in starts—1968, 1969, and 1971—and in complete games for two seasons, 1970 and 1971!

Fergie became the first Chicago Cub to ever win the coveted Cy Young Award for the National League Best Pitcher-of-the-Year in 1971. On five occasions he finished in the top three for the Cy Young Award. In addition, as a batter in 1971, he hit .243 with 6 home runs and 20 RBIs!

After being traded to the Texas Rangers in 1974, he won 25 games for the Rangers, becoming the first 20-game winner ever in a Rangers uniform. In 1983 he completed his sterling career while posting career numbers of 284 wins, 3,192 strikeouts, 49 shutouts, .557 winning percentage and a 3.34 lifetime ERA!

Fergie became the first baseball player to ever win the Lou March Trophy, recognizing Canada's top athlete. He was the first unanimous selection for Canada's Baseball Hall of Fame in 1987! Soon afterwards, in 1991, Cooperstown's Baseball Hall of Fame inducted the modest and humble Ferguson Jenkins. In 1999, The Society for American Baseball selected Ferguson as one of the top 100 players in the major leagues in the 20th century.

Currently the quiet and humble Ferguson Jenkins resides in central Arizona with his wife, Lydia!

Ferguson Jenkins quietly went to the pitcher's mound and dominated an era like very few others had. On the baseball diamond he accomplished a great deal, living a Hall-of-Fame career. In life, he more importantly has shared his life by serving others unselfishly, reflecting the character of a Hall-of-Fame person!

Ferguson Jenkins

The element that sets Fergie apart from most is his cheerful attitude and huge heart with his willingness to help others. Ferguson Jenkins is a definite Hall-of-Famer in every way!

In My Own Words

Big Mac

ONE OF MY FAVORITE STORIES involves Willie McCovey. Willie was tough on a lot of right-handed pitchers, but he would light me up. One time when the Cubs were playing on a west coast trip, we were staying in San Francisco at the team hotel. The first day of our series opener, I was down in the lobby and a chauffeur approached me and said that he and the car were ready to take me to Candlestick Park. I was baffled as I had no idea what the chauffeur was talking about. I later found out that Willie McCovey had sent a Cadillac for me to assure that I made it on time to the ball park. He was very much looking forward to my presence on the pitching mound facing him later that day! That would classify as a hitter owning a pitcher.

Me & Ray?

When I first went to the American League, most umpires did not think I could consistently keep the ball down in the strike zone for strikes. Jim "Sunny" Sundberg was the Rangers rookie catcher that year, and he was worried that I was going to get upset at the umpires for not calling my low pitch for a strike. In the American League, pitchers were not allowed to approach the umpires to speak the way we could in the National League. So I called Sunny out to the mound and said, "You stay right here, and don't leave, because I want to talk to the umpire when he comes out here to break up our conversation!" In the National League I would have had the opportunity to at least plead my case. However, that was not permitted in the American League. So I simply arranged an unofficial business meeting near my office, the pitching mound!

I was standing out on the mound as the ump arrived, and he said, "Come on, guys. Let's go! Come on, let's go!" I said, "Hey. Ray. I need that pitch! Ray, they don't swing at that pitch, because they can't hit it! But believe me, it is a strike!" The umpire said, "My name is Dick Stello, not Ray!" I said," It will be Ray Charles, it can be Stevie Wonder if you want it to be, or Jose Feliciano, I don't care! But, that pitch is a strike!" All three of us were laughing hysterically. Billy Martin, our fiery Manager in the Rangers dugout, was trying to figure out what the heck was going on. When we went to our dugout after the third out, Billy Martin asked me what went on out at the mound. I said to Billy, "Can you believe it? I called that umpire Ray Charles, and he did not throw me out of the game!" Later on, I did get that pitch consistently called a strike and rightfully so! But it was definitely a strike; Dick Stello finally realized it!

The Knockdown

Two people you never wanted to knockdown, or wakeup as the ballplayers use to say, were Frank Robinson and Willie Mays! If you were to knock down either one of those guys with a pitch, they would become more determined and focused! Leo Durocher would order for Willie to receive a little chin music and invariably he would get back up, dust himself off, and whack the ball out of sight. I knocked a few guys off of the plate; in fact I hit 84 guys in my big league career. That was only six a year though—not bad! The guy I had to really focus to keep him honest was Dick Allen, just to let him know I was out there.

Others I had to concentrate on with no letting up were Orlando Cepeda and Willie Mays. I wouldn't necessarily hit them, but I had to throw the ball high, hard and tight. One guy I never threw at intentionally was Jerry Grote, but Tom Seaver accused me of it. Grote was real mouthy! More chirpy than anything else! To me, throwing at a guy meant throwing behind the hitter or at his head. I never did that! I may throw under the chin, or towards the inside portion of the torso, but never to intentionally hit a batter! To earn his respect and keep the hitter off of the plate, I had to send subliminal messages at times! Yeah, I pitched to keep everyone honest!

Bobby Bonds

Bobby was a great player who had a sincere desire to win. When he first came up to the majors he had a lot of difficulty hitting the breaking pitch. But later in his career he overcame that deficiency and was pretty good at hitting the breaking ball. Twice we were teammates: in Texas with the Rangers and in Chicago with the Cubs. Believe me, he had my respect as a player and as a person, because he was a real competitor. In Texas I didn't hang out with Bobby very much because his running mate was Doc Ellis. Bobby was incredible though, because, as everyone knows, he could do it all. He could hit with power, was excellent on defense, he was great at stealing bases, and had an exceptional throwing arm from right field. Bobby was just an all-around good guy that I enjoyed as a player and a friend.

Ferguson Jenkins

Ferguson Jenkins
Lifetime Statistics

Year	Age	Tm	Lg	W	L	W-L%	ERA	G	GS	GF	CG	SHO	SV	IP	H	R	ER	HR	BB	SO
1965	22	PHI	NL	2	1	.667	2.19	7	0	6	0	0	1	12.1	7	3	3	2	2	10
1966	23	TOT	NL	6	8	.429	3.32	61	12	22	2	1	5	184.1	150	77	68	24	52	150
1966	23	PHI	NL	0	0		3.86	1	0	22	0	0	0	2.1	3	2	1	0	1	2
1966	23	CHC	NL	6	8	.429	3.31	60	12	22	2	1	5	182.0	147	75	67	24	51	148
1967	24	CHC	NL	20	13	.606	2.80	38	38	0	20	3	0	289.1	230	101	90	30	83	236
1968	25	CHC	NL	20	15	.571	2.63	40	40	0	20	3	0	308.0	255	96	90	26	65	260
1969	26	CHC	NL	21	15	.583	3.21	43	42	1	23	7	1	311.1	284	122	111	27	71	273
1970	27	CHC	NL	22	16	.579	3.39	40	39	1	24	3	0	313.0	265	128	118	30	60	274
1971	28	CHC	NL	24	13	.649	2.77	39	39	0	30	3	0	325.0	304	114	100	29	37	263
1972	29	CHC	NL	20	12	.625	3.20	36	36	0	23	5	0	289.1	253	111	103	32	62	184
1973	30	CHC	NL	14	16	.467	3.89	38	38	0	7	2	0	271.0	267	133	117	35	57	170
1974	31	TEX	AL	25	12	.676	2.82	41	41	0	29	6	0	328.1	286	117	103	27	45	225
1975	32	TEX	AL	17	18	.486	3.93	37	37	0	22	4	0	270.0	261	130	118	37	56	157
1976	33	BOS	AL	12	11	.522	3.27	30	29	1	12	2	0	209.0	201	85	76	20	43	142
1977	34	BOS	AL	10	10	.500	3.68	28	28	0	11	1	0	193.0	190	91	79	30	36	105
1978	35	TEX	AL	18	8	.692	3.04	34	30	3	16	4	0	249.0	228	92	84	21	41	157
1979	36	TEX	AL	16	14	.533	4.07	37	37	0	10	3	0	259.0	252	127	117	40	81	164
1980	37	TEX	AL	12	12	.500	3.77	29	29	0	12	0	0	198.0	190	90	83	22	52	129
1981	38	TEX	AL	5	8	.385	4.50	19	16	2	1	0	0	106.0	122	55	53	14	40	63
1982	39	CHC	NL	14	15	.483	3.15	34	34	0	4	1	0	217.1	221	92	76	19	68	134
1983	40	CHC	NL	6	9	.400	4.30	33	29	1	1	1	0	167.1	176	89	80	19	46	96

19-Year Totals

W	L	W-L%	ERA	G	GS	GF	CG	SHO	SV	IP	H	R	ER	HR	BB	SO
284	226	.557	3.34	664	594	37	267	49	7	4500.2	4142	1853	1669	484	997	3192

"Did You Know"

"It never ceases to amaze me how many of baseball's wounds are self-inflicted." — Bill Veeck

Gaylord Perry HOF pitcher completed 197 games in the 1970s decade.

"I remember one time going out to the mound to talk with Bob Gibson. He told me to get back behind the plate; that the only thing I knew about pitching was that I could not hit it." — Tim McCarver

Willie Stargell slugged 296 Homers for the most home runs in the decade of the 1970s.

"They say some of my stars drink whiskey. But I have found that the ones who drink milkshakes don't win many ballgames." — Casey Stengel

Al Kaline

Born December 19, 1934, Baltimore, Maryland
Height 6'2"   **Weight** 180 lbs.
Bats Right   **Throws** Right
Debut June 25, 1953   **Final game** Oct. 2, 1974

ALBERT WILLIAM KALINE made his major league debut with the Detroit Tigers June 25, 1953. He was right out of Baltimore's Southern High School and was only 18 years old. Immediately, Al was targeted as a five-tool player, and he was a bonus baby who signed for the astronomical sum of $35,000, which was rare in the 1950s!

In 1955, Al became the youngest player in major league history to win a batting title, and he did so with an amazing .340 batting average at the age of twenty!

Al bypassed the Tigers' minor leagues and reported directly to the parent club in Detroit. During his career he often was referred to simply as 6, which was the number he wore for the last 21 years of his illustrious career. Al is more commonly known as, and affectionately referred to, as Mr. Tiger!

As an outstanding right fielder with a cannon for an arm, it did not take long for the American League runners to learn not to attempt to take an extra base, or to run when the baby-faced Tiger was in right field. In 1956 he led the league with 18 assists, and again in 1958 with 23 assists. His throwing arm became legendary. He once played in 242 consecutive games without an error. In one game, Al threw out two base runners in the same inning at home plate. In the outfield, Al Kaline was unsurpassed!

However, it was his batting prowess that won Al the most acclaim and the major accolades from baseball fans and baseball purists throughout the country. In 1955 he had an outstanding season with a .340 batting average, 27 homeruns, and 102 RBIs and came in second place in the MVP voting to Yogi Berra of the New York Yankees. Again in 1963, Al finished second in the MVP voting to Elston Howard of the Yankees, compiling a .312 batting average, 27 home runs, and had 128 RBIs. Al Kaline was one the most accomplished and proficient hitters of his era!

At times, however, he seemed besieged by injuries. In 1954, while chasing a fly ball, he ran into a wall, landing him in the hospital for five days. He also fractured his right collarbone diving for a catch in 1962 and was lost for two months. Injuries continued to plague Kaline throughout his career, sidelining the hitter for some 200 games over fifteen years. In 1962 Kaline broke his hand after jamming his bat into a bat rack after striking out. That mishap called for him to miss twenty-eight games.

1968 was the most memorable year for Al in more ways than one. Al missed two significant months with a broken arm in that championship season. The Tigers were thrashing American League opponents with abandon while advancing to the American League pennant. It was an incredible season for the Tigers. Later in the season Manager Mayo Smith decided to play his fleet-footed center fielder Mickey Stanley at shortstop in order to create a valuable spot for Mr. Tiger upon his return from the broken arm! The decision paid the expected dividends. The Tigers were on their way to participating in their first World Series since 1945! Al Kaline as expected would play a monumental role!

Once the Tigers accomplished their rightful place in the 1968 World Series, they were to play the powerful Cardinals of St. Louis, the previous World Champions having defeated the Boston Red Sox in 1967. The St. Louis Cardinals were a perennial powerhouse in the 1960s, but the Tigers were not intimidated. Most in baseball considered the Cardinals the favored team. After losing three of the first four games to the Cardinals, Al came to bat with the bases loaded in the seventh inning of game 5 and the Tigers trailing 3-2, and as usual delivered a clutch single to drive in the two go-ahead runs for the necessary win in game 5. The Tigers went on to the next two games, astonishing the baseball world by winning the World Series.

Mr. Al Kaline hit an impressive .379 with two home runs and eight runs batted in for his only World Series appearances. The 1968 Detroit Tigers were themselves a legitimate powerhouse with Willie Horton, Jim Northup, Norm Cash, and

Al Kaline

of course Mr. Tiger. That magical year though belonged to Denny McLain who won 31 games with a 1.96 ERA and went on to win the American League Cy Young Award and MVP! However, Al Kaline's team was a true team of balance, focus, and camaraderie.

In the last season of Al's fabulous career, he collected his historic 3000th hit on September 24 with a double off of Dave McNally of the Baltimore Orioles. Al finished his career with 3007 hits, 1583 RBIs, and 399 home runs. Nine times in his career he batted .300 or better! He won 10 Gold Gloves for his outstanding defense, and played in 15 All-Star games.

When I asked Al Kaline about today's players, he said, "Some of the players in today's game that I would pay to watch play are Justin Verlander, Rick Porcello, Derek Jeter, Albert Pujols, Miguel Cabrera, and Ichiro Suzuki. Of course, there are several more, but these are the ones who come to mind who are outstanding players today with bright futures!"

In 1980, Al Kaline became the tenth player in history to be elected into Cooperstown's Baseball Hall of Fame in his first year of eligibility! The Detroit Tigers named a street after their legend and retired his famous #6!

Of all of the great baseball accomplishments and accolades that Al has deservedly earned, none can compare to the reputation amongst his peers. They agree that Mr. Tiger epitomizes humility while always being first and foremost a true gentleman!

The Best of the Best
Al Kaline

Best Fastball
Nolan Ryan

Best Curveball
Camilo Pascual

Most Intimidating Pitcher
Nolan Ryan

Best Right-Handed Pitcher
Denny McLain, Nolan Ryan

Best Left-Handed Pitcher
Mickey Lolich

Best Left-Handed Reliever
John Hiller, Sparky Lyle

Best Right-Handed Reliever
Rollie Fingers

Overall Most Challenging Pitcher
Stu Miller

Best Right-Handed Hitter
Frank Robinson

Best Left-Handed Hitter
Ted Williams

Overall Best Clutch Hitter
Frank Robinson

Best Catcher
Yogi Berra, Bill Freehan

Best First Baseman
Harmon Killebrew, Norm Cash

Best Second Baseman
Rod Carew, Nellie Fox

Best Shortstop
Luis Aparicio

Best Third Baseman
Brooks Robinson

Best Left Fielder
Carl Yastrzemski

Best Center Fielder
Mickey Mantle

Best Right Fielder
Frank Robinson, Dwight Evans

Fastest Base Runner
Luis Aparicio

Best Base Runner
Luis Aparicio

Best Overall Player
Frank Robinson

Player Who Didn't Reach Maximum Potential
Norm Cash

Strongest Outfield Arm
Dwight Evans

Al Kaline

Best Team Rival
New York Yankees

Best Opposing Manager
Dick Williams

Best Manager I Played For
Mayo Smith, Fred Hutchinson

Most Trusted Friend
Norm Cash

My Favorite Team Mate
Jerry Lumpe, Ed Brinkman

Funniest Player
Norm Cash

Most Heart
Nellie Fox

Most Courageous
John Hiller

Best Work Ethics
Several

Most Flamboyant
Reggie Jackson

Most Congenial
Brooks Robinson

Most Zany
Jimmy Piersall

My Favorite Team
Detroit Tigers

Player I Most Admired
Mickey Mantle

**Player I Would Have Liked
as a Team Mate**
Ted Williams

My Favorite Stadium
Fenway Park

My Favorite City
Boston

Best Baseball Announcer
Ernie Harwell

**My Favorite Baseball
Announcer**
Ernie Harwell

The Best Umpire
Nestor Chylak

Umpire with The Best Attitude
Nestor Chylak

**Most Respected Baseball
Personality**
Yogi Berra

Al Kaline
Lifetime Statistics

Year	Age	Tm	Lg	G	PA	AB	R	H	2B	3B	HR	RBI	SB	CS	BB	SO	BA	OBP	SLG
1953	18	DET	AL	30	30	28	9	7	0	0	1	2	1	0	1	5	.250	.300	.357
1954	19	DET	AL	138	535	504	42	139	18	3	4	43	9	5	22	45	.276	.305	.347
1955	20	DET	AL	152	681	588	121	200	24	8	27	102	6	8	82	57	.340	.421	.546
1956	21	DET	AL	153	693	617	96	194	32	10	27	128	7	1	70	55	.314	.383	.530
1957	22	DET	AL	149	636	577	83	170	29	4	23	90	11	9	43	38	.295	.343	.478
1958	23	DET	AL	146	607	543	84	170	34	7	16	85	7	4	54	47	.313	.374	.490
1959	24	DET	AL	136	595	511	86	167	19	2	27	94	10	4	72	42	.327	.410	.530
1960	25	DET	AL	147	629	551	77	153	29	4	15	68	19	4	65	47	.278	.354	.426
1961	26	DET	AL	153	665	586	116	190	41	7	19	82	14	1	66	42	.324	.393	.515
1962	27	DET	AL	100	452	398	78	121	16	6	29	94	4	0	47	39	.304	.376	.593
1963	28	DET	AL	145	616	551	89	172	24	3	27	101	6	4	54	48	.312	.375	.514
1964	29	DET	AL	146	608	525	77	154	31	5	17	68	4	1	75	51	.293	.383	.469
1965	30	DET	AL	125	474	399	72	112	18	2	18	72	6	0	72	49	.281	.388	.471
1966	31	DET	AL	142	572	479	85	138	29	1	29	88	5	5	81	66	.288	.392	.534
1967	32	DET	AL	131	550	458	94	141	28	2	25	78	8	2	83	47	.308	.411	.541
1968	33	DET	AL	102	389	327	49	94	14	1	10	53	6	4	55	39	.287	.392	.428
1969	34	DET	AL	131	518	456	74	124	17	0	21	69	1	2	54	61	.272	.346	.447
1970	35	DET	AL	131	555	467	64	130	24	4	16	71	2	2	77	49	.278	.377	.450
1971	36	DET	AL	133	501	405	69	119	19	2	15	54	4	6	82	57	.294	.416	.462
1972	37	DET	AL	106	314	278	46	87	11	2	10	32	1	0	28	33	.313	.374	.475
1973	38	DET	AL	91	347	310	40	79	13	0	10	45	4	1	29	28	.255	.320	.394
1974	39	DET	AL	147	630	558	71	146	28	2	13	64	2	2	65	75	.262	.337	.389

22-Year Totals

G	PA	AB	R	H	2B	3B	HR	RBI	SB	CS	BB	SO	BA	OBP	SLG
2834	11596	10116	1622	3007	498	75	399	1583	137	65	1277	1020	.297	.376	.480

"Did You Know"

The Pittsburgh Pirates were the first team to field an all-black starting lineup in a major league game on September 1, 1971.

Vin Scully stated that Bob Gibson pitched so quickly, it was as though he were double parked!

"The only thing worse than a Mets game, is a Mets double-header."
— Casey Stengel on the Mets' 1962 inaugural year

"Trying to sneak a fastball past Henry Aaron is like sneaking a sunrise past a rooster." — Joe Adcock and Curt Simmons

First former major league player to become inducted into the Radio Hall of Fame, was Bob Uecker, Mr. Baseball.

My mother, Aude and me with the bat Orlando Cepeda had just hit two home runs with. Wrigley Field, 1966.

The author as a bat boy at Dodger Stadium, 1971.

Little Tito 23 Fuentes in Havana. For once, he appears serious.

Tito 23 Fuentes with three friends in Havana, 1952.

Tito 23 Fuentes with his Mom and Dad in Havana.

Bill Russell not straying TOO far from second base while trying to nail Tito.

Orlando Cepeda, "The Baby Bull" creating havoc once again. Orlando was my first baseball hero.

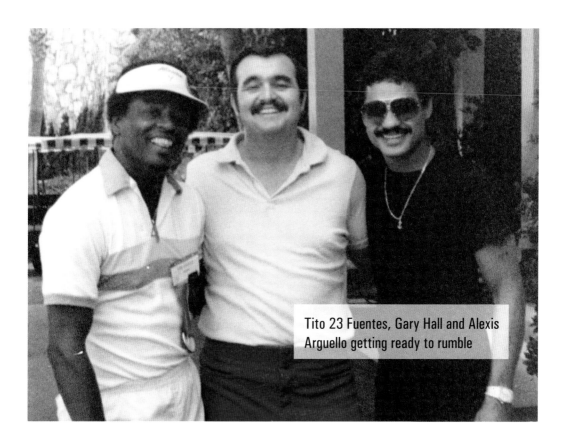

Tito 23 Fuentes, Gary Hall and Alexis Arguello getting ready to rumble

Tito 23 Fuentes, Gary Hall and Orlando Cepeda at Orlando's house recently.

My new buddy, Juan Marichal at Wrigley Field in 1966.

Gary and Juan Marichal in 2009, dos amigos.

Hall of Fame National League umpire Doug Harvey early in his career (at left) and recently (below).

My brother, Bobby Bonds with me at the Giant's hotel in St. Louis.

Fred Lynn

Born February 3, 1952, Chicago, Illinois
Height 6' 1"   **Weight** 190 lbs.
Bats Left   **Throws** Left
Debut September 5, 1974   **Final game** October 3, 1990

FRED LYNN was born in Chicago, Illinois, February 3, 1952. He was an outstanding athlete who played baseball. But he was far more than a baseball player; he excelled in multiple sports. Fred was an All-American baseball player at USC for the legendary Rod Dedeaux. Later he was inducted into USC's Baseball Hall of Fame. It was baseball's good fortune that he was adopted into baseball and chosen by the Boston Red Sox in the second round of the 1973 amateur draft.

Fred Lynn had one of the most impressive major league first year in baseball history! He was the first major league player to achieve both the Most Valuable Player Award and the Rookie of the Year Award in his first year! He led the American League in doubles, runs scored, and slugging percentage. He had 21 home runs and finished second in the batting race with an incredible first year average of .331 all the while winning his first Gold Glove!

His outstanding first year was a mere glimpse into the bright future the Red Sox were counting on for their investment. He was severely hampered by serious and nagging injuries, and eventually the injuries took their toll on the mega-talented centerfielder. Fred was a gritty blue-collar type player whose approach was more like that of a linebacker than that of a gifted centerfielder who roamed the majestic outfield of the major leagues for 17 years. He constantly chased balls into fences with his fierce and competitive demeanor.

His best friend, Jim Rice, came up through the minor league system of the Red Sox at the same time, and they arrived the same year in Boston. Both Fred and Jim Rice became affectionately known as the "Gold Dust Twins!" To this day, they are best of friends.

Fred was an excellent baseball player with great accomplishments. If you were to compare his career numbers based on games played and career at bats to Hall of Famers, Fred Lynn deserves to be gracing the hallways of Cooperstown's illustrious Baseball Hall of Fame!

Fred was an unselfish player whose only wish was to win championships for his teams; he never fixated on selfish numbers for himself. He was a true team player who had an insatiable desire to win for the team! In 17 seasons and only 6925 career at bats, Fred slugged 306 home runs, 1111 runs batted in, 72 stolen bases, and a career batting average of .283. He also earned 4 Gold Gloves, 9 All-Star appearances, and won the Rookie of the Year Award while capturing the American League Most Valuable Player Award! One interesting tidbit regarding the Most Valuable Player Award is that his name was misspelled on the trophy!

Fred's greatest passion is his beautiful wife, Natalie. According to Natalie, Fred is an outstanding gourmet cook who has a flair for the extraordinary in the kitchen.

In conclusion, Fred impressed on me that his only desire as a major leaguer was to win for his team, for his city, and, of course, for his fans. Fred is just as incredible of a person as he was as an extraordinary major leaguer!

Fred Lynn

In My Own Words

I'VE HAD MANY GREAT MEMORIES, but my first game jumps out as one of the most memorable. Jim Rice and I came up to the big leagues at the end of 1974. Sitting on the Red Sox bench was Hall-of-Famers Orlando Cepeda, Juan Marichal and Luis Aparicio. You have to remember I grew up as a San Francisco Giants fan, and to be sitting on the same bench with my heroes Cepeda and Marichal was very special. The first time I entered a game was at Fenway. We were playing the Tigers, and I was brought in to pinch run at third base with one out. Juan Beniquez was the hitter, and Aurelio Rodriguez was the third baseman for the Tigers. Rodriguez had the best arm of any third baseman in the American League at the time. Bill Freehan was the All-Star catcher for the Tigers.

This play was actually my fault. Juan Beniquez often hit the ball to the opposite field. I expected Beniquez to hit the ball to the opposite field, right field. He laid down a bunt along the third base line which surprised me. Rodriguez was pretty quick at third and he had that great arm. He threw a perfect strike in one motion to the catcher Freehan. They threw me out by such a huge distance, Freehan almost would have had time to finish a cup of coffee in the time it took me to arrive at home. I never had an opportunity to even sniff home plate as Freehand literally moved me towards the third base side dugout and tagged me out! Here I was this rookie pinch running at third base, thrown out in front of my heroes Orlando Cepeda and Juan Marichal! I should have stayed at third or at least bluffed the defense. Anyway, my first experience in a game was somewhat embarrassing.

However, my first start was in Milwaukee at County Stadium, and Jim Slaton was pitching for the Brewers. He threw me a fastball which I hit hard; it had home run length but it went foul. I thought I should have waited just a little longer on my swing; I had been a little too anxious. The next pitch Slaton threw was a curve ball that I hit out of the park over the right field wall, and as I was rounding the bases, I thought how fortunate I was that my first hit in the big leagues was a homer. My next at bat, I hit a double off of Slaton. I was two for two, and as I stepped to the plate around the fourth inning or so, the Brewers brought in a left handed pitcher and the Red Sox manager took me out of the game. I felt weird as I had never been taken out of a game before. When I reached the dugout, Cepeda said, "Way to go kid! Go take a shower!"

From Milwaukee, we went to Detroit. The first game in Detroit I went four for five, and after I scored my first run, Tiger catcher Bill Freehan said, "Hey, kid. When the reporters interview you after the game, don't tell them I was telling you what the pitches were." I thought that was pretty funny!

The Amazing Dick Allen

I was pretty seasoned coming out of the USC baseball program with Rod Dedeaux. However when I was 21, my dad really encouraged me to go to Florida to attend the instructional league; I listened to my dad. When I arrived in Florida, the Red Sox were sharing their baseball facility with the Chicago White Sox. Dick Allen was there for some reason, and I remember something I still find very impressive! Dick was taking batting practice off the old Iron Mike pitching machine. What was shocking was that he was standing ten feet closer to Iron Mike in front of home plate and he was swinging a solid lead pipe hitting the baseballs! Boy, was he strong and quick! I never forgot that!

Oh! It's the Spaceman!

After the Red Sox had played the Orioles in Baltimore, we had a charter flight about to leave Baltimore at the airport. Red Sox Manager Don Zimmer told the players when the plane would leave and we dispersed around the airport. Bill "Spaceman" Lee, Bernie Carbo, Jim Willoughby, and I were messing around the video arcade area. Some of these guys were not Zimmer's favorites. About ten minutes before the plane was scheduled to leave, the four of us went back to the gate to board. We saw that the plane was rolling backwards preparing for takeoff! We told one of the airline employees at the gate, "Hey! We are supposed to be on that plane!" She called the pilot to tell our manager Zimmer that they had just left four of their players in the airport. When Zimmer found out one of the players was Bill "Spaceman" Lee, he said, "Just keep going–they'll figure out a way to get there!" They left us, and we had to pay our own way on a commercial flight. Not so funny back then, but hilarious now! Bill Lee was not popular with Don Zimmer, but he was a fierce competitor and an accomplished pitcher. Believe me, Bill Lee earned his nickname as the "Spaceman!"

The Not So Funny, Carlton Fisk!

One time when we were in New York, Carlton (Pudge) Fisk, Jerry Remy, Rick Burleson, and I went to a watering hole called P.J Clarks. We decided to have a drink or two while waiting for a table. I was wearing a cashmere sweater that I was pretty proud of! Pudge picked me up off of the ground and hung me on a coat rack hook, hanging by my beautiful sweater. My feet were dangling about six inches off the ground! I tried to get off of the coat rack and people were snickering! My "friends," of course, left me for the dining room. Finally, I wriggled out of my sweater, and noticed there was now a gaping hole in it. After we had dinner and were ready to leave, we hailed a cab to go our hotel. I ended up giving the cab driver my sweater! Maybe I had said something to Pudge that prompted him to hang me on the hook like a rag doll. Whatever my comment was, it cost me a great sweater and created another public embarrassing moment at the hands of Carlton Fisk!

1978 Playoffs

In 1978 the Red Sox played the Yankees in the playoffs to determine who was going to the World Series. For the most part, we had a lead throughout the season, and, going into September, the Yankees overtook us to lead the American League East. The Red Sox won eight games in a row at the end of September to tie the Yankees. Then they lost the last game of the season, forcing the rivals to play each other for a World Series title. The Red Sox won the coin flip, so we were to play at Fenway in Boston. Ron Guidry was pitching for the Yanks and the Red Sox had Mike Torrez starting.

Early in the game, Yastrzemski hit a two-run homer and the Red Sox went up two runs quickly. In about the third or fourth inning, we had two runners on base, and I never pulled Guidry as I always hit him the other way. If we could have gotten into their middle relief, we would have steam rolled over them! The next pitch from Guidry I pulled, and Lou Pinella, the Yankees right fielder, snow cones it, robbing me of at least a double and keeping us from scoring two more runs off of Guidry which would have made a four-run lead. I threw my helmet down to the ground in disgust, which was a rare occurrence for me, as I seldom displayed my emotions! I was aggravated also because Pinella was so far out of position he was playing me to pull the ball. I wasn't able to hit the other way to left field as I almost always did off of Guidry. There is no way he should have been there in that area for even a chance at that catch. It was a day game and the sun is brutal that time of the year in Fenway, especially in right field. The Yankees had put Pinella out in right field as a defensive replacement for Reggie Jackson, or we would have definitely had a four-run lead instead of the two we had from Yaz's homer. We ended up losing that game 5 to 4, but that play Pinella made cost us at least two runs!

Pinella made another play later in that same game. Jerry Remy hit a ball to right and Pinella was blinded by the ball and it hit him in the chest. That kept Burleson from scoring. Later I was announcing for ESPN and Pinella was the manager for the Seattle Mariners. I couldn't wait to talk to Pinella about the time he robbed the game from the Red Sox in that 1978 game. I asked Pinella, "Lou, was there a good looking blonde down in the right field corner, or something? Because there was no logical reason for you to play me to pull the ball to right off of Guidry!" Pinella answered me, "Yeah, I had a hunch. It looked like Guidry might have gotten a little fatigued, so I acted on my gut feelings that you might have been able to pull Guidry late in the game!" The amazing part of this famous game is that everyone remembers Bucky Dent's three-run homer, when in reality, Lou Pinella was the hero or there would never have been an opportunity for the Yankees to win–he robbed the

Red Sox with two great plays in the outfield. The Yankees were a very smart team that knew how to play the game. But Red Sox Pitcher Mike Torrez was dominating until the late in the game. Believe it or not, I still think about that game. It haunts me! I believe we would have been the World Champions instead of the Yankees! This stands out in my memory and it is still tough to digest!

1982 Angels

In 1982, when I was with the California Angels, we had an incredibly talented team; we won 95 games. We had virtually an All Star at each regular position. That year the Angels consisted of Rod Carew, Bobby Grich, Doug DeCinces, Don Baylor, Reggie Jackson, me, plus a very good, solid pitching staff! We had the team that really should have won it all! The Angels were playing the Milwaukee Brewers, commonly referred to as "Harvey's Wallbangers," in the playoffs. Harvey Kuenn was the Brewers manager and they had a very good team with a lot of power! But I truly believe we were the better team. In game five of the playoffs, the score was tied 3 to 3, and the series was tied 2 to 2 late in game five. The Angels manager Gene Mauch had a talented left-handed reliever in our bullpen, Andy Hassler. He was afraid to bring Hassler into the game with Cecil Cooper coming to the plate because Hassler was erratic, but he had a 2.78 ERA. Cooper was batting left handed, and Hassler was just wild enough to be a little unpredictable, but hitters rarely got comfortable against him. Anyway, it was the correct move to bring Hassler in to face Cooper, and Mauch did not have the confidence in Hassler to do it. When Mauch did not bring in Hassler, I was shocked, and Cooper naturally got a hit off of our right-hander for the game winner. The result was that the Brewers went to the World Series in our place against the St. Louis Cardinals. The Angels owner Gene Autry fired Gene Mauch on our flight home to California–that was an interesting flight! Gene Mauch was excellent with Xs & Os, but he did not handle pitching staffs well. I believe it cost us the opportunity to participate in the World Series, a shot at being champions of baseball!

I was the first player to have the dubious honor of winning the ALCS Most Valuable Player Award on the losing team! I was so angry, I didn't even want to talk to the presenter of the award. It is amazing to me that a player could even win the MVP while playing for the losing team, no matter how well he may have played! Looking back on it now, I am proud to have won the MVP. However, my preference would have been to win the Series.

The Best of the Best

Best Fastball
Nolan Ryan

Best Curveball
Bert Blyleven

Most Intimidating Pitcher
Nolan Ryan
(Nolan was unbelievable!)

Best Right-Handed Pitcher
Jim Palmer

Best Left-Handed Pitcher
Frank Tanana
(He struck me out three consecutive times for the first time in my life! Frank struck out 17 Red Sox. I do not know how we got 2 hits.)

Best Left-Handed Reliever
Sparky Lyle

Best Right-Handed Reliever
Rollie Fingers &
Dan Quisenberry

Overall Most Challenging Pitcher
Nolan Ryan

Best Right-Handed Hitter
Jim Rice

Best Left-Handed Hitter
George Brett

Overall Best Clutch Hitter
George Brett &
Thurman Munson
(We hated to see Thurman come to bat against us!)

Best Catcher
Carlton Fisk

Best First Baseman
George Scott & Cecil Cooper
(George was great defensively with his glove and quick as a cat.)

Best Second Baseman
Rod Carew & Bobby Grich
(Second baseman were mostly glove men back then.)

Best Shortstop
Robin Yount

Best Third Baseman
George Brett

Best Left Fielder
Jim Rice
(Jim worked hard on his fielding
& he threw out several runners.)

Best Center Fielder
Fred Lynn
(I'm not being egotistical here, but I
was the best in center field.)

Best Right Fielder
Reggie Jackson
(He was not good defensively, but he
had a great arm. What a hitter!)

Fastest Base Runner
Willie Wilson
(Willie could outrun the baseball
and therefore the outfielders had
to be aware of knocking down the
baseball)

Best Base Runner
Bert Campaneris

Best Overall Player
George Brett (In his era!)

Player Who Didn't Reach Maximum Potential
Bo Jackson
(More raw talent than anyone!
Overpowered aspects of the game of
baseball.)

Strongest Outfield Arm
Dwight Evans

Best Team Rival
New York Yankees
& Boston Red Sox
(Both teams were the beast of the
east. We were each others'
competition along with the
Baltimore Orioles.)

Best Opposing Manager
Billy Martin

Best Manager I Played For
Gene Mauch &
Sparky Anderson

Most Trusted Friend
Jim Rice
(We came up through the minors
together, and were the Gold Dust
Twins. Great Guy!)

My Favorite Team Mate
Tom Burgmeier

Funniest Player
Luis Tiant
(No one was funnier than El
Tiante!)

Most Heart
Rick Burleson

Most Courageous
Jim Eisenreich

Fred Lynn

Best Work Ethics
Jim Rice & Rick Burleson
(Rice worked diligently on his defense every day!)

Most Congenial
Fred Stanley

My Favorite Team
Boston Red Sox
(My first year was great!
The mid 70s were most
memorable)

Player I Would Have
Liked as a Team Mate
George Brett

My Favorite City
Chicago
(No doubt about this one!)

My Favorite
Baseball Announcer
Vin Scully

Umpire with The Best
Attitude
Steve Palermo
(I personally liked Ron Luciano
because he was kind & funny!)

Most Flamboyant
Oscar Gamble

Most Zany
Bill (Spaceman) Lee

Player I Most Admired
Willie Mays & Roberto
Clemente

My Favorite Stadium
Fenway Park & Wrigley Field
(Remembering where we sat as a
kids in Wrigley was awesome!)

Best Baseball Announcer
Vin Scully

The Best Umpire
Rich Garcia

Most Respected Baseball
Personality
Al Kaline

Fred Lynn
Lifetime Statistics

Year	Age	Tm	Lg	G	PA	AB	R	H	2B	3B	HR	RBI	SB	CS	BB	SO	BA	OBP	SLG
1974	22	BOS	AL	15	51	43	5	18	2	2	2	10	0	0	6	6	.419	.490	.698
1975	23	BOS	AL	145	605	528	103	175	47	7	21	105	10	5	62	90	.331	.401	.566
1976	24	BOS	AL	132	566	507	76	159	32	8	10	65	14	9	48	67	.314	.367	.467
1977	25	BOS	AL	129	564	497	81	129	29	5	18	76	2	3	51	63	.260	.327	.447
1978	26	BOS	AL	150	627	541	75	161	33	3	22	82	3	6	75	50	.298	.380	.492
1979	27	BOS	AL	147	622	531	116	177	42	1	39	122	2	2	82	79	.333	.423	.637
1980	28	BOS	AL	110	478	415	67	125	32	3	12	61	12	0	58	39	.301	.383	.480
1981	29	CAL	AL	76	302	256	28	56	8	1	5	31	1	2	38	42	.219	.322	.316
1982	30	CAL	AL	138	545	472	89	141	38	1	21	86	7	8	58	72	.299	.374	.517
1983	31	CAL	AL	117	500	437	56	119	20	3	22	74	2	2	55	83	.272	.352	.483
1984	32	CAL	AL	142	600	517	84	140	28	4	23	79	2	2	77	97	.271	.366	.474
1985	33	BAL	AL	124	508	448	59	118	12	1	23	68	7	3	53	100	.263	.339	.449
1986	34	BAL	AL	112	456	397	67	114	13	1	23	67	2	2	53	59	.287	.371	.499
1987	35	BAL	AL	111	438	396	49	100	24	0	23	60	3	7	39	72	.253	.320	.487
1988	36	TOT	AL	114	432	391	46	96	14	1	25	56	2	2	33	82	.246	.302	.478
1988	36	BAL	AL	87	334	301	37	76	13	1	18	37	2	2	28	66	.252	.312	.482
1988	36	DET	AL	27	98	90	9	20	1	0	7	19	0	0	5	16	.222	.265	.467
1989	37	DET	AL	117	406	353	44	85	11	1	11	46	1	1	47	71	.241	.328	.371
1990	38	SDP	NL	90	223	196	18	47	3	1	6	23	2	0	22	44	.240	.315	.357

17-Year Totals

G	PA	AB	R	H	2B	3B	HR	RBI	SB	CS	BB	SO	BA	OBP	SLG
1969	7923	6925	1063	1960	388	43	306	1111	72	54	857	1116	.283	.360	.484

"Did You Know?"

The first time in major league history two black pitchers started an all-star game to face each other was in 1971. Vida Blue started as a representative of the Oakland A's in the American League and Doc Ellis was the starting pitcher for the Pittsburgh Pirates representing the National League.

"Son, we would like to keep you around, but we have decided to try win a pennant instead." — Casey Stengel

The first film on baseball was in 1898 by the Edison Manufacturing Company called, "The Ball Game."

The only brother trio who played at the same time was Matty Alou, Felipe Alou and Jesus Alou who played the three outfield positions in the same game for the San Francisco Giants in 1962.

"Career Highlights you ask, I had three! I got an intentional walk from Sandy Koufax. I escaped a run down against the Mets. The third highlight was in 1967 with St. Louis, I walked with the base loaded to drive in the winning run in an intersquad game at spring training."
— Bob Uecker

Juan Marichal

Born Oct. 20, 1937, Laguna Verde Monte Cristi, Dominican Republic

Height 6'0"   **Weight** 185 lbs.

Bats Right   **Throws** Right

Debut July 19, 1960   **Final game** April 16, 1975

JUAN MARICHAL was born in Laguna Verde Monte Christi, Dominican Republic. As a little boy, he was completely focused on becoming a professional baseball player, so much so that in the eleventh grade, he quit to play baseball full-time. He signed a professional contract with the Escogido Leones, a team that had a working agreement with the New York Giants. It was in 1957 that he signed on as an amateur with the New York Giants.

At twenty-two years of age, Juan was called up to the major leagues by the Giants who had moved across the United States to San Francisco from New York.

Juan was easily distinguished from other pitchers as he had an exaggerated motion when pitching the baseball towards home plate. He kicked his left leg high above his head which would provide exceptional velocity while concealing the ball from the opposing batters until it was on its way. He delivered his pitches with the accuracy similar to that of a surgeon.

Tom Sheehan was the manager for the Giants at the time of Juan's first game in San Francisco. After several days of throwing batting practice, the "Dominican Dandy" finally got his wish when, on Tuesday, July 19, 1960, he proudly took the mound for his first start. The poised twenty-two year old from the Dominican Republic mowed down the Philadelphia Phillies by pitching with his unique delivery and pinpoint accuracy. The 13,279 fans at Candlestick Park enthusiastically cheered their future superstar. The Phillies managed only one hit off of the future Hall-of-Famer as Juan, pitching with what would soon become his trademark high kick, struck out twelve and walked one. The National League caught a glimpse of what they would encounter for the next several years. Juan Marichal made his entrance into major league baseball with a strong message for his future opponents: "Life just got tougher!"

In fact, on Saturday June 15, 1963, Juan threw a no-hitter against the Houston Colt 45's at Candlestick Park in front of 18,869 San Francisco fans.

Pitching in the 1960s and 1970s was incredible, but what separated Juan from everyone else was the fact he had excellent command of all of his pitches—the fastball, the curve, the slider, and the screwball! Juan was an incredible pitcher and a disciplined student of the game. He knew how to pitch in every situation. In addition, he threw his pitches from different arm angles and from different release points! The hitters were off balance because they never could get comfortable with any particular situation or pitch count. He had sensational control and confidence combined with pinpoint accuracy. Juan even had the courage to throw pitches inside on the hitters to keep them uncomfortable and off of the plate, often taking the bat out of the hitter's hands!

Some pitchers like Sandy Koufax, Don Drysdale, Ferguson Jenkins, and Bob Gibson may have had a slight edge in one particular area of pitching, but no one had the entire arsenal of the grand master, Juan Marichal! He won more games in the dominant 1960s than any other pitcher with 191 wins! In 1968, Juan completed 30 games for the San Francisco Giants! That number is staggering.

Three times in Juan's career he pitched over 300 innings! Six times he won 20 games or more! His lifetime winning percentage is a mind boggling .631! Juan Marichal dominated his era of the 1960s and the 1970s, and, without question, he was one of the greatest pitchers of all time and was arguably the overall best in his era.

Severe back pain which sidelined the Dominican Dandy in 1970 carried over for the next few years. However, he bounced back to win 18 games in 1971 with an outstanding 2.91 ERA to lead the National League's Western Division Champion San Francisco Giants!

Juan Marichal

Juan was selected for nine All-Star games and was the winning pitcher for the National League twice—in 1962 and 1965. That same year, 1965, he also won the Most Valuable Player in the 1965 All-Star game!

In 1983 Juan Marichal took his rightful position amongst baseball's elite in Cooperstown,New York, as he became the first baseball player from the Dominican Republic inducted into the magnificent Baseball Hall of Fame!

Recently, Juan was added to the fifteen-member panel of the Veterans Selection Committee for the Baseball Hall of Fame.

The San Francisco Giants honored him by erecting a statue showing his famous high kicking pitching motion. That same day, the Giants players wore jerseys with the "Gigantes" name and logo. In a pre-game ceremony on July 20, 2003, Juan was inducted into the Hispanic Heritage Baseball Hall of Fame.

I've had the pleasure of knowing Juan since we first met in 1966 at Wrigley Field in Chicago. Years later, I became his batboy in San Francisco with the Giants. At times I visited his home with my friend Tito Fuentes. The one thing that has most impressed me about Juan is that he has always been, and still is, a considerate, kind, and a very respectful gentleman. No one surpasses his sense of grace and hospitality!

Juan currently resides in his beautiful Caribbean country of the Dominican Republic with his lovely wife, Alma.

In My Own Words

Dominican Republic and the Air Force Team

WHEN GROWING UP in my beautiful country of the Dominican Republic, at a very early age I realized how special my country was. My family lived in a poor village and we were a typical family from our area. In those days my belief in God sustained me and gave me the vision and strength to play baseball which has always been my passion. Throughout my life, my faith in God has truly placed the strength within my heart to withstand some of my life's darkest moments.

When I was nine years old, I found the time and ways to play baseball. My position was shortstop until I watched our exceptional Dominican National team play. They had an outstanding pitcher named Bomo Ramos. Ramos was incredible! He threw the ball sidearm. From the first time I saw him, I mimicked everything about my new hero Bomo Ramos, and he inspired me to pursue my career as a pitcher, not as a shortstop.

My mother did not understand my passion at first, as she wanted me to advance to a higher level of education. One time when I was nine years old, she caught me skipping school to play baseball. She said, "Mijo, why are you not in school and instead are playing baseball?" I told her, "Mommy, I am going to be a baseball player!" She did not understand. It was much later in my life when she actually watched me playing winter ball in the Dominican after I had signed my contract as a professional with the San Francisco Giants that she learned that I could make a living. I promised to send her some money, which I was able to do because of my profession. I thank God for those opportunities!

In the Dominican Republic, not only is baseball loved by just about everyone, but at times they have taken baseball to the extreme, as illustrated in this story. Before I was a professional player, I played amateur baseball in the town of Manzanillo in the Dominican Republic. We were playing a game against the powerful Dominican Republic Air Force team. The National Air Force team had the best players of the entire Dominican Republic, and they were very good. Our small town team in Manzanillo defeated the Air Force National team 2-1!

The next day a lieutenant from the Air Force knocked on my door and informed me that I was being drafted into the Air Force immediately. My recruiter was Ramfis Trujillo, son of the then political dictator of the Dominican Republic!

My new Air Force teammates and I returned to play my former team of Manzanillo just a few days later, which was a little strange for me as I had only been in the Air Force, and on the team, a few days. I pitched that day against my former team and lost in a very low-scoring game. We went on to lose a doubleheader to my former team. That became a controversial issue!

Rafael Trujillo, the dictator of Dominican Republic, directed an investigation to discover how it was possible that we lost two games! He was so displeased that we had lost two games that he threw the entire team into jail for several days. There I was—in jail for five days! At seventeen years of age, it was a very unpleasant, daunting and embarrassing experience. I then came to the full realization that my country took baseball far more seriously than I ever could have imagined. Our Air Force team resolved to never lose two games in a doubleheader again!

United States and the Major Leagues

In 1957 I was signed my professional contract from the amateur draft by the New York Giants. I made my way in the Giants' farm system to play for the Michigan Whitecaps in Michigan City. When I arrived; I was really shocked at some of the peculiarities of the new culture. This was the first time I experienced being separated by ethnic background. When we traveled, the four black and three Latino players took seats in the last two rows of the bus. I had never seen that before, and I was surprised. When we were on the road, the rest of the team would stay at a hotel, and the blacks and Latinos would have to stay at a black family's home as previously arranged. I was not angry or bitter, just confused. I did not understand the reasoning behind these divisions.

My first appearance in the major leagues was on July 19, 1960. The Giants were playing against the Philadelphia Phillies in Candlestick Park. It was a great day: in my debut game, I pitched a one-hitter and struck out twelve. It is difficult to express my feelings, emotions, and thoughts of that day. My dreams were coming true! From the very first time I arrived at Candlestick Park, Orlando Cepeda and Felipe Alou met me at the door of the clubhouse and introduced me to everyone on the club. Orlando and Felipe were so kind and considerate to me, and to this day we are very good friends! I remember clearly the first time I met Willie Mays. I thought, "How fortunate I am to actually make my dream a reality." In my mind and at that moment, I learned that my dreams, hard work, and passion had paid the dividends to produce what I so badly wanted!

I had learned from my hero Bomo Ramos to be a sidearm pitcher. Later on I learned to throw over the top and three quarters. I wanted to learn how to throw a screwball to make my pitches break the opposite direction from my curveball. Early in my career, the San Francisco Giants had a pitching coach named Andy Gilbert. Gilbert told me about Ruben Gomez who also played with the Giants in New York until 1958. Gomez had a pretty good screwball. Andy taught me the basic principles until I finally became comfortable. With lots of experimenting and practice, I finally accomplished the screwball and added it to my pitching arsenal! That gave me four legitimate pitches to show the batters to keep them off balance and guessing.

The Classic Pitching Duel

One of my most memorable games was on Tuesday, July 2, 1963. The Giants were playing the Milwaukee Braves in San Francisco at Candlestick Park. Warren Spahn was pitching for the Braves and I was pitching for the Giants. Both Spahn and I hooked up in a real pitchers' duel. The game was 0-0 in the ninth inning, and the Giants manager Alvin Dark wanted to take me out of the game. I looked at our manager and I said, "Alvin, do you see that man over there in the Braves dugout?" Alvin said, "Of course I do. What's your point?" I said (referring to Spahn), "Well, that man over there is forty-two years old! And if he can still pitch, then, since I am only twenty-two years old, I'll stay in the game until he stops pitching!" The game went into the fifteenth inning, still tied up at 0-0. I came into the Giants' dugout after pitching the fifteenth inning and I told Alvin Dark that he could take me out now. So Alvin got a Giants' reliever up in the bullpen to warm up for the sixteenth inning. However, Spahn went out and got the Giants out in a quick one, two, three innings! Before Alvin could motion or signal for our reliever to come in, I changed my mind and grabbed my glove and ran to the pitching mound. Alvin was not happy! But Alvin let me stay in and finish the sixteenth. Once I retired the Braves quickly in a one, two, three order, we went into our dugout. Willie Mays was the leadoff hitter for the Giants in the sixteenth inning. Willie came over to me before he went to the batter's box and said, "Chico, relax. I'm going to end this thing and win the game for us!" The very first pitch, Willie hit a rocket for a home run over the left field wall for the game winner! That day, I threw 227 pitches. After this game, Warren Spahn came over to me in the tunnel by the two clubhouses and gave me some valuable advice on how to prepare and take care of my arm for my next game I was going to start. I always appreciated that gesture and thought he was nice for being concerned. Without question, that game is one of my fondest memories in baseball.

My Most Embarrassing Moment

This brings me to my most embarrassing and least favorite game played on August 22, 1965. This game against the Los Angeles Dodgers was also played in San Francisco at Candlestick Park. A couple of games prior to this Sunday game, there was some chatter and something brewing as there were knockdown pitches, brush backs and hard slides. Every time our two teams played there was more excitement and enthusiasm amongst the fans and players. During Friday's game, after a couple of rough plays, I noticed Johnny Roseboro yelling from the Dodger dugout across the diamond at our Giants manager Herman Franks. I was standing up at the front of our dugout and I also was yelling towards the Dodgers' dugout. The 42,807 screaming fans were so loud that neither team could understand or even hear what the opposing team was chattering about. You could just tell by observing the body language that there was some animosity and these were not pleasantries being exchanged! After that Friday game, it came to me with messages from the Dodger catcher Johnny Roseboro that their team was going to get me on Sunday when I pitched.

Before Saturday's game I was sitting on the bench out in the right field bullpen near the door that lead to both teams clubhouses. Roseboro came out from the tunnel onto the field and walked towards me. Roseboro was cordial and not threatening in any way, and I thought that everything from the night before was forgotten. During Saturday's game there had also been some rough plays with hard slides and so forth, but nothing outlandish. But there were still some comments from both teams.

On Sunday, the day I am to face Sandy Koufax, the game started, and immediately I threw the baseball high and tight in on the first batter, Maury Wills. Maury hit the dirt! The next batter was Jim Gilliam; he also received some inside pitches. The game was intense as the players in the Dodgers' dugout were on me from my opening pitch. I was surprised as I thought that all had been forgotten from the brief conversations that Roseboro and I had the day before in the bullpen. When I came up to bat in the bottom of the Giants' third inning, Koufax threw the first pitch; it was a ball that was low. I looked over my right shoulder and saw Roseboro drop the ball and position himself more directly behind me and when he threw the ball back to Koufax, Roseboro nicked my right ear with the ball. I immediately looked back at Roseboro with my bat resting on my shoulder. I told him, "Don't hit me with that ball!" Roseboro replied with comments I did not appreciate, and he came up out of his catchers' crouch. Roseboro had his full catcher's equipment on and he was a big strong imposing man. As he stepped towards me, both of us were making unpleasant comments at each other, and, without even thinking, I did the unthinkable! I hit Roseboro on his head with the bat! It was a terrible incident, and Roseboro ended up with seventeen stitches in his head.

I've never made excuses. I was wrong, and, like Roseboro, I was caught up in the tension and heat of the previous three days. My act of aggression was 100% reaction. I had no prior intent or even thought of hitting Roseboro! Later in our lives, after our careers had ended, I invited Roseboro and his family to my first golf tournament in the Dominican Republic. Roseboro was very gracious and accepted my invitation. Our families, (Roseboro and Marichals) enjoyed each other's company along with our families! When Roseboro died, his wonderful wife invited me to the funeral to speak and memorialize him. It truly was an honor and I have always been very grateful for the opportunity. Johnny Roseboro and I had become friends!

It was a very unfortunate incident, and I have suffered from remorse ever since. That one incident is so far from my true character. Yet, when we do a terrible act, even when it is reaction, we can be remembered forever for that one wrong. That is why I am so appreciative of the good times the Roseboro and Marichal families shared, and of having that last opportunity at Johnny's funeral to talk about the type of man he really was.

August 22, 1965 was a terrible and dark day, not only for me, but for baseball also. I know that Roseboro, his family and God have forgiven me, and that is sufficient.

Gratitude

Baseball has always been wonderful to me and my family as it has provided a life beyond anything I could have ever imagined. Truly I have a grateful heart and I am appreciative of what baseball has provided

My desire is that history will also recognize and remember me for being a man of humility with a sincere desire to extend grace to others.

Juan Marichal

The Best of the Best

Best Fastball
J.R. Richard

Best Curveball
Camilo Pasqual

Most Intimidating Pitcher
Don Drysdale

Best Right Handed Pitcher
Bob Gibson

Best Left-Handed Pitcher
Sandy Koufax

Overall Most Challenging Pitcher
Ferguson Jenkins

Best Right-Handed Hitter
Roberto Clemente

Best Left-Handed Hitter
Rod Carew

Overall Best Clutch Hitter
Tony Perez

Best Catcher
Johnny Bench

Best First Baseman
Orlando Cepeda

Best Second Baseman
Julian Javier

Best Shortstop
Maury Wills

Best Third Baseman
Brooks Robinson

Best Left Fielder
Lou Brock ·

Best Center Fielder
Willie Mays

Best Right Fielder
Roberto Clemente

Fastest Base Runner
Willie Davis

Best Base Runner
Maury Wills

Best Overall Player
Hank Aaron

Player Who Didn't Reach Maximum Potential
Cesar Cedeno

Strongest Outfield Arm
Roberto Clemente

Best Team Rival
Dodgers

Best Opposing Manager
Walter Alston

Best Manager I Played For
Alvin Dark

Most Trusted Friend
Orlando Cepeda

My Favorite Team Mate
Orlando Cepeda

Funniest Player
Tito Fuentes

Most Heart
Orlando Cepeda

Most Courageous
Orlando Cepeda

Best Work Ethics
Orlando Cepeda
(Orlando taught others exercises)

Most Flamboyant
Tito Fuentes

Most Zany
Dave Kingman

Most Congenial
Matty Alou

My Favorite Team
1962 San Francisco Giants

Player I Most Admired
Roberto Clemente

Player I Would Have Liked as a Team Mate
Roberto Clemente

My Favorite Stadium
Dodger Stadium

My Favorite City
New York

Best Baseball Announcer
Vin Scully

My Favorite Baseball Announcer
Lon Simmons

The Best Umpire
Doug Harvey

Umpire with The Best Attitude
Doug Harvey

Most Respected Baseball Personality
Horace Stoneham

Juan Marichal
Lifetime Statistics

Year	Age	Tm	Lg	W	L	W-L%	ERA	G	GS	GF	CG	SHO	SV	IP	H	R	ER	HR	BB	SO
1960	22	SFG	NL	6	2	.750	2.66	11	11	0	6	1	0	81.1	59	29	24	5	28	58
1961	23	SFG	NL	13	10	.565	3.89	29	27	2	9	3	0	185.0	183	88	80	24	48	124
1962	24	SFG	NL	18	11	.621	3.36	37	36	1	18	3	1	262.2	233	112	98	34	90	153
1963	25	SFG	NL	25	8	.758	2.41	41	40	1	18	5	0	321.1	259	102	86	27	61	248
1964	26	SFG	NL	21	8	.724	2.48	33	33	0	22	4	0	269.0	241	89	74	18	52	206
1965	27	SFG	NL	22	13	.629	2.13	39	37	2	24	10	1	295.1	224	78	70	27	46	240
1966	28	SFG	NL	25	6	.806	2.23	37	36	1	25	4	0	307.1	228	88	76	32	36	222
1967	29	SFG	NL	14	10	.583	2.76	26	26	0	18	2	0	202.1	195	79	62	20	42	166
1968	30	SFG	NL	26	9	.743	2.43	38	38	0	30	5	0	325.2	295	106	88	21	46	218
1969	31	SFG	NL	21	11	.656	2.10	37	36	1	27	8	0	299.2	244	90	70	15	54	205
1970	32	SFG	NL	12	10	.545	4.12	34	33	0	14	1	0	242.2	269	128	111	28	48	123
1971	33	SFG	NL	18	11	.621	2.94	37	37	0	18	4	0	279.0	244	113	91	27	56	159
1972	34	SFG	NL	6	16	.273	3.71	25	24	1	6	0	0	165.0	176	82	68	15	46	72
1973	35	SFG	NL	11	15	.423	3.82	34	32	1	9	2	0	207.1	231	104	88	22	37	87
1974	36	BOS	AL	5	1	.833	4.87	11	9	1	0	0	0	57.1	61	32	31	3	14	21
1975	37	LAD	NL	0	1	.000	13.50	2	2	0	0	0	0	6.0	11	9	9	2	5	1

16-Year Totals

W	L	W-L%	ERA	G	GS	GF	CG	SHO	SV	IP	H	R	ER	HR	BB	SO
243	142	.631	2.89	471	457	11	244	52	2	3507.0	3153	1329	1126	320	709	2303

"Did You Know?"

Willie Mays was the first rookie of the year winner to be elected into Cooperstown's Hall of Fame.

"Reggie Jackson would give you the shirt off of his back. Of course he would call a press conference to announce it." — Jim "Catfish" Hunter

While playing for the Philadelphia Phillies in 1976 catcher Tim McCarver came to bat with the bases loaded and hit the ball over the wall for what appeared to be a grand slam. However, McCarver took off running and at one point put his head down and ran past teammate Garry Maddox who was on base at first. McCarver was called out for passing another runner. When asked about how something like that could ever happen, McCarver said, just pure speed.

In 1970 Rico Carty was the first player selected to an all-star game with a write in vote.

"Being with a woman all night never hurt any baseball player. However, it's staying up all night looking for a woman that is what does him in." — Casey Stengel

Jon Miller
Hall-of-Fame Broadcaster

JON MILLER, the golden voice of the Giants and of ESPN, was born in San Francisco on October 11, 1951. After graduating Hayward High School and the College of San Mateo, Jon worked as the sports director for KFTY Santa Rosa, California. In 1974 the Oakland A's hired Jon, providing him his first opportunity as a major league play-by-play baseball announcer. Fortunately for him, that year the Oakland A's played the Baltimore Orioles for the American Championship which the A's won handily, three games to one. That was the same year he broadcast his first World Series, when once again the Oakland A's defeated the Los Angeles Dodgers in five games to capture the World Championship. Since then, Jon has eloquently broadcast 12 World Series, including the last 11 for ESPN Radio.

In his distinguished career Jon has broadcast games for the California Golden Seals hockey team, the University of San Francisco, University of Pacific basketball, Golden State Warriors, and the original San Jose Earthquakes of the Northern American Soccer League. Jon broadcast major league games for the Texas Rangers from 1978–1979, the Boston Red Sox from 1980–1982, and the Baltimore Orioles from 1983–1996. From 1986–1989, Jon occasionally worked NBC's Game-of-the-

Week with both Tony Kubek, and Joe Garigiola. After the 1996 season with the Orioles, Jon was hired by his favorite team, the San Francisco Giants to broadcast games in the Bay Area.

He is beginning his 13th season as the "Voice of the Giants" and he is acknowledged as one of the most distinguished broadcasters in baseball. In addition to the San Francisco Giants, Jon enters his 21st season as the fine play-by-play announcer for ESPN Sunday Night Baseball Game-of-the-Week.

Jon Miller has the silky golden tones that most baseball fans immediately recognize and acknowledge as one the games' truly great play-by-play announcers. He displays his quick wit, analogies and finesse while narrating the game in a lively and descriptive manner. Listening to Jon Miller eloquently paint the details of a game is similar to watching a grand master purposefully apply each brush stroke to the canvas as a masterpiece comes to life.

The most famous call in Jon Miller's career came when he called Barry Bonds' record breaking 756th home run when Bonds broke the record of legendary Hank Aaron. His call will go down in history as one of the most famous calls in the history of baseball! Here's a transcript of that call:

> "Three and two to Bonds. Everybody standing here at 24 Willie Mays Plaza. An armada of nautical craft gather in McCovey Cove beyond the right field wall. Bonds is one home run away from history. [Crack of the bat] And he swings, and there's a long one, deep into right center field, way back there! It's gone!!! *A HOME RUN!* Into the centerfield bleachers to the left of the 421-foot marker. An extraordinary shot to the deepest part of the yard! And Barry Bonds, with 756 home runs, has hit more home runs than anyone who has ever played the game!"

Jon Miller was nominated for a national Emmy twice—once in 1995 and again in 1996. He was also nominated six times for an "ACE" award, emblematic of cable television excellence; he won the award in 1991 and 1996 for his play-by-play work. Jon was selected as the Sportscaster-of-the-Year by the National Sportswriters Association in 1988, and that same year he was inducted into the Hall of Fame of the National Sportscasters Association of America.

In addition to being a famous and fabulous play-by-play announcer for baseball, Jon Miller is a genuine, honest and gracious gentleman who enjoys being kind and hospitable to people. Jon is very considerate, and deserves his Hall-of-Fame status as an announcer, but more importantly, as a person!

Jon currently resides with his wife Janine in a gorgeous oceanside hamlet just south of San Francisco. They are the proud parents of daughters Michelle, Holly, and Emilie, and son Alexander.

In My Own Words

O NE OF MY GREAT MEMORIES as a kid growing up in the East Bay was watching Willie Mays play for my favorite team, the San Francisco Giants. Then, when the A's left Kansas City for Oakland in 1968, I also became an Oakland A's fan!

In 1968, during what proved to be Mickey Mantle's last year, the Yankees came to Oakland to play the A's, and I naturally I wanted to see Mickey play. 1968 was also the year of the pitcher as they dominated the hitters! There was only one hitter in the entire American League who hit .300: Carl Yastrzemski won the batting title with a .301 average! Danny Cater of the Oakland A's was the second leading hitter behind Yaz in the league with a .290 batting average. The entire New York Yankees as a team only batted .214!

Although Mickey Mantle finished his last season with a .237 batting average, remember that he actually batted over 20 points higher than the entire Yankees team! While I sat at the Oakland Coliseum during that memorable August 1968 game, I witnessed the Mick hit one of his last home runs ever! Bobby Cox once told me that his own claim to fame was that he was leading the Yankees in hitting at the break in that 1968 All-Star game. I asked him, "What were you hitting at the break?" He smiled and said, ".260!"

Willie and the Giants Return

The following story was conveyed to me by the New York sports writer Ron Angel, who was at the 1962 game and witnessed the evening's events. When the Giants first returned to New York to play the Mets at the Polo Grounds in 1962, the atmosphere was almost like that of a World Series. Lindsay Nelson, the first Mets broadcaster, introduced both teams one at a time, just like it is done at a World Series. At that point, the Mets were terrible! They had lost over 100 games their first four consecutive years. Even before the game started, the New Yorkers in the bleachers were obviously rooting for the San Francisco Giants—they had not fully accepted the Mets as their new team.

In spite of the New Yorkers who were rooting for the Giants, there was a handful of enthusiastic fans out near the bleachers rooting for the Mets. One guy in the outfield seats had a horn and would periodically play one single note. It sounded almost like a foghorn. Every time he blew the horn, a handful of fans would yell, "Go!" This went on for a couple of innings! Out of that game grew the Mets' cult following, later identified as "The Breed!"

Late in that game, with the Giants still leading 9-1, the Mets put together a rally. As they came back, the Mets were embraced by the fans. A new phenomenon was born with the chant "Let's go, Mets!" Other teams have since adopted the "Let's go, Mets!" chant for their team, but it happened first during that game in 1962.

There is another humorous side note to that game. Jimmy Davenport, the Giants defensive wiz at third base, hit his first grand slam ever. The outfield foul pole at the Polo Grounds was only 257 feet down the right field line, but the upper deck protruded back towards the infield another 15-20 feet, so that a home run to the upper deck had to be hit approximately 237 feet. The ball that Davenport hit barely landed in the upper deck. The funny part is that originally when the ball was hit, the Mets second baseman went back on the ball as it appeared to be just another popup. He actually thought that he had a chance to make a catch. It's not often an infielder thinks he has a play on the ball, and it leaves the yard for an upper deck home run!

About Willie

Willie Mays once told me that when Herman Franks was the manager of the Giants, he would ask Willie's opinion about making out the lineup card. Willie made the selections and Franks would pencil their names as Willie told him. If a Giants player was batting second or sixth in the lineup, and that player failed to advance the runners, Willie would move them down in the batting lineup the next day!

Bobby Bonds told me a story about Willie Mays during the time when Bobby was playing with the Texas Rangers and I was the Rangers broadcaster. Bobby said that once the Giants were playing a game when a couple of the Giants got upset about how the opposing catcher was intentionally throwing at the Giants base runners. Willie got on base, and later in the inning he had an opportunity to slide into home plate. Willie was a remarkable base runner and he had an uncanny knack for perfectly timing every move on the base paths. When he was striding towards home plate, he knew there would be a collision. He hit the catcher very hard with his slide, taking out the catcher's knee. The catcher had to be removed from the game and taken to the hospital. Bobby told me that if Willie thought one of the Giants' opponents was playing dirty, Willie would at some point balance the books!

Willie Mays served in the armed forces and he missed 128 games in 1952, and the missed the entire 1953 season. When he returned in 1954, he slammed 41 home runs. It's interesting to think about how many more home runs he might have hit at the Polo Grounds if he had not missed those 290 games.

Willie Mays was far more than a superstar! As an example, Willie would bait outfielders to throw towards his base by speeding up, or delaying, just enough to draw the outfielders' throw so his team mates could advance another bag. According to his peers, Willie Mays was the most cunning, clever and astute player in the game!

You Gotta Have Heart

In the Best of the Best section I mention that Ron Hunt had a tremendous heart. In 1971, Hunt got hit by fifty pitches while playing for the Montreal Expos. Steve Carlton once told me what a real pain in the neck Ron had become to him. Carlton always had the desire to go the distance and complete his starts. When playing against Ron Hunt's team, that was less likely as the pesky Hunt would constantly foul pitch after pitch, then take several pitches, get hit with a pitch, and end up on base anyway. Carlton said that if it was in the later innings with two outs and no runners on base, he would drill Hunt with a pitch. By hitting Hunt, he would save on his pitch counts and also speed up the game. If Carlton did that, surely there were other pitchers who had thought of the same tactic. Ron Hunt had to be respected. He was a player who maximized his talent and always found ways to reach base!

Classic Mickey Mantle & Whitey Ford

Here's a story direct from Whitey Ford to me. Mickey Mantle and Whitey Ford were selected for the 1961 All-Star game to be played in San Francisco's new Candlestick Park. Both Mickey and Whitey were avid golfers, and Giants owner Horace Stoneham asked his brother Charles to take care of the two legends while they were in San Francisco. The day before the All-Star game, Mantle and Ford golfed at the Olympic Club. Charles told them, "If you need clubs, gloves or shoes, just charge it to my brother's account and you can pay him tomorrow when you get to the ballpark." They charged all kinds of things to Horace Stoneham's account.

Mantle and Ford were well known for their drinking escapades, and after they played their rounds of golf, they headed towards the country club's bar to have a few toddies. They are now also charging their cocktails to Stoneham's account, racking up some serious dough! Charles Stoneham proceeded to take Mantle and Ford to another club and yet another club, going all over San Francisco. Horace knew about all of the charges as his brother Charles had kept him informed. After several hours of this, Mantle looked at his buddy Ford, and said, "You better go home and get some sleep as you may have to pitch in the All-Star game." Ford looks at Mantle and said, "Nah! I'm not going to pitch tomorrow. I just pitched on Sunday. There's no way they would pitch me on two days rest!"

Both Mantle and Ford had gotten about two hours' sleep, and it's a day game! Just before the game, Ford said to Mantle, "We owe Horace $600, so give me $300 and I will settle up with him." Ford goes up to Horace's office at Candlestick and Mantle heads to the clubhouse. Horace knows the whole story, and he told Ford to hang onto the money for now. "I'd like to make you a proposition. If you get Willie Mays out today, then you keep your money and don't owe me anything. But if Willie gets on base, then you owe me double!" Ford looked at Horace and said, "If I get Willie out today, Mantle and I don't owe you anything?" "That is correct" said Horace. Ford is beaming as he and Horace shake hands on it because Ford is thinking he's not even pitching today. This is a cinch bet!

Ford is jubilant when he got to the clubhouse. He said to Mantle, "We won't owe Horace a penny! I just made the bet of the century!" Mantle asked, "What's the bet?" Ford replied, "I just saved us both three hundred big ones!" Mantle kept asking Ford, "What's the bet?" Ford then told Mantle the bet that he and Horace had just shaken hands on. "If Willie doesn't get on base against me, we owe nothing!" Mantle looked at Ford and said, "Of course Willie is going to get on base, because he owns you! Remember, you cannot get Mays out!" Ford replied, "He can't get a hit off of me because I'm not pitching!" Mantle told Ford, "You sure are! You are not only pitching today, but you are the starter!"

Ford then went to his manager, Ralph Houk, to plead his case. Ford said, "I can't pitch. I just pitched day before yesterday on Sunday. Remember?" Houk responded to Ford, "The league president is insisting that you pitch because you are Whitey Ford of the New York Yankees, for goodness sake!"

Mays was up in the first inning, and Ford could not even walk him or Mays would get on base and both Mantle and Ford would lose the bet. So Ford threw an off-speed pitch down in the dirt outside and Mays golfs it about four hundred feet foul down the right field line. Next time Ford threw a fastball way inside on Mays' hands. Mays opened up and launched this pitch about fifteen feet foul down the left field foul line. Ford thought to himself, "I can't possibly throw a more unhittable pitch than those last two." He now had two strikes on Mays. Ford said that if you throw at Mays, he will definitely hit the deck. He decided to throw an illegal pitch to Mays by cutting the ball. The pitch danced and moved like a butterfly! This pitch went right at Mays, and he hit the deck as the ball came back over the plate. Strike three! Mays jumped and started yelling at Jocko Conlan. Then he stared at Whitey Ford on the mound, screaming, "What the hell kind of pitch was that, you cheating no good so-and-so?" As Mays went into a verbal tirade, he looked out in centerfield and saw Mickey Mantle clapping his hands. Then Mays again directed his verbal assault on Ford. He asked, "What the heck is he clapping his hands at out there for, you lousy cheaters?" Finally Whitey Ford yelled back at him, "Willie, I will explain later. It has nothing to do with you! Give me a chance to explain after the game. Okay?" After the game, both Mantle and Ford went to Mays and explained the bet with Horace Stoneham. In the end Horace honored the bet and Mantle and Ford got off without owing a nickel—at the expense of Willie Mays in his hometown!

Later, Willie Mays explained more to me so I really put this story together about Mantle, Mays, and Ford. He told me that Jocko Conlan had a thing for him, and was not fair with his calls towards Willie. Because of the attitude Jocko had towards Willie, the ball Ford threw at Willie in the All-Star game only had to be in the vicinity of the plate. Then this crazy story really made sense!

The Best of the Best

Best Fastball
Nolan Ryan

Best Curveball
Bert Blyleven

Most Intimidating Pitcher
Nolan Ryan

Best Right-Handed Pitcher
Catfish Hunter

Best Left-Handed Pitcher
Sandy Koufax

Best Left-Handed Reliever
Sparky Lyle

Best Right-Handed Reliever
Rollie Fingers

Overall Most Challenging Pitcher
Bob Gibson, Mike Cuellar

Best Right-Handed Hitter
Willie Mays
(I'm a Giants' fan!)

Best Left-Handed Hitter
Willie McCovey, Rod Carew

Overall Best Clutch Hitter
Sal Bando, Eddie Murray
(A lot of times the superstars like
Mays and McCovey were pitched
around.)

Best Switch Hitter
Mickey Mantle, Reggie Smith
(In the 60s and 70s Reggie Smith
was the best!)

Best Catcher
Carlton Fisk, Johnny Bench

Best First Baseman
Willie McCovey, Orlando
Cepeda,
(McCovey was also good as a left
fielder with quite an arm.)

Best Second Baseman
Joe Morgan
(Joe played in an era of the pitcher
and dominated his era!)

Best Shortstop
Maury Wills, Mark Belanger
(Bert Capaneris was also
outstanding!)

Best Third Baseman
Brooks Robinson, Mike Schmidt,
(Jimmy Davenport was the best S.F.
Giants, & excellent fielder!)

Best Left Fielder
Joe Rudi, Willie Stargell
(Joe Rudi made the catch of the
World Series three years!)

Best Center Fielder
Willie Mays
(Paul Blair was a great
centerfielder!)

Best Right Fielder
Hank Aaron, Frank Robinson,
(Reggie Jackson once told me he
would choose Bobby Bonds)

Fastest Base Runner
Willie Davis, Willie Wilson,
(Bobby Bonds certainly was in that
class with his speed!)

Best Base Runner
Maury Wills, Willie Mays,
(Maury revolutionized baseball
with the running game!)

Player Who Didn't Reach Maximum Potential
Mark "The Bird" Fidrych
(Not because of a lack of effort, but
because of injuries)
(Joe Charboneau played two years
& won Rookie of the year!)

Strongest Outfield Arm
Roberto Clemente

Best Team Rival
Giants & Dodgers
(The Cubs & Cardinals is great!
Cub fans hate the Cardinals!)

Best Manager
Earl Weaver, Dick Williams

Funniest Player
Dick Green (Dick would get on
everybody)

Most Heart
Ron Hunt (He maximized his talent! He was hit fifty times in one
year with the ball by pitchers!)

Most Courageous
Frank Linzy, Stu Miller,
(Linzy won 14 games with the
Giants in 1969 as a reliever!)

Best Work Ethics
Hank Aaron

Most Flamboyant
Willie Montanez

Most Congenial
Ray Fosse
(In 1974, when I was new as a
broadcaster, Ray went above and
beyond to assist me!)

Most Zany
Jimmy Piersall

My Favorite Team
San Francisco Giants

Jon Miller

Player I Most Admired
Willie Mays
(I emulated everything I could about
Willie, including the way
he walked!)

My Favorite Stadium
The old Tiger Stadium in Detroit,
From a broadcasters' perspective,
in Detroit you were the closest to
the field! However, Fenway Park
in Boston is incredible as a fan!)

My Favorite City
New York
(What a thrill, my first visit! Chicago, Toronto, & Seattle are also fabulous!)

Best Baseball Announcer
Vin Scully
(I now understand how sensa-
tional Vin is as a broadcaster, and
I believe he's probably the best
ever!)

My Favorite Baseball Announcer
Russ Hodges & Lon Simmons
(Always my favorites and the best!)

The Best Umpire
Satch Davidson
(Great guy! He worked game 6 of
the 1976 Red Sox & Reds World
Series)

The Best Umpire
Satch Davidson
(Great guy! He worked game 6 of
the 1976 Red Sox & Reds World Series)

Umpire with The Best Attitude
Nester Chylak

Most Respected Baseball Personality
Hank Aaron, Sandy Koufax,
& Willie Mays!

Players I would be willing to pay to watch play today
Tim Lincecum, Pablo Sandoval,
Jacoby Ellsbury, Prince Fielder,
and Joe Mauer!

Recommendations for future broadcasters
Study & know the game. Study good literature, and set yourself apart.

"Did You Know?"

The most seasons spent with one ball club is twenty three, held by Hall of Famers Carl Yastrzemski of the Boston Red Sox, and Brooks Robinson of the Baltimore Orioles.

"The difference from the old ballplayers and the new players are, the old ballplayers played the game for the name on the front of the jersey. The new ball player cares about the name on the back of his jersey." — Steve Garvey

1963 was the only time in the history of baseball that an entire starting infield of the all-star game consisted of players from the same team. The St. Louis Cardinals all-stars consisted of Bill White at first base, Julian Javier at second base, Dick Groat at shortstop, and Ken Boyer at third base.

Hall of Fame pitcher Gaylord Perry while pitching for the San Francisco Giants, stated in 1963, "they will put a man on the moon before I ever hit a home run." On July 20, 1969 the Apollo 11 landed with Neil Armstrong walking on the moon. The same day, moments later, Gaylord Perry hit the first home run of his illustrious career just as he had predicted.

Tug McGraw on how to he would recommend pitching to Henry Aaron? "I'd recommend pitching to Aaron like you would everyone else, except don't release the ball."

Tony Oliva

Born July 20, 1938, Pinar del Rio, Cuba

Height 6'2   **Weight** 190 lbs.

Bats Left   **Throws** Right

Debut Sept. 9, 1962   **Final game** Sept. 29, 1976

ANTONIO LOPEZ HERNANDES (JAVIQUE) OLIVA was born in Pinar del Rio, Cuba, on July 20, 1938. Tony was signed as a free agent by the Minnesota Twins scout Joe Cambria on July 24, 1961.

Tony excelled in every aspect as a professional major leaguer. He could run very well, had a strong and accurate throwing arm, was an efficient outfielder, and was an exceptional hitter. Several major league players have told me that Tony Oliva was the best left-handed hitter in the 1960s and 1970s! He was definitely one of the most proficient hitters from either side of the plate in his era. He frequently dominated the game with his bat.

In 1964, his first full season in the majors, Tony finished with a .323 batting average, 217 hits, 32 home runs, 43 doubles, 94 RBIs, and he collected the Rookie of the Year Award. The Minnesota Twins and the fans experienced firsthand what the future would hold for Tony Oliva and the Minnesota Twins.

He won the American League batting title the first two seasons of his illustrious career. In total, Tony won three American League batting titles, one of only fourteen major leaguers to have won three batting titles!

His prowess as a feared hitter was demonstrated on five different occasions as he led the American League with hits for the seasons: in 1964, 1965, 1966, 1969, and 1970!

On nine occasions he had better than a .300 batting average for the Twins. American League pitchers winced when Tony came to bat; they knew he was a master with the bat who could hit to all fields with exceptional control.

After 15 successful seasons, Tony's career marks are 1917 hits, 220 home runs, and an outstanding career batting average of .304!

In addition, he played in eight All-Star games, and, in 1966, he won a Gold Glove playing right field. On two separate occasions, Tony finished second in the American Most-Valuable-Player voting.

Tony suffered greatly with the severe injuries he sustained in his career, and in 1973, due to his severe knee injuries, he was relegated to the designated hitter role.

When examining his career totals, it is significant to look at his 6301 career at bats. Compared to other extraordinary players, Tony's numbers are very impressive and certainly Hall-of-Fame caliber!

On July 14, 1991, the Minnesota Twins honored him by retiring his number 6!

Tony Oliva and his wife, Gordette, reside happily in Bloomington Minnesota.

Tony Oliva

In My Own Words

IN 1976, THE DESIGNATED HITTER RULE had been in effect only a couple years, but that new rule benefited both me and the Minnesota Twins. By 1973, the first year of the DH rule, I had missed a lot of time due to injuries, particularly to my knees. The DH rule was a good fit as I could use my hitting skills without any further injury on the field on defense. Sometimes, I even platooned in the DH role and would also pinch hit.

One time in 1976, I pinch hit for the DH about halfway through the game. I did not get on base and returned to the dugout where I picked up my things and headed to the clubhouse, as I usually did when I would pinch hit and came out of a game. I got to the clubhouse, took off my uniform, and took a shower. When I got out of the shower, ready to dry off and get into my street clothes. Bobby Randall came in and said to me, "Tony, what are you doing? You're on deck!" I then realized that I wasn't out of the game—I was still in the game as the designated hitter! That day I proved to myself just how fast I could get into my uniform. I broke all records getting dressed, and I flew back to the dugout just in time. I was able to get to hit at my turn, and there was a runner on first who stole second, so they intentionally walked me.

Man, was I embarrassed! You are not supposed to forget you're the hitter and you're not supposed to forget you're still in the game! My teammates goofed on me relentlessly, laughing and joking about my forgetting to "stay in the game!"

The manager, Gene Mauch, was a stern, business type of manager. He didn't say anything, but boy, I knew what he was thinking. I was afraid to ask, or, for that matter, say anything to him. Incidentally, that runner ahead of me on the intentional walk scored, tying up the game, which we later won. But I never forgot that day. This happened later in my career, in 1976. Maybe it was my first senior moment!

My Most Memorable Moment!

For certain, my most memorable moment was in 1965 when we clinched in the American League. Starting in spring training, every player's dream is to go all the way to the Word Series. That was the year we did it as we faced the Los Angeles Dodgers. It was also the only year I played in a World Series. The Minnesota Twins won 102 games that year, we had an awesome group of players.

Stepping Up & Speaking Out

Gary Hall, the author of this book, recently asked me to describe my thoughts and perspective about me and my career, especially with respect to others and their Hall-of-Fame credentials.

The Hall of Fame is a real sore topic for me personally. They need to revise the so-called Veterans Committee rules. Yes, again! These rules simply do not work properly or effectively.

In those years when selections are made, it is ridiculous to pick veteran members. Most of us are in our sixties, seventies, and eighties, and electing us late in life or even posthumously does not serve us at all. We should be able to savor the honor in this lifetime! It hurts even more so because the election is done exclusively by living Hall-of-Famers. Most of us candidates have played with these guys, but they refuse to give us the respect that we have earned and deserve. Indeed, it seems that these guys have formed little "clubs" based on league loyalty, or even overall loyalty to each other, to the exclusion of us candidates. This club of certain living Hall-of-Famers for the most part does not want any new members for fear that the newcomers may threaten or dilute their influence!

I believe that I absolutely belong in Cooperstown's Hall of Fame. My friend Lou Galgano and I could literally write a book on this topic alone! Many of my friends, family, baseball writers, announcers, and others have spent much time and effort trying to convince the so-called experts that I truly belong in the Hall of Fame. For some reason, those listening have deaf ears, and they have prevailed. The determining criteria and process is more than baffling! In my opinion, the system is in need of greater clarity and less politics!

Pete Rose

Pete Rose, without question, deserves his plaque on his record alone as a player. However, his issues after his playing career were over are his own and not for me to judge. Pete Rose was an incredible hitter!

What Should Change in Baseball

If I were Commissioner, I would like to change back to the old rule on World Series home field advantage, alternating the field where the series is played between the National League and American League. I do not believe the winner of All-Star game should determine home field advantage. When I played the All-Star game, we always played to win. We thought our American League players were better than the National League players; and we did not want them to beat us or think otherwise. The current rule does not change how the real All-Star players play the game. The rule should be changed back to the old way and left that way!

What Has Changed

There are three main areas of the game of baseball that have changed since I last played.

The first is in pitching. There are no more complete games and complete game doubleheaders by the same pitcher! Now we have pitch counts, inning counts, starters (for five innings anyway), long relievers, short relievers, mop-ups, setups, and closers. A quality start now is six innings regardless of the outcome. It used to be a complete game win!

The second is in corner positions—left field, right field, first base and third base. These positions used to be dominated by high-average hitters with power. Now they seem to be dominated by defense.

The third is designated hitters. This has changed the game and permitted weak-fielding, strong-hitting players to prevail as well as prolonging the careers of older and injury-prone players. But the position needs to be dominated by really good hitters—the top of the lineup hitters—not the seventh, eighth or ninth slots. Remember, a quality at bat used to be when you got a hit or moved the runner up a base. Now it's when you foul off a certain amount of pitches, take full counts, or make the pitcher work, regardless of the results of the at bat.

There is an old saying: "If it is not broken, don't fix it!" Years ago, baseball was oppressive, racist and at times dangerous to play, the wealth was not shared, and it was a difficult way to make a living. We have a lot to be thankful for in present baseball—nice parks, good food, good crowds, good game security, and good money! We should take some time to "smell the roses" today. Some things are meant to be left alone and enjoyed, not necessarily improved upon.

Ridiculous Record

Cal Ripken, Jr., holds the "Iron Man" record for the most consecutive games played: for being at the park every day, ready to play, no excuses, no days off, no injuries, playing hurt, playing tired, playing every day with no "rest" day, playing under tremendous pressure. It is amazing to me that someone would simply avoid taking days off so that he would be in a position to break this ridiculous milestone. You also have to remember that Lou Gehrig did the same thing. His streak ended when he became too sick to play. This record is meaningless because it hurts teams more than it helps them.

Today's Players

There are some wonderful, gifted and talented players in today's game. Among those player with enormous talent, here are three of my favorites that I would be willing to go out and pay to watch play!

First is Joe Mauer! He is a pure hitter and people love to watch him hit. When he is at bat, you always know that something good and exciting is about to happen.

Second is Albert Pujols. He is probably the number one most dangerous hitter in the game today. He can always make something happen in the game.

Third is C.C. Sabathia who is probably the best in his league. He is big, strong, tough, and good defensively. He will go out 95% of the time and throw a good, solid game!

In Closing

I'm very thankful for the opportunities baseball has provided in my life with all my experiences, former teammates, opponents and my fabulous fans. Baseball truly is the greatest game!

The Best of the Best

Best Fastball
Nolan Ryan
(100 mph fastball speaks for itself!)

Best Curveball
Camilo Pasqual
(Nasty dip down hook)

Most Intimidating Pitcher
Nolan Ryan
(Very deceptive)

Best Right-Handed Pitcher
Luis Tiant
(My pick from the AL based upon my personal experiences; others include Juan Marichal, Jim Palmer, Bert Blyleven, Bob Gibson, Jim "Catfish" Hunter, Don Drysdale, & Tom Seaver. Each had their own power points, & it's difficult to label one as the "best!")

Best Left-Handed Pitcher
Sandy Koufax
(I only faced him in the World Series & All-Star games but a great lefty indeed! Others were Mickey Lolich, Mike Cuellar, & the toughest lefty I faced on a regular basis was without a doubt, "Sudden" Sam Mc-Dowell!)

Best Left-Handed Reliever
Terry Foster
(Very nasty, hard throwing lefty!)

Best Right-Handed Reliever
Rich "Goose" Gossage
(He would cook your goose in a hurry!)

Overall Most Challenging Pitcher
Nolan Ryan
(I knew it was coming 100 mph, & I still could not hit it!)

Best Right-Handed Hitter
Willie Mays, Hank Aaron, Roberto Clemente, Frank Robinson!
(All equally great hitters!)

Best Left-Handed Hitter
Rod Carew,
Carl Yastrzemski,
George Brett
(Present company excluded as I always thought I was pretty good too!)

Overall Best Clutch Hitter
Harmon Killebrew
(Always seemed to come through when we needed him to step up and do some damage.)

Best Catcher
Earl Battey
(My teammate who did it as well as anyone.)

Best First Baseman
Vic Power
(Grossly underrated at his position!)

Best Second Baseman
Rod Carew
(Underrated defensively, but very smooth and more than capable!)

Best Shortstop
Luis Aparicio
(I also have to mention my team-mate, friend, and MVP Zoilo Ver-sailles. Very good!)

Best Third Baseman
Brooks Robinson
(A literal vacuum cleaner at the hot corner!)

Best Left Fielder
Carl Yastrzemski
(Another one who could play good defense as well as an outstanding hitter!)

Best Center Fielder
Willie Mays
(No question on this one!)

Best Right Fielder
Al Kaline
(One of my idols and mentors, but don't forget that I also was a Gold Glove recipient!)

Fastest Base Runner
Ron Leflore
(He could literally outrun the ball!)

Best Base Runner
Maury Wills
(Not necessarily the fastest, but the smartest and overall the best!)

Best Overall Player
Willie Mays
(He could do it all – run, throw, field, hit for average & power. Willie was the five-tool player before anyone else could count that high!)

Player Who Didn't Reach Maximum Potential

Mickey Mantle

(Mick certainly was the most gifted player talent-wise who was hampered by injuries. Who knows what a healthy Mickey Mantle would have accomplished? Also, I always thought the same about myself and my dear friend Orlando Cepeda if we had been healthy through our careers.)

Best Team Rival

Minnesota Twins
& Chicago White Sox

Best Manager I Played For

Sam Mele

(The special one who gave me my first opportunity! Billy Martin was the best I ever played for as he got 110% from his players and always out-managed his opponents!)

My Favorite Team Mate

Rod Carew

(My roommate)

Most Heart

Cesar Tovar

(At all nine positions. You could play him anywhere & he would play exceptionally, without complaining!)

Strongest Outfield Arm

Rocky Colavito

(One time in Kansas City, Rocky caught a ball against the wall and nearly threw me out tagging up at second base to advance to third base! He could throw a baseball 400 feet, farther than a lot of players could hit the ball! He absolutely had the strongest arm I ever witnessed!)

Best Opposing Manager

Earl Weaver

(Always seemed to have the best team.)

Most Trusted Friend

Lou Galgano

(Always close to me like a brother)
Julio Becquer
(My best baseball friend!)
Also, Mike Day!

Funniest Player

Bert Blyleven

(A clown with jokes, but very smart. He knows how & when to pull the laugh trigger!)

Most Courageous

Pete Rose

(He was daring, fearless, & courageous. He often played hurt!)

Best Work Ethics
Tony Oliva
(I'm wanting to be humble, but I feel no one worked harder than me!)

Most Flamboyant
Reggie Jackson
(He started a trend by dropping his bat with a flair as he watched his home runs sail into the blue sky!)

Most Zany
Lou Pinella
(Mad & crazy! Once in Kansas City, he hit a smoking hot line shot, but we got him out on a very good defensive play. Lou was still heated when he walked out to field on defense in left field. All of a sudden, Lou attacked and beat up the foul pole!)

My Favorite Team
Minnesota Twins
(49 years & counting, none better!)

Player I Most Admired
Gordette Oliva and Cesar Tovar
(My wife, a true player, who has put up with me for 45 years! Cesar Tovar is the player I most admired on the field!)

Player I Would Have Liked as a Team Mate
Orlando Cepeda
(A good friend & great player. He played hard, was a very good hitter, and has a great personality. Orlando had great influence as my senior and mentor; I especially remember his help and influence at All-Star games and winter ball in Puerto Rico. We still share a good friendship!)

My Favorite Stadium
The original Yankee Stadium

My Favorite City
Minneapolis
(Home sweet home! My favorite city to visit was always New York!)

Best Baseball Announcer
Mel Allen (Overall)
Herb Carneil (Locally)

My Favorite Baseball Announcer
Herb Carneil

The Best Umpire
Nestor Chylak

(An overall good umpire who worked very hard and was funny. One time I took a knuckle ball that I thought was over my head. Nester said, "Strike one!" I said, "That ball was way high." Nestor said, "No Tony, that ball came back into the strike zone when you weren't looking!" Another time I'm at the bat and the catcher complains to Nestor, "That ball was right over the plate." Nester said, "No way. You know if that ball was close, Tony would have swung at it!")

Umpire with The Best Attitude
Nester Chylak & Ron Luciano

Most Respected Baseball Personality
Harmon Killebrew

(I played with him many years. He was a true professional, even tempered, never got mad, never over-reacted, never showed or played his emotions. Just a nice guy with a good attitude, a genuine person that you could not shake up or get under his skin!)

Tony Oliva
Lifetime Statistics

Year	Age	Tm	Lg	G	PA	AB	R	H	2B	3B	HR	RBI	SB	CS	BB	SO	BA	OBP	SLG
1962	23	MIN	AL	9	12	9	3	4	1	0	0	3	0	0	3	2	.444	.583	.556
1963	24	MIN	AL	7	7	7	0	3	0	0	0	1	0	0	0	2	.429	.429	.429
1964	25	MIN	AL	161	718	672	109	217	43	9	32	94	12	6	34	68	.323	.359	.557
1965	26	MIN	AL	149	647	576	107	185	40	5	16	98	19	9	55	64	.321	.378	.491
1966	27	MIN	AL	159	677	622	99	191	32	7	25	87	13	7	42	72	.307	.353	.502
1967	28	MIN	AL	146	615	557	76	161	34	6	17	83	11	3	44	61	.289	.347	.463
1968	29	MIN	AL	128	528	470	54	136	24	5	18	68	10	9	45	61	.289	.357	.477
1969	30	MIN	AL	153	692	637	97	197	39	4	24	101	10	13	45	66	.309	.355	.496
1970	31	MIN	AL	157	674	628	96	204	36	7	23	107	5	4	38	67	.325	.364	.514
1971	32	MIN	AL	126	518	487	73	164	30	3	22	81	4	1	25	44	.337	.369	.546
1972	33	MIN	AL	10	30	28	1	9	1	0	0	1	0	0	2	5	.321	.367	.357
1973	34	MIN	AL	146	624	571	63	166	20	0	16	92	2	1	45	44	.291	.345	.410
1974	35	MIN	AL	127	494	459	43	131	16	2	13	57	0	1	27	31	.285	.325	.414
1975	36	MIN	AL	131	515	455	46	123	10	0	13	58	0	1	41	45	.270	.344	.378
1976	37	MIN	AL	67	128	123	3	26	3	0	1	16	0	0	2	13	.211	.234	.260

15-Year Totals

G	PA	AB	R	H	2B	3B	HR	RBI	SB	CS	BB	SO	BA	OBP	SLG
1676	6879	6301	870	1917	329	48	220	947	86	55	448	645	.304	.353	.476

"Did You Know?"

Richard Nixon was the first president to be an eyewitness to a triple play. On July 15, 1969 the Detroit Tigers performed a triple play against Washington Senators.

George Foster lead the major leagues with RBI's in back to back seasons.

"The designated hitter rule is like letting someone else shoot free throws for Wilt Chamberlain." — Rick Wise

Rick Wise is the last pitcher to hit a home run while pitching a no-hitter.

"The pitcher has to find out if the hitter is timid. And if the hitter is timid, he has to remind the hitter he's timid." — Don Drysdale, July 1979

James "Pags" Pagliaroni

Born December 8, 1937, Dearborn Michigan
Height 6'4"   **Weight** 210 lbs.
Bats Right   **Throws** Right
Debut   Aug. 13, 1955
Final game   Sept. 30, 1969

JIM PAGLIARONI played major league baseball from 1955 – 1969 as a catcher with the Boston Red Sox, Pittsburgh Pirates, Oakland Athletics and the Seattle Pilots. Jim, who was often affectionately called Pags by his peers, was fortunate in getting to catch two no-hitters in his major league career. The first was with teammate Bill Monbouquette of the Boston Red Sox in 1962. The Red Sox beat the Chicago White Sox one to zero on that August 1, 1962.

The second no-hitter Pags caught was with his good friend with the Oakland Athletics, Jim "Catfish" Hunter. That no-hitter is a sterling memory for Pags, as it was also a perfect game! Catfish pitched his perfect game on May 8, 1968 at the Oakland Coliseum.

179

Pags had a successful major league career playing with some the greatest players the game has ever known. The Hall-of-Famers that Pags played with were Ted Williams, Carl Yastrzemski, Willie Stargell, Roberto Clemente, Bill Mazeroski, Reggie Jackson and Jim "Catfish" Hunter!

Three of the greatest Hall-of-Fame catchers of all time were Johnny Bench, Yogi Berra, and Carlton Fisk. To give you an idea how accomplished Jim Paglironi was as a major league catcher, consider the following lifetime fielding percentages!

Johnny Bench:	.990
Yogi Berra:	.989
Carlton Fisk:	.988
Jim Pagliaroni:	.991

Pags was an excellent defensive big league catcher, with a career defensive percentage of .991 behind the plate. Offensively, Pags had a lifetime batting average of .252 in 11 seasons.

Pags was a very accomplished receiver behind the plate who was also a great teammate. He was a blue collar player with an outstanding work ethic. Pags played baseball the way it was meant to be played – to win, but as a game.

In addition, Pags was very well respected and popular with his major league peers – he was very popular, and one of the true delights of the great game of baseball! I'm honored to have called Pags my friend!

Unfortunately my dear friend Pags was called home to be with the Lord, April 3, 2010, while the book was being produced.

Jim Pagliaroni

In My Own Words

I WAS SEVENTEEN when I first arrived to join the Red Sox in 1955, and now, Ted Williams, my childhood hero, was my teammate! Ted took an interest in me. He encouraged and instructed me into the art of becoming a more complete hitter, instead of a dead pull hitter that I was, and he had a huge impact on my first full year of service with the Red Sox. I needed more than one year's instruction from even the great Teddy Ballgame (the players' affectionate name for Williams), but Ted invested time for my benefit and, because of this, I became a more proficient hitter.

Boston

In 1960, Ted's last year with the Red Sox, he was verbally accosted with funny insults in a good natured manner by the flamboyant and bizarre Red Sox outfielder Jimmy Piersall. Williams and Piersall had a love-hate relationship which was often hilarious. One particular time, Ted was striding towards the Red Sox on deck circle preparing to bat. Piersall, in his typical and condescending manner, initiated a funny and sarcastic attack toward Ted that was absolutely merciless. Piersall started yelling to Ted that if he was half the hitter he thought he was, he would break the exaggerated Williams shift by hitting the ball to the opposite side, which was left field. Piersall went on to say how overrated Williams was as a hitter, and because of his pride he never could be the games' greatest hitter because he failed to hit the ball to the opposite direction in left field. The good-natured ribbing was certainly for entertainment purposes only.

Piersall shouted what a loser Ted was, and that if he would hit to the opposite field he could hit closer to a .500 batting average instead of the mere .400 batting average Ted had accomplished in 1946. Of course Piersall's comments were all a bunch of hog wash, and merely verbal outbursts for Piersall's personal delight and anyone else within earshot. Ted was glaring and growling at Piersall. Ted, however, was an absolute masterful hitter, capable of waving his bat like a magic wand to place the ball consistently in any and every direction that he chose.

The opposing players must have been howling with laughter as just about everyone within two hundred feet of Piersall could clearly hear his screams of lunacy directed at Williams. When Ted finally approached his comfort zone in the batter's box, he glared one more time at Piersall as the pitcher unleashed the ball towards home plate. Ted, with one of his 521 career bombs, deposited the ball directly over the left fielder's head for a deep opposite field homer. The entire time he circled the base paths, Ted sarcastically shouted a question: "Teddy Ballgame could not hit the other way, huh? Teddy Ballgame could be a .500 hitter if he were not so stubborn?" The entire time he circled the base paths, Ted gestured towards Piersall with his fingers pointed making hand signals with sexual connotations!

181

After watching the barrage of insults hurled between Piersall and Williams, I was completely overcome with uncontrollable laughter along with the entire Red Sox bench. I have no idea what took place with our opponents on the field. The opposing team must have felt as though they were part of a side show as most did not realize what had just taken place. But, along with the fans, there must have been complete disbelief; everyone was filled with insane uncontrollable laughter. Piersall was the beloved Red Sox nut case, but the great Teddy Ballgame answered the often funny and zany Piersall the way he responded to all criticism and opposition—with skewered success! Make no mistake about it. Ted Williams was the John Wayne of baseball! Ted Williams was the Red Sox! While in a Red Sox uniform, Ted Williams was larger than life, frequently producing what others on the field could only dream of. What a fabulous first year I had experienced!

Roger Maris

During my playing career with the Red Sox, the single greatest event I witnessed was Roger Maris's home run number 61 against the Red Sox. The home runs of Roger Maris and Mickey Mantle in 1961 were front page headline news items, not only for sports reporters but for news agencies all across the entire country. Rog and Mick were both depositing baseballs at a record speed never before witnessed at the major league level by two players in the same year. Roger was a quiet, dignified gentleman from North Dakota who truly displayed the values of his rural Midwestern heritage. For some unknown reason, the news media in New York were unfair and harsh with Roger in 1961 while chasing Babe Ruth's record of 60.

The brutal pressure and stress that the New York media created for this gentleman became sad and overwhelming for Maris and the Yankees. The day Roger finally displayed his power and delivered his majestic number 61 homer came as a major relief and blessing for him. Most of his peers were thankful for his sake that finally it had come to a merciful end. To witness that monumental blast truly was a memory I will never forget. Fortunately for baseball, a humble man with dignity and respect broke the game's greatest home run record previously set by baseballs' first and foremost loved icon, the immortal Babe Ruth! I've always been proud to have played with Roger, he was a great person.

Pittsburgh

When I was traded to the Pittsburgh Pirates from the Boston Red Sox in 1963, Stan Musial asked me how I liked playing with Ted Williams. I told him that I loved playing with Ted, and that I learned a lot about hitting. I told Stan how everyone I knew compared both him and Ted. Stan then asked me how many check swings I could remember from Ted at bat. After thinking long and hard about it, I said "Stan, I cannot recall any check swings by Ted. Why?" Stan replied that no one ever remembers a check swing by the great Teddy Ballgame because he never held up on his swings! Stan said the difference between him and Ted as hitters was that Ted was so accomplished and committed to each and every swing that he never had a check swing. After I thought about it, I was even more amazed by Ted Williams! The great Stan Musial who had a .336 lifetime batting average just confirmed to me that he, Stan Musial, was convinced that Ted Williams was the greatest hitter!

I believe the era of baseball of the 1960s and 1970s definitely was a golden era and I was privileged to have the opportunity to play with some of the greatest players of all time. In addition to playing on the Red Sox with Ted Williams, I also played with the Pittsburgh Pirates and as a teammate for five years with the legendary Roberto Clemente, Willie Stargell, and Bill Mazeroski!

Without question, I believe Roberto Clemente was one the greatest all around players of all time; he had the strongest and most accurate throwing arm of any outfielder I ever witnessed! In fact, one time I said to Clemente, "Roberto, when you make your throws to home plate, you must either make the ball bounce on the infield dirt area between first and second base, or throw it all the way to home on the fly." Roberto's throws were so strong, they literally would handcuff the catcher—me. His throws were low and straight as an arrow with unbelievable velocity; I was very pleased to be catching Roberto's throws with my full catcher's equipment on!

Pirate Pranksters

The Pirates were like family at that time. Once while visiting San Francisco, we had just played the Giants at their wind tunnel stadium, Candlestick Park. We went back to the San Francisco Palace Hotel where the Pirates stayed, taking over an entire floor of the hotel. Steve Blass, Gene Alley, Bob Bailey, Bill Mazeroski and I decided to have a couple of beers up in Maz's room. We had decided to stay in the hotel and get comfortable and we ordered room service. We were in our under shorts and, as usual, acting the fool and just having some good old fun with our buddies drinking a few beers! All of a sudden the four of them jumped me, grabbed a playpen that had been left in the hotel hallway, put me in the playpen, and tied me up with bath towels. Then they proceeded to push me into the hallway towards the elevator, then inside the elevator, and promptly punched the hotel lobby button. When the doors opened in the lobby, I was in my under shorts, tied to the playpen! I meekly asked for the manager's assistance and said to the people in the lobby who had seen me as the elevator door opened, "You folks just wouldn't understand!" As you might imagine, even after a couple of beers that was an embarrassing moment.

There was another funny event on a road trip, and this time it was in Houston. The Pirates were playing the Houston Astros. Joe Morgan was a budding star, and future Hall-of-Famer. Joe was absolutely killing the baseball against the Pirates that particular year! As usual, the Pirates held our team meeting before the first game of that series with the Astros. Our manager Danny Murtaugh and the pitching coach said that Joe Morgan was batting .467 against the Pirates. Murtaugh told the team no matter how we pitch to Morgan, we have not been successful in getting Morgan out, and asked if anyone had any ideas. I looked around the room as it was silent, and said perhaps we should just tell Joe what pitch is coming next. Murtaugh said, "Are kidding me, Pagliaroni?" "Look, Skip," I said. "He is already hitting .467 off of our pitchers. Maybe it will mess with his psyche!" Everyone chuckled and agreed. At the very least we would have some fun with Joe!

The first time Joe came into the batter's box, I said, "Joe! Hey, do you realize that you are absolutely killing us?" Joe very humbly responded, "Yeah, I'm having some pretty good success against you guys, and getting lucky." I responded, "Some success and getting lucky? You are hitting .467 against us, Joe! We have decided that since we can't get you out, we are going to tell you the pitch that is coming and help you—that way maybe you can hit .500." Joe immediately replied that was unfair and he did not want the Pirates to do that. I said, "Joe, we have made up our minds and that is exactly what we are going to do!"

Joe looked back at the umpire, who had heard every word, and protested to the umpire, asking him to stop us from telling him the next pitch. The umpire looked at Joe and said, "There is nothing in the rule book to stop the Pirates from telling an opposing player the next pitch." Joe was upset. I asked, "Joe, what would you like— a fastball?" Joe said, "Don't tell me! I do not want to know what pitch is coming!" The Pirates pitcher Bob Veale yelled back to me behind the plate, "What does Joe want?" I said, "He can't make up his mind. Throw him a fastball." "Strike one!" Then I asked Joe, "What do you want now?" Joe was more upset. I told our pitcher Bob Veale to throw another fastball. "Strike two!" Morgan looked back at me behind the plate, and said, "Pags, I mean it. I want you to stop telling me the pitches!" I told our pitcher, "Bob, give Joe another fastball." "Strike three!" Joe disgustedly gave me a dirty look over his shoulder as he walked back to the Astros dugout. For that entire series, the Pirates told Joe what the pitches were that we would throw, and if memory serves me correctly, I believe Joe only got maybe one or two hits the entire series! The great Joe Morgan temporarily had been neutralized!

Tim McCarver

Another story with the same results happened to me against the St. Louis Cardinals. Tim McCarver, the Cardinals colorful catcher, and I were friendly to each other. The Cardinals and Pirates were both out of the playoffs late in September and playing a doubleheader. McCarver asked me if I wanted to know the pitch I would see from his pitcher? I said, "Sure, and I'll tell you the pitches that we will throw to you when you come up to bat!" McCarver said, "Great!" The first game was an absolute offensive fireworks display for both teams. The final score of the first game

Jim Pagliaroni

was something like 12-10. Ironically, McCarver and I were the only ones from each team who did not get a hit! Now, the second game was an offensive display as well! I think McCarver and I both had one hit between us. I said to McCarver, "My, that worked out well! Let's be sure never to have that kind of fun ever again!" Boy, you talk about funny circumstances! Baseball truly is a peculiar game!

Bob Uecker

Speaking of funny, the Pirates were playing in Atlanta against the Braves. Bob Uecker was catching for the Braves. Late in the game the Pirates were leading 3-1. When the Pirates came up in the seventh inning, I was digging into the batter's box preparing to hit. Bob said, 'Hey, Pags! Ueck here! We may not see each other again. I just wanted to wish you and your wife, Linda, a Merry Christmas and a Happy New Year! I said, "Thanks, Ueck." When I came to bat in the ninth inning, the Braves had tied the game. I'm preparing to get into the batter's box, and Bob says, "Hey, Pags! Ueck here! I just wanted be sure to wish you and Linda a Merry Christmas and a Happy New Year." I said, "Thanks, Ueck. You too!" In the twelfth inning, the Pirates came to bat again! It was my turn to hit again, and Ueck says, "Hey, Pags! Ueck here! I just wanted to wish you and Linda a Merry Christmas and a Happy New Year!" I said, "Look, you silly son of a gun. I know who you are! I know where you are! And I plan on having a great Christmas and New Year's with my wife, Linda! Now leave me alone so we can both go home!" Bob Uecker was, and still is, unbelievably funny! Without question, Bob Uecker was one of the most colorful and funny players of our era! I really enjoyed Bob Uecker!

Embarrassing Moments on the Field

There were two times that were the most embarrassing moments in my baseball career. The first happened in Atlanta while playing the Braves. The Pirates were in the field, Hank Aaron was on second base, and Joe Torre was at the plate. Bob Veale was pitching for the Pirates. Veale got strike one on Torre! Then came another quick second strike. I knew that I was the first batter to lead off when the Pirates came up to bat, so I had in my mind to hustle to the dugout to remove my catchers' gear. So our ace pitcher throws a beautiful pitch for strike three on Torre! I rolled the ball slowly towards the pitching mound about half way. I immediately ran to our dugout to take off my chin guards to bat first. Just as I'm removing my gear, I heard a loud commotion. As I looked over my shoulder towards home plate, Bob Veale had run towards the ball I had rolled and he dove towards home plate just in time to tag Hank Aaron out who had run like a gazelle to attempt to score all the way from second base. There was a huge cloud of dirt over the home plate area! I realized my major goof-up. Our fiery manager, the frequently funny Danny Murtaugh, looked at me and said, "Hey, Diego! You do know that there are still three outs up here in

185

the big leagues, don't you?" I was very embarrassed to say the least! When I came to the plate to bat, the Atlanta fans gave me a standing ovation! That did not make me feel any better!

The second embarrassing time happened in Chicago while the Pirates were playing the Cubbies at Wrigley Field. It had rained the night before, and the grass was still wet. There was a routine popup behind home plate. I waltzed under the popup and at the very last moment my feet slid out from under me and I landed squarely on the numbers of my jersey. The ball hit me on the forehead and bounced eighteen to twenty rows up into the famed Wrigley Field box seats. Our Irish second baseman Bill Mazeroski, yelled at me, "Hey, Diego! If that ball had hit anyone other than an Italian, it would have bounced only two or three rows into the seats!" There is nothing like being surrounded by out-of-work comedians!

Oakland A's Memories

December 3, 1967, I was purchased by the Oakland Athletics from the Pittsburgh Pirates. Here's one humorous story about the Athletics owner, eccentric Charles O. Finley. The A's had just finished a road trip on the east coast. On the team flight back to Oakland, some players had been talking about how ridiculous it was for Mr. Finley to be making baseball decisions on the telephone from his downtown office in Chicago during games. Mr. Finley would call the A's dugout during the games and give directives during the course of our games! Somehow the chatter on that team flight back to the west coast was conveyed by one of the reporters directly to Charles O. Finley. Mr. Finley immediately flew from his Chicago office to Oakland to conduct a post-game meeting with the entire Athletics team in our clubhouse. As Mr. Finley walked into the A's clubhouse after the game, he said, "Gentleman, I understand some of you may be disappointed that I make some decisions regarding the team from my Chicago office. I want you to know that the team is for sale to you members only tonight. You who want to purchase the Oakland Athletics are to place $35 million in cash by midnight tonight on the manager's desk in less than two hours. If you decide not to buy the A's, then please remember that Charles O. Finley still owns the team. The O between Charles and Finley stands for the only one! That means as long as I own this 'blankety blank' team, I will do exactly what I want to with all future decisions!" As Mr. Finley started to exit by the clubhouse door, he turned to look at his stunned players and said, "By the way, gentleman. Congratulations on beating the New York Yankees this evening!" He walked out. Never again did I hear mention of Mr. Finley calling the A's dugout to make suggestions or decisions for the manager from any of the players.

Jim Pagliaroni

Perfect Catfish

My most memorable game with the Oakland Athletics was on Wednesday evening, May 8, 1968! One of the premier players of the golden era of the 1960s and '70s was Jim "Catfish" Hunter. Catfish threw his perfect game, and I had the distinguished honor of being his catcher for that historic evening against the Minnesota Twins. The Twins had a killer lineup with Tony Oliva, Rod Carew, & Harmon Killebrew. When the A's went to the dugout in the bottom of the seventh inning, I'm sitting down by the bat rack on the bench. Cat is at the other end of the dugout and Hunter yells down at me, "Hey. Diego, let's not start thinking now as we have a no-no going!" Everyone on the dugout bench started laughing! That comment broke the ice, and loosened everyone from any anxiety that may have existed. In the ninth inning, Cat didn't know that it was a perfect game, When Jimmy Reese struck out for the last out, Sal Bando ran towards Cat on the mound yelling, "Perfect game! Perfect game!" That's the first time it dawned on Cat that he just pitched a perfect game! Some interesting side notes: Cat's perfect game was Joe Rudi's first big league game! Joe Rudi replaced Tony LaRussa on the roster to start in left field. One fact of that game that goes unnoticed is that Catfish got three hits himself that day, two of which were doubles with three RBIs, and eleven strikeouts!

On that Friday, Charlie O, the A's owner, announced to the press that he was going to give Catfish a $10,000 bonus for pitching his brilliant perfect gem! Charlie was great at marketing, and he had several motives for his timing of presenting Cat's check. He made arrangements to present the check to Cat on the mound before Saturday's game on the national game-of-the-week that would be televised. Saturday morning when I arrived at the A's clubhouse, I found out about the $10,000 to be presented, and I went to Hunter's locker and congratulated him on getting the bonus from the old man, Charlie O! Cat said, "You're going to be with me on the mound in front of the national television audience also." I said, "Why do I have to go to the mound with you on the presentation?" Cat said, "You are going to receive a bonus check also!" I said, "What for?" Cat chuckled and said, "That is exactly what Charlie O' asked!" Mr. Finley told me he already had made the announcement to the press and television crew. So Cat asked Charlie O. "What about Pags, my catcher?" Charlie said. "What about your catcher? Catchers don't get anything!" Cat told Charlie O., "If my catcher is not rewarded with a bonus check, neither will I!" Catfish knew he had the old man in a predicament as he had already made all of the arrangements with the media. When we strode to the pitching mound with Charlie O., Cat handed me a box with a beautiful new Longine watch inscribed on the back "To Jim Pagliaroni, battery mate, perfect game, May 8, 1968, Jim "Catfish" Hunter." Catfish Hunter was a class act and a dear friend.

Today's game has some terrific talent! Players I would pay money to watch play are Derek Jeter, Albert Pujols, and Alex Rodriguez.

The Best of the Best

Best Fastball
Sandy Koufax

Best Curveball
Juan Pascual

Most Intimidating Pitcher
Bob Gibson

Best Right-Handed Pitcher
Juan Marichal, Bob Gibson

Best Left-Handed Pitcher
Sandy Koufax

Best Left-Handed Reliever
Ron Perranoski

Best Right-Handed Reliever
Rollie Fingers

Overall Most Challenging Pitcher
Sandy Koufax
(Overwhelmingly so!)

Best Right-Handed Hitter
Willie Mays, Roberto Clemente

Best Left-Handed Hitter
Ted Williams

Overall Best Clutch Hitter
Orlando Cepeda

Best Catcher
Johnny Bench

Best First Baseman
Willie McCovey, Willie Stargell

Best Second Baseman
Bill Mazeroski

Best Shortstop
Maury Wills

Best Third Baseman
Brooks Robinson, Ron Santo

Best Left Fielder
Lou Brock

Best Center Fielder
Mickey Mantle

Best Right Fielder
Hank Aaron, Roberto Clemente

Fastest Base Runner
Willie Davis

Best Base Runner
Willie Mays,
Roberto Clemente,

Player Who Didn't Reach Maximum Potential
Joe Pepitone, Bo Belinsky,
(Mickey Mantle once said that
Joe Pepitone had the
quickest bat in baseball)

Jim Pagliaroni

Strongest Outfield Arm
Roberto Clemente

Best Opposing Manager
Walter Alston,
(For respect and integrity)

Most Trusted Friend
Bob Bailey, Don Gile

Funniest Player
Gene Freese, Bob Uecker
(Both had minds like popcorn
machines! Gene Freese wanted to
video our Yorkshire Terriers mating
and charge for viewing in the
clubhouse.)

Most Courageous
Mickey Mantle
(Played in tremendous pain. Mickey was literally taped before each
game from his crotch to his ankles!)

Most Flamboyant
Tito Fuentes, Vic Power

Most Zany
Jimmy Piersall
(Actually went to bat with a
woman's wig on under his ball cap!)

Player I Most Admired
Al Kaline
(Quiet strength and presence)

My Favorite Stadium
Fenway Park

Best Team Rival
New York Yankees
(Mantle, Maris, Berra)

Best Manager I Played For
Danny Murtaugh

My Favorite Team Mate
Rick Monday, Catfish Hunter

Most Heart
Pete Rose
(Because of his passion)

Best Work Ethics
Ted Williams, Roberto Clemente
(Ted took more BP than anyone,
Clemente practiced in front of
mirrors)

Most Congenial
Sandy Koufax
(Great gentleman)

My Favorite Team
Pittsburgh Pirates

Player I Would Have Liked as a Team Mate
Ron Santo

My Favorite City
San Francisco

Best Baseball Announcer

Vin Scully

My Favorite Baseball Announcer

Harry Carey

The Best Umpire

Doug Harvey

Umpire with The Best Attitude

Doug Harvey

Most Respected Baseball Personality

Joe DiMaggio

(Great integrity and heart!)

Jim "Pags" Pagliaroni
Lifetime Statistics

Year	Age	Tm	Lg	G	PA	AB	R	H	2B	3B	HR	RBI	SB	CS	BB	SO	BA	OBP	SLG
1955	17	BOS	AL	1	1	0	0	0	0	0	0	1	0	0	0	0			.000
1960	22	BOS	AL	28	77	62	7	19	5	2	2	9	0	0	13	11	.306	.434	.548
1961	23	BOS	AL	120	440	376	50	91	17	0	16	58	1	1	55	74	.242	.342	.415
1962	24	BOS	AL	90	303	260	39	67	14	0	11	37	2	1	36	55	.258	.359	.438
1963	25	PIT	NL	92	294	252	27	58	5	0	11	26	0	0	36	57	.230	.330	.381
1964	26	PIT	NL	97	346	302	33	89	12	3	10	36	1	0	41	56	.295	.383	.454
1965	27	PIT	NL	134	452	403	42	108	15	0	17	65	0	0	41	84	.268	.337	.432
1966	28	PIT	NL	123	435	374	37	88	20	0	11	49	0	5	50	71	.235	.329	.377
1967	29	PIT	NL	44	118	100	4	20	1	1	0	9	0	0	16	26	.200	.314	.230
1968	30	OAK	AL	66	227	199	19	49	4	0	6	20	0	0	24	42	.246	.330	.357
1969	31	TOT	AL	54	160	137	11	33	5	1	6	16	0	0	18	18	.241	.327	.423
1969	31	OAK	AL	14	33	27	1	4	1	0	1	2	0	0	5	2	.148	.303	.296
1969	31	SEP	AL	40	127	110	10	29	4	1	5	14	0	0	13	16	.264	.333	.455

11-Year Totals

G	PA	AB	R	H	2B	3B	HR	RBI	SB	CS	BB	SO	BA	OBP	SLG
849	2853	2465	269	622	98	7	90	326	4	7	330	494	.252	.344	.407

"Did You Know?"

"I became a good pitcher when I stopped trying to make them miss the ball and started trying to make them hit it." — Sandy Koufax

"There are two theories on hitting the knuckleball. Unfortunately, neither of them work." — Charlie Lau

In 1966 Frank Robinson won the triple-crown with the Baltimore Orioles.

"The best way to catch a knuckleball is to wait until the ball stops rolling and then pick it up." — Bob Uecker

"Baseball is ninety percent mental. The other half is physical." — Yogi Berra

Dave Phillips
Outstanding America League Umpire

D AVID ROBERT PHILLIPS was born October, 1943, in St. Louis, Missouri. His career followed closely that of his father, Bob Phillips, who was a professional umpire in the minor leagues. Dave always idolized his father and eventually also chose to be a professional umpire.

When Dave attended umpiring school, there were three others there who also made it to the major league level: Larry Barnett, Jake O'Donnell, and the fun-loving and gregarious Ron Luciano. However, Dave not only made it to the major leagues, but was one the most accomplished and respected umpires in the American League.

His career as a major league umpire lasted 32 years, from 1971 through 2002, mostly in the American League, until, in 1999, the umpires from both leagues merged into one group called the MLB umpires.

Dave umpired four different World Series and two All-Star games and several championship games. He also toured both Japan and Germany, representing major league baseball as an umpire.

One of Dave's fondest memories was the 1982 World Series. He participated as part of the umpire crew in his hometown of St. Louis as the Cardinals played the

Royals of Kansas City. In addition to being chosen as part of the umpire crew for the battle for bragging rights in the show-me state, Dave's father, Bob, attended the World Series, and was able to see his son on baseball's grandest platform and in one of his greatest moments as an umpire, the World Series!

For some unknown reason, Dave was either in the right place or wrong place several times, umpiring in some of major league baseball's most memorable and bizarre games, including Disco Demolition Night, Pine Tar Incidents, and many more! Dave also ejected Hall-of-Fame pitcher Gaylord Perry from a game when none of his colleagues had ever gathered the required evidence or proof that Perry was throwing illegal spitballs.

Be sure to collect a copy of Dave's intriguing first-hand accounts found in his book, *Center Field on Fire.*

Dave Phillips

In My Own Words

Becoming a major league umpire at the age of 26 in 1970 had its advantages and disadvantages. Someone once said that umpires have the best seat in the house, but you have to stand. I admit that sounds like a pretty good job description, but there is much more to being an umpire than fans understand or appreciate. Most fans watching the game might think it's about making the basic calls: safe, out, fair, foul, strike or ball. What most fail to realize are the intangibles needed to be successful and the sacrifices to family and personal life a major league umpire has to make. Still, I would never trade my experiences and life with anyone—I was very lucky! A lot of people go through life and never find a job that they like. But I not only found a job I liked, but it was in a profession I truly loved!

After umpiring in the minor leagues for 7 years, in 1970 the American League purchased my contract. Major league baseball decided that there should be more longevity in the umpiring profession and started bringing umpires in at a younger age. I was only 26 years of age when I arrived to umpire my first major league game – one of the first guinea pigs!

The first few years I worked in the majors were difficult for me because I looked so young. In fact, Joe Cronin, the American League President, had a rule that no rookie umpire could work the home plate position if he had never worked in that ballpark before! He wanted the umpire to become familiarized with the ballpark and the ground rules of that stadium. So the first year, every time I entered a new ballpark, Larry Napp, the crew chief of my umpire team, would walk me around the ballpark. Often during our inspections the players were taking batting practice, and it was as if I had huge neon sign on my back that read, "I am a rookie and don't know what I am doing." It was embarrassing! I hated it because I was the new kid everywhere we went! I could get 100 calls right, and Larry get 100 calls wrong, and, since I was the rookie, I would be the one they would argue with! But, I knew I had to earn their respect. You cannot buy creditability at the local Wal-Mart.

In the 1950s and 1960s, a lot of umpires ruled by intimidation but I didn't like that. In the 1920s and 1930s it was common for players and umpires to settle their disputes under the stands with fistfights. I'm glad that practice stopped; I would have lost the fights because of my lack of size compared to size of the players back then.

My job as umpire was to expedite the game as fairly as I could and let the chips fall where they may. If I had to argue or eject a player or manager, so be it! Tomorrow is a new day, and all is forgotten, from my perspective. I believe that, for the most part, today's umpires follow that same theory. I also believe people skills are a very important part of umpiring. It does not matter what profession an individual may choose, show me someone who has good people skills, and I will show you a successful person!

Memories of Several Firsts

Then there's Fenway Park, and the infamous "Green Monster." I had many memorable games there. One was my first ejection in the major leagues and it just so happened to be "Mr. October," Reggie Jackson. Reggie was playing for the Oakland A's then, and the game was May 28, 1971. I had worked third base the night before, my first game umpiring at Boston's Fenway Park. Dick Williams was the fireball manager of the A's, and Williams was very difficult to deal with anytime, to say the least, but he was even more difficult and arrogant when he returned to Boston, a team that he managed into the 1967 World Series.

Before I left my hotel room that night to go to Fenway, I realized I had truly made it to the big leagues when the weatherman said on television that Vida Blue was pitching for the A's and Sonny Siebert was pitching for the Red Sox. Both pitchers were going into the game undefeated. The weatherman said, "It will be a cool, crisp evening, but regardless of the temperature, the game will be Sonny and Blue!" I thought "Man, that didn't happen in the International League." The game was everything it was billed as, well pitched and very well played.

The next day was the game-of-the-week on television. I was at second base and it was an absolute television nightmare of a game. The score was 12-8, 3 hours and 11 minutes long. It seemed everything that could go wrong did go wrong: the wind was blowing, the pitching was bad, balls were dropped, and errors were made. It was a bad game for both teams. Reggie Jackson was not having a good day, either. In the seventh inning, Reggie was on first base and was going to third on a hit. He was going to be out by plenty. Luis Aparicio cut the ball off and ran Reggie back towards second when Aparicio flipped the ball to Griffin, the Red Sox second baseman, and I called Reggie out. I was the rookie umpire and Reggie wanted to vent his anger on somebody and he directed his tirade towards me. Everyone in the park knew he was out, but he kept arguing with me. I had to eject him, and on national television no less!

Sometimes I had to go toe to toe with intimidating managers such as Billy Martin or Earl Weaver, but I never backed down! In today's game, more managers are like Tony LaRussa or Joe Torre, who are well educated, articulate and are good teachers of the game, exercising patience. They argue their point, and then they get on with the game.

Not Always What It Seems!

One of the questions I'm asked most is what players and managers say when they come out to the umpire to argue a call. A lot of managers are so upset they really are not speaking in sentences that can be understood. It's more like grunts and curse words all mixed together. One particular time, I called a player out at second base, and the player started arguing with me. Chuck Tanner, the manager, came running onto the field. I think Tanner knew I had made the right call, but he also knew he had to protect his player from being ejected. When Tanner reached me, he got right in my face and started screaming, "Have I told you about the new restaurant downtown? They have great steaks and lobsters and they are reasonably priced!" Tanner kept on screaming, jumping up and down, and pointing his finger. The crowd was loving it because they thought he was really giving an earful about my call!

Larry Barnett was my umpire partner in that game, and later he asked me why I had not ejected Tanner for his seemingly out of control antics. When I explained to Barnett what Tanner had done, he had a hard time believing that it was just a show for the benefit of Tanner's players and fans. It was bizarre! The next day when the managers came to home plate to exchange lineup cards before the game, Tanner asked, "Hey, did you guys try that new restaurant?" and then Tanner smiled and winked at me. "See, what did I tell you?" I said to Barnett. Barnett just looked at me and shook his head. He was shocked!

The Bizarre and Unusual!

Believe me when I say I have had my share of experiences that were very unusual occurrences. The most unexpected occurred because of a poorly planned promotion at Chicago's Comiskey Park on July 12, 1979. The White Sox innovative owner, Bill Veeck, teamed up with the Chicago radio station WLUP-FM to hold a promotion called "Disco Demolition Night." Even before it started, it had disaster written all over it. And that's exactly what it became—a disaster!

The White Sox were playing the Detroit Tigers in a doubleheader. Umpires never pay much attention to promotions that are planned at a game unless it affects our efforts. I might have read something in the paper about the Disco Demolition Night promotion, but never gave it much thought. Even if I had, it certainly would not have prepared me for what was about to unfold.

I was working home plate in the first game and about the fifth or sixth inning I noticed an unusually large crowd in the ball park. The bleachers were full and the upper decks were filling up with fans also. Suddenly, some of the fans starting sailing music records onto the playing field like Frisbees. The umpires were forced to halt the game several times to pick up and remove the records. I had asked the public address announcer to make a plea to the fans not to throw any more records onto the field. I should have been aware of the potential problems this posed for the second game, but, at that point I was just trying to make sure we finished the first

197

game: the Tigers won the first game 4-1. The umpires left the field along with the players and we told both the Tigers and the White Sox to be ready to start the second game in thirty minutes.

I took a quick shower, got something to eat, and relaxed for a couple of minutes until it was time to go back onto the field for the second game. In the umpire's dressing room we could not hear what was happening in the stadium and no one came to tell us that there were major problems on the playing field. What ensued will go down as the most bizarre and worst promotion in the history of baseball!

Fans that brought a disco record with them were to be admitted to the game for 98 cents. Everyone who brought a record was then permitted on the field where they could put their record into a dumpster in center field to be blown up or demolished. To this day, I'm not sure the White Sox or the radio station personnel knew what kind of crowd they were expecting, but more than 50,000 fans showed up.

When the other umpires and I walked out onto the field for the second game, there was nothing but utter chaos! A police officer met us and said, "Where do you guys think you are going?" When we told the officer that we were the umpires, he just shook his head and said, "Good luck! Have you guys seen the field? There's no way you're going to play this game today on time." He told us we would be better off going into the stands to see what was transpiring. To our shock, no one was in the stands—the fans were all on the field. I had never seen anything like it. Center field was literally on fire!

The dumpster full of records was on fire! Some of the fans who had not put their records in the dumpster started their own small fires to burn their records. Home plate had been dug up and removed as had all of the other bases. Some of the people were actually lying down on the field smoking marijuana—we could smell it from the stands. We sat down, shook our heads in utter disbelief and watched.

Harry Carey, the popular White Sox announcer, came on the video board and pleaded with fans to clear the field so the second game could start. But the rancorous fans ignored Harry's pleas and yelled back at him, and some even gave him the finger!

The promotion that was supposed to take fifteen minutes was now more than hour long. The police finally appeared in riot gear with police dogs, and the fans began to disperse. Finally the field was cleared, but Tigers manager Sparky Anderson said he did not want to play the game under those conditions because, not only was the outfield scorched, but the fans were in a riotous mood from being drunk and or high on marijuana. Sparky was right, and we cancelled the game.

We went back to our dressing room, and soon after the White Sox owner Bill Veeck came in the umpire's room and asked if we would give him fifteen minutes to get the field into playing shape. "Sorry, Bill. We just can't do it!" I told him. We dressed and left the stadium as quickly as we could. The next morning, Lee MacPhail, the American League President, called to ask me what had happened. I told MacPhail there was no excuse for what took place at Comiskey Park, and that I thought that the White Sox should be held liable and should be held accountable. MacPhail agreed with me and declared the game a forfeit, giving the Detroit Tigers the victory in the second game.

A total of 37 people were arrested during the marketing folly, and to tell you the truth, I was surprised there were not several serious injuries.

The First Pine Tar Incident!

The pine tar incident involved the then California Angels and the Kansas City Royals, managed by Whitey Herzog. Bill Kunkel was the umpire behind the plate and I was at first base. Kunkel always tried to defuse any situation he had by acting as if it was something else. Well, that theory did not quite work in this instance. In fact, it put Kunkel in the middle of a gigantic mess.

Dave Chalk led off the inning for the Angels, and Kunkel called a strike that Chalk did not agree with. The same thing happened on the very next pitch also. Kunkel did not want fans or the media to think that Chalk or anyone else would question his strike calls, so he reached out for Chalk's bat as though he wanted to check it for excessive pine tar. Kunkel laid the bat down on the plate and measured it to see if it had too much pine tar. This was Kunkel's way of showing the fans and the media that Chalk was not arguing strikes, but rather checking for an illegal bat.

After Kunkel checked the bat, he had the batboy bring out a towel to wipe the bat off a little bit. Angels manager Dick Williams and Chalk made a note of the pine tar fiasco that Kunkel created. The game continued and John Mayberry of the Royals hit two home runs. His second homer in the tenth inning won the game for the Royals. I had gone down the right field line to watch the second home run ball, and when I turned around and started back towards the infield, I saw Dick Williams standing at home plate. Williams was there to challenge Mayberry's bat, saying it had too much pine tar on it because Kunkel had done that very thing to Williams' player, Dave Chalk, earlier! The bat was measured, and Kunkel declared the bat was legal. Williams immediately said he was protesting the game.

After the game, Williams came into the umpire's room where the Angels executive Red Patterson was waiting, which is highly unusual. Williams said he was supposed to wait for a call from the American League President. Sure enough, the phone rang. It was Lee MacPhail asking to speak with Kunkel. After several minutes of conversation about everything except the pine tar, the talk got around to Mayberry's bat. Kunkel said he had measured the bat and everything was fine at which point Williams exploded, calling Kunkel every name in the book. I seriously thought that Kunkel and Williams were going to come to blows.

MacPhail could hear Williams screaming and asked to speak with the fiery manager's executive manager, begging Patterson to get Williams out of the umpire's room. Nothing happened after this incident, but it was totally created by Kunkel who did not want people to think his strike calls were coming into question.

More Pine Tar Please!

The most famous pine tar incident happened in 1983 when Kansas City's George Brett was called out for having too much pine tar on his bat after he had hit a home run against the New York Yankees. Brett always used an excessive amount of pine tar on his bat as he did not wear batting gloves and the pine tar helped him get a better grip on his bat. I was not at the original game, but the replays of Brett charging out of the dugout after home plate umpire Tim McClelland ejected him made all of the highlight shows.

After the home run was overturned and Brett was declared out, the Royals protested the game. League President MacPhail upheld the protest, ruling that the home run should have been allowed to stand, and that the game should be won or lost on the field, not through technicalities of the rules. I agreed! Besides, I do not think there has ever been any scientific evidence to prove that pine tar aided the distance a ball was hit.

That was not the end of the incident, because MacPhail ruled that the game should be resumed at the point of Brett's home run. MacPhail wanted my umpiring crew to oversee the completion of that game which had been rescheduled for a off day for the Yankees, Royals, and my umpiring crew. Kansas City had to charter a plane back to New York, and Brett did not even leave the plane. But, it got more interesting!

Bob Fishel, one of the American League officials, was there to greet my crew, saying that the Yankees might protest the game by claiming that Brett had missed first base. The Yankees knew my umpire crew was not the same crew that umpired the original game. Fishel said he was going to give me a court affidavit in case the protest happened. The court document said the umpires who worked the original game saw Brett touch not only first base, but second, third and home plate in order, and legally.

Fishel assured me he did not really think the Yankees would protest, but when we went out to start the game, I put the affidavit in my pocket, just in case. On the very first pitch, sure enough, Yankee's pitcher George Frazier stepped off of the pitching rubber and threw to first base while appealing that Brett had missed first base two months ago. First base umpire Tim Welke gave the safe sign and Yankees manager Billy Martin came racing out of the dugout. Martin headed straight for Welke, but I intercepted him. Martin knew I was not at the original game, so when he got to me he said, "Davey, you were in Seattle, not at the original game!" I replied, "Billy, you are absolutely right. I have no idea whether Brett touched all of the bases or not, but I have this affidavit." Billy said, "An Affa...f----ing what?" And I showed it to Billy. Billy just stood there, not believing he had lost an argument so quickly. He said, "I'll be a S.O.B!" as he stormed off towards the Yankees dugout. That became a very famous photograph and was the only time an affidavit has been used in a major league game.

Points to Ponder

From the time I started umpiring until today, there are several issues that have changed.

One is the designated hitter. I have often emphatically stated that I do not like the rule! I remember the first meeting the umpires had about the designated hitter rule in Tampa ,Florida, in 1973. Joe Cronin, the American League President, instigated putting in the DH because there was very little offense in the American League. In 1968, only Boston's Carl Yastrzemski batted over .300, leading the entire league with a .301 batting average. The next batting leader behind Yaz was Danny Cater of the Oakland A's who hit .290. That was the same year Bob Gibson set the major league record with a 1.12 ERA playing for the St. Louis Cardinals.

The offensive part of the game was down. Major league baseball was very concerned and looking for ways to generate more offense in the game. The mound was lowered after that season and talk about the DH had begun to take serious points. At the initial conversations supporting the DH rule, I did not really care one way or another. After several years I came to be opposed to the DH rule because it creates longer games and is much more difficult for pitchers facing another hitter who can potentially hit 30-50 home runs. If I were a pitcher, I would want to pitch in the National League because hurlers face a much less offensive lineup every day.

The DH has also changed the strategy of the game. If I were a fan, I would have liked to see Stan Musial, Willie Mays, Ted Williams and Mickey Mantle just to hit and extend their careers. But to me it changes the strategy of the game, because managers do not use the bunt as much, no one pinch hits for a pitcher, and pitching changes are made during an inning creating longer games. If it were up to me, I would abolish the DH rule! However, I doubt that will ever happen because it allows players to extend their careers and make large sums of money. The player's union would never allow the DH to be eliminated.

Another thing that has to change is to complete the World Series at an earlier date. I remember in the 60s that the World Series was over the first week in October. In 2009, the series did not even start until October 28th, the latest start in World Series history. For the first time ever, the series was scheduled to end in November and the winning game 6 took place on November 4th!

Baseball is now sitting on a time bomb by playing the World Series, especially in the eastern portion of the country, so late. It is my belief that World Series should be completed no later than October 20. This could be accomplished easily. I know doubleheaders are a thing of the past because the owners do not want to give anything away anymore. However, if a split doubleheader could be played on Saturdays during a two-month period in June and July, that would save a minimum of eight days during the season. Then the World Series could be completed by the October 20.

Inter-league play has been fun, but I think it has lost its luster. In addition, it's ridiculous to make an exhibition game like the All-Star game the criteria for home field advantage in the World Series. Bud Selig, who has done a fantastic job of marketing baseball in a number of positive ways, determined several years ago that the change would make the All-Star game more meaningful. This happened after the All-Star game ended in a tie because the managers ran out of players. However, the league with the best inter-league record would make more sense as criteria for determining who would possess home field advantage for the World Series, not an exhibition game. The All-Star game is an exhibition game and is played to allow every team to be represented. Making the game so meaningful places each manager in a very difficult position because he has the responsibility to use all of his players but still has the pressure to win the game to gain home field advantage for his league.

Shameful

Tony Oliva belongs in the Hall of Fame. You speak with any one who was on the field in any professional capacity as a player or umpire, and I'm certain they would also concur that Tony Oliva was a great player. How this man is not in the Hall of Fame is beyond me.

Never To Be Broken

They say records are made to be broken, but something happened in my first year as a major league umpire that we will never experience again!

We rarely see one 20-game winner today. But in 1971, the Baltimore Orioles had four 20-game winners: Jim Palmer (20), Mike Cuellar (20), Dave McNally (21), and Pat Dobson (20). I umpired in Baltimore the final four game series. I don't remember if any of them won their 20th game in that final series, but I worked home plate when Jim Palmer won his 20th. Think about it! Four 20-game winners! Of course that came with a four-man rotation, something that all teams used at the time. Now they use five-man pitching rotations. Trust me, we will never again witness four 20-game winners on the same major league team in the same year!

Today's Players

Some of today's players I would pay to watch are Albert Pujols, Alex Rodriguez

& C.C. Sabathia. Of the young players, I'd pay to watch Grady Sizemore, Tim Lincecum, Pablo Sandoval, and Colby Rasmus

The Best of the Best

These selections were what I personally witnessed!

Best Fastball
Nolan Ryan & Goose Gossage

Best Curveball
Nolan Ryan
(Tough finding the strike zone)
Bert Blyleven

Most Intimidating Pitcher
Nolan Ryan
(Ryan was just wild enough to be intimidating and dangerous.)

Best Right-Handed Pitcher
Jim "Catfish" Hunter
(More than a thrower. He knew how to control his pitches.)

Best Left-Handed Pitcher
Ron Guidry & Frank Tanana
(Tanana hurt his arm. Other wise he would have a lot better statistics and numbers! In Tanana's hey day he was phenomenal!

Best Left-Handed Reliever
Sparky Lyle
(Dominating with both his fastball and curveball)

Best Right-Handed Reliever
Goose Gossage, Dennis Eckersley, & Rollie Fingers!
(Goose had a killer instinct look which separated him from the others, and Goose would challenge anyone!)

Overall Most Challenging Pitcher
Nolan Ryan
(Difficult to work as an umpire because of his inconsistency. He threw a lot of pitches! He could bust a curveball!)

Best Right-Handed Hitter
(1) Frank Robinson (2) Al Kaline (3) Dick Allen could also flat hit!

Best Left-Handed Hitter
Rod Carew, George Brett, Tony Oliva, Carl Yastrzemski! (Oliva should be in the Hall of Fame!)

Overall Best Clutch Hitter
Rod Carew

Best Catcher
Carlton Fisk & Bob Boone
(These guys were superior receivers who could hit and with power!)

Best First Baseman
Cecil Cooper
(Underrated & under appreciated!
Great defensively and at the plate!)

Best Shortstop
Luis Aparicio & Bert Campaneris
Defensively only, Mark Belanger
was terrific!

Best Left Fielder
Carl Yastrzemski & Joe Rudi
& Jim Rice
(These three were awesome and really worked hard at their craft!)

Best Right Fielder
Frank Robinson & Al Kaline

Best Base Runner
Willie Wilson

Player Who Didn't Reach Maximum Potential
Dick Allen
(Hall-of-Fame talent!)

Best Team Rival
New York Yankees & Boston Red
Sox

Best Second Baseman
Rod Carew & Bobby Grich

Best Third Baseman
Brooks Robinson & Graig Nettles
(Nettles was often overshadowed by
Brooks, but Nettles was just as outstanding defensive third baseman as
Brooks!)

Best Center Fielder
Fred Lynn & Lyman Bostock
(Nobody came close to Fred Lynn as
a centerfielder in the 1970s for every aspect, hitting, power, defense,
arm strength, & speed! Bostock was
incredible for his three years with a
.311 batting average.)

Fastest Base Runner
Willie Wilson

Best Overall Player
George Brett would be my number
one selection.
Frank Robinson was quiet, but absolutely an incredible talent and would
be my second selection!

Strongest Outfield Arm
Reggie Smith & Al Kaline
(Didn't get any better than Reggie
Smith!)

Best Manager
Billy Martin, Whitey Herzog &
Ralph Houk
(In my estimation these managers
were outstanding)

My Favorite Manager
Chuck Tanner
(I had Tanner in the minor leagues at every level, and he was the kind of manager I would have liked to play for, with great people skills!)

My Favorite Umpire
Shag Crawford & Bill Haller
(Shag worked with my father, Bob Phillips, in the minor leagues as umpire!)

Most Heart
Frank Robinson!
(No pads! Never gave ground to anyone, played hard, and was tough!)

Best Work Ethics
Jim Rice & George Brett
(These guys made themselves far better with their work ethics! I'm certain there are several, but I have first-hand knowledge of these two.)

Most Congenial
Harmon Killebrew

My Favorite Team
My umpire team

My Favorite Stadium
Kauffman (Royals Stadium), Fenway & Yankee Stadiums

Best Baseball Announcer
Vin Scully

Most Trusted Baseball Friend
Rocky Roe & Larry Barnett. Ron Luciano was an absolute character. He was not the best umpire, but was fun loving, and I really enjoyed him! Fans loved Luciano because of his charisma and great people skills!

Funniest Player
Tommy John
(I enjoyed him a lot! George Brett was also jovial and funny as was Freddy Patek!)

Most Courageous
There were several! I cannot single one out.

Most Flamboyant
Reggie Jackson

Most Zany
Bill "Spaceman" Lee

Player I Most Admired
There are too many to mention!!

My Favorite City
Chicago

My Favorite Baseball Announcer
Harry Carey

Dave Phillips

Most Respected Baseball Personality
Joe Garagiola & Bob Costas

"Did You Know?"

During the 1960s Juan Marichal (HOF) won the most games with 191 wins.

Sandy Koufax had the highest winning percentage of (.695%) during the 1960s.

"Work like you don't need the money. Love like you've never been hurt. Dance like nobody's watching." — Satchel Paige

"Just give me 25 guys on the last year of their contracts; I'll win a pennant every year." — Sparky Anderson

"There is a world of difference between a count of one ball and two strikes which is a lot different situation than hitting with two strikes and one ball." — Tim McCarver

Joe Rudi

Born Sept. 7, 1946, Modesto, California

Height 6'2" **Weight** 200 lbs.

Bats Right **Throws** Right

Debut April 11, 1967 **Final game** October 3, 1982

JOSEPH ODEN RUDI was born in Modesto, California, on September 7, 1946. He was signed by the Kansas City A's out of high school in 1964. However he did not play much due to a broken hand. In the winter of 1965, he joined the Marine Corps reserves and missed spring training totally. In 1966 while playing single A ball in Modesto, Joe played with a total of fourteen guys who eventually made it to the major leagues.

His breakout year happened in 1967, when Alvin Dark, the manager of the A's, promoted Joe as the opening day left fielder in Kansas City. Joe was only 20 years old. He played in 19 games before being sent back to the minor leagues. At the time of his initial promotion, Joe had not played 100 games as an outfielder at any level of baseball since he was originally signed out of high school as an infielder.

It did not take Joe long to adapt to playing left field. His hard work and tenacity paid dividends as he became one of the premier outfielders in all of major league baseball.

During the prime of his career he served six consecutive years in the Marine Corps reserve for which he missed approximately 50 games each year.

Joe's major league career consisted of 16 outstanding seasons: the Kansas City and Oakland Athletics, 1967–76 and 1982; the California Angels, 1977–1980; and the Boston Red Sox, 1981.

Rudi's 1970 year earned him a .309 batting average. In 1972 he collected 181 hits for the season. The same year he made a highlight game-saving catch in game 2 of the 1972 World Series to preserve a victory. He also hit a home run in that same game!

However, 1974 proved to be Rudi's career year: he hit 22 home runs and knocked in 99 runs for the Oakland A's. In game 5 of the memorable 1974 World Series against the Los Angeles Dodgers, Joe hit a game-winning home run off Dodger relief specialist, Mike Marshall, clinching the championship for the A's! Rudi's Oakland Athletics became the first team since the New York Yankees of the early 50s to win 3 consecutive championships!

When Rudi retired from baseball, he finished with an outstanding career of 179 home runs, 810 RBIs, and a respectable .264 batting average.

Joe earned 3 consecutive Gold Gloves for his outstanding defense in 1974, 1975, and 1976. In addition he played in the 1972, 1974, and 1975 All-Star games.

Joe Rudi was the consummate team player who earned the respect of his peers. Joe Rudi was a gifted professional athlete and one of the more likeable players in the game.

Joe Rudi

In My Own Words

Oakland Thoughts & Memories

WHEN I FIRST PLAYED with the A's in Oakland, there were numerous times when there were screaming ground balls splitting the shortstop and third baseman on the way to me in left field. I literally had to run as hard as I could to get to the ball before it would stop rolling. You could see water in the air just streaming off the ball. And these were games when there had been no rain for days—there was that much moisture in Oakland. Especially between 1968–1976 in the Oakland Coliseum it was almost impossible to hit a ball out at night. It was like trying to hit a ball over the Grand Canyon.

One guy who never had a hard time hitting the ball hard was Willie Horton. He was immensely strong! Willie would literally hit the ball so hard that at times he would hit a one-hopper and it could almost handcuff me if it wasn't played just right.

Best Single Season

The best single season I ever personally witnessed was that of Vida Blue in 1971. The year he had was the most dominating I have ever seen for an entire season. Vida won 24 games and lost only eight for a winning percentage of .750! That is incredible! In addition he pitched 312 innings striking out 301 and walking only 88. His microscopic 1.82 ERA tells a portion of the story. The opposing hitters were intimidated and off balance for the entire season. Vida Blue was as dominating as any who ever played the game in our 1971 magical season. Besides Vida was a good fit on the team. Our entire club was special, but Vida Blue was the definition of green, or money in the bank!

Words of Encouragement

Our manager during the A's championship years was Dick Williams. He was an outstanding manager who had a no nonsense attitude. He knew how to win, and he taught us how to conduct ourselves and win as a team. In 1972 I had a fairly decent year with a .305 batting average. Early in the 1973 season when the A's were playing on the road somewhere, I came to bat early in the game and hit a pretty weak popup to the opponent's third baseman. I came back into the dugout and wasn't feeling particularly good about my last at bat. As I walked past Dick Williams, he mumbled just loud enough for me hear, ".300 hitter, my ass!" I quickly turned to look at him but he was staring towards the field. Well, later in the game I did get a couple of hits. Williams had different approaches for different people, but he did know how and when to motivate us individually and as a team. Now, he can read about how I felt that moment forty years later in this book!

Ken Holtzman, Forgotten Hero

It is unbelievable to me when I speak with people about the glory years of the Oakland A's during the early seventies that Ken Holtzman's name never comes up. People always mention Reggie Jackson, Campy Campaneris, Sal Bando, and frequently Jim "Catfish" Hunter and Vida Blue. But Ken Holtzman is almost never mentioned—that is shocking to me! Holtzman was a huge part of our success—as much as anyone except maybe Catfish! People have forgotten that Holtzman won 59 games in three years! He won 19 with a 2.51 ERA in 1972, 21 with a 2.97 ERA in 1973, and 19 games with 3.07 ERA in 1974! His strikeout-to-walk ratio was way better than 2 to 1! Holtzman was very dominant and hardly anyone ever stole bases on him as his pickoff move was great. Besides, he was fun in the clubhouse as he and Rollie Fingers would go at each other. Both Rollie and Holtzman provided a lot of entertainment for the rest of the mustache gang! Thanks, guys!

El Tiante

Luis Tiant was always a character who brought humor to players, fans and the game. One time early in my career, Luis threw me his stupid Eephus pitch. Anyway, Luis threw this pitch high in the air and as it was dropping into the batter's box at about forty miles per hour I was laughing, and I took a mighty swing at this silly thing. My right hand slipped off the bat and caught my left thumb. Believe it or not I tore the tendons in my left thumb badly and ended up missing about three weeks of the season because of the goofy pitch by the great El Tiante! I could not believe that I fell prey to his prank, and I've often thought of how silly I must have looked swinging at that pitch. Luis was great as a competitor. As a person he always kept things light hearted! And I remember falling to one of his famous pitches. Tiant must still chuckle about hitters swinging at that goofy pitch.

Earl Weaver & Ron Luciano

It was always a pleasure for me personally to play against the Baltimore Orioles—they were an elite team in the early seventies. Earl Weaver, of course, was their fiery manager, and he always had his guys ready to play championship-caliber baseball, and the A's were his nemesis.

Ron Luciano, an umpire, was one of the fun characters of the American League. Ron had a great sense of humor and always delighted the fans and even some of the players. He was unique, to say the least, and I enjoyed Ron's jovial attitude and fun spirit.

Joe Rudi

It was common knowledge around the American League that Weaver and Luciano hated each other. Weaver was constantly giving Luciano a hard time, and Luciano I'm certain also had Weaver in his sights. The Athletics were in the play-offs against Weavers' Orioles, and late in one of the playoff games I got either the tying hit or game-winning hit late in the game. I headed down the line for first base. As I arrived I looked up and saw Luciano give a wink and put his hands together for a soft clap of the hands like a little boy. I remember thinking how funny and un-usual that was to see an umpire applaud a player. I'm not sure Weaver ever noticed, but if he did, I'm sure he was disgusted. Those two were bitter rivals, and at times it was humorous to observe from afar. A lot of times it was fun to be an observer of the crazy nuances of baseball.

The Best of the Best

Best Fastball
Nolan Ryan (speed & velocity)
Jim Palmer (deceptive and
difficult to hit solid – his pitch had
extra hop!)

Most Intimidating Pitcher
Bob Gibson &
Don Drysdale that I saw!
With Nolan Ryan you would pray he
wouldn't hit you!

Best Left-Handed Pitcher
Ron Guidry was nasty!
Vida Blue was a challenge for
almost everyone! Thankfully he was
a team mate

Best Right-Handed Reliever
Rollie Fingers was one of the best of
all time. He was old school. I'm
fortunate we were teammates.

Best Right-Handed Hitter
Harmon Killebrew
(He hurt the Oakland A's more frequently than almost anyone.
Killebrew owned Rollie Fingers.)
Al Kaline & Frank Robinson were
the most consistent and were tremendous hitters! It's a toss up between these three.

Best Curveball
Bert Blyleven would
buckle my knees!
Camilo Pasqual & Juan Marichal
had really great curves!

Best Right-Handed Pitcher
Jim Palmer
Ferguson Jenkins absolutely owned
me! Fergie and I both would chuckle
as I came up to bat, we both knew I
was dead meat!

Best Left-Handed Reliever
Terry Forester stands out as the
toughest lefty I ever saw. He would
run the cutter in on me.
Daryl Knowles was excellent when
he pitched with the A's!

Overall Most Challenging Pitcher
Nolan Ryan & Gaylord Perry (Umpires looked the other way – with
Gaylord there was no way an umpire
could not tell the difference between
a spitter & a sinker!)

Best Left-Handed Hitter
Carl Yastrzemski first comes to
mind as a pure hitter!
**Tony Oliva & Rod Carew were
fabulous to all fields and constantly made contact as they were great
hitters!**

Joe Rudi

Overall Best Clutch Hitter
Carl Yastrzemski and
Frank Robinson
(They were the best I faced with the
game on the line.)

Best First Baseman
Boog Powell **was dominating in
the American League offensively**!
Offensively & defensively George
Scott was solid!

Best Shortstop
Bert Campaneris
(#1 all-around – as a leadoff hitter,
base stealer, offense and defense)
Mark Belanger
(defensively he could not be beat.)

Best Left Fielder
Carl Yastrzemski
(I was glad he moved to first base
otherwise I never would have won
a Gold Glove! Yaz was the best left
fielder I ever saw!)

Best Right Fielder
Al Kaline was the best I played
against! Reggie Jackson was an incredible force all around and my
personal favorite, who also is my
great friend

Best Catcher
Johnny Bench would be number #1.
(I played just a few games against
Bench.)
Thurman Munson & Carlton Fisk
(They were best I played against
often. They were #1 & #2!)

Best Second Baseman
Bobby Grich
(Best all-around second baseman)
Dick Green
(Defensively was fabulous!)

Best Third Baseman
Brooks Robinson
(I use to get a lot of bunt hits, but
could never get a bunt hit off of
Brooks!)
Sal Bando was solid in the field, a
clutch hitter, but as a captain of a
team they should have his picture
next to the word "captain," Bando
was the best!

Best Center Fielder
Paul Blair
(An incredible defensive center
fielder. You could not hit the ball
over his head.)
Ken Berry with White Sox
(could cover as much ground as anyone.)

Fastest Base Runner
Mickey Mantle
(The fastest I ever saw!)

Best Base Runner
Campy Campaneris
(The best I saw!
Lou Brock and Willie Mays are
obvious, but I never saw Lou and
Willie play very much.)

Player Who Didn't Reach Maximum Potential
Tony Conigliaro
(Because he was beaned!)
Ray Fosse
(He had his career cut short in an
All-Star game with Pete Rose. That
play was over the top and senseless.
That play Rose created was
ridiculous!)

Best Team Rival
San Francisco Giants & Los Angeles Dodgers
(As a Giants fan growing up).
As a professional it would have to be
the Oakland A's & Baltimore Orioles! The A's played Baltimore in
the playoffs 1971, 1973 & 1974!

Best Manager I Played For
Dick Williams
(He taught us how to win, and made
us grow up as individuals
& as a team.)
Bob Kennedy
(He taught me the most for my
personal benefit
as a defensive player.)

Best Overall Player
Mickey Mantle & Willie Mays
(The best I played with were Al Ka-
line & Frank Robinson)

Strongest Outfield Arm
Al Kaline
(He got rid of the ball quickly & was
very accurate, very strong and he
was the best I played against! Obviously Clemente was great, but he
played in the National League.
Reggie Jackson was also excellent.)

Best Opposing Manager
Earl Weaver!
(He was a show in himself, and I
loved playing against him & his
Baltimore teams.)

Most Trusted Friend
Reggie Jackson, Gene Tenace & Sal
Bando are the ones I spend the most
time with today!

Funniest Player
Ken Holtzman & Rollie Fingers
(We would try to figure out ways for those two to get going at each other, which would break up the entire A's team! Holtzman & Fingers were a riot when they would focus on each other.)

Most Heart
Jim "Catfish" Hunter.
(He was the heart and soul of the Oakland A's during our glory days! When we lost Cat it changed the dynamics of our team. Great player and great guy!)

Most Courageous
Jim "Catfish" Hunter

Best Work Ethics
Reggie Jackson &
Jim "Catfish" Hunter
(Ray Fosse was also incredible)

Most Flamboyant
Reggie Jackson
(It was show business, and he was a genuine superstar who knew how to market himself!)

Most Congenial
Harmon Killebrew
& Brooks Robinson

Most Zany
Bill "Spaceman" Lee &
Mark "Bird" Fidrych

My Favorite Team
New York Yankees
(When I was growing up)
As a player the 1974 Oakland A's was probably our best team and most memorable team

Player I Most Admired
Mickey Mantle

Player I Would Have Liked as a Team Mate
I would have liked to have been a fly on a wall with the Yankees in the early 1960s. Mickey Mantle would have been my first choice!

My Favorite Stadium
Fenway Park
(I loved the ballpark, city and the people)

My Favorite City
Boston is the greatest! Most knowledgeable fans!

Best Baseball Announcer
Vin Scully

My Favorite Baseball Announcer
Monte Moore

The Best Umpire

Ed Runge
(He rang me up on a pitch that was outside. I apologized to him for popping off to him. He tested me though! Runge was a great umpire.)
Dave Phillips
(an outstanding umpire who had my respect and a great human being!)

Umpire with The Best Attitude

Dave Phillips & Nester Chylak
I really liked Ron Luciano! Luciano was a breath of fresh air!

Most Respected Baseball Personality

Joe DiMaggio
(He was the Oakland A's coach in 1968 & 1969. He was accommodating, delightful, a fun character, and, most of all, a true gentleman!)

Joe Rudi
Lifetime Statistics

Year	Age	Tm	Lg	G	PA	AB	R	H	2B	3B	HR	RBI	SB	CS	BB	SO	BA	OBP	SLG
1967	20	KCA	AL	19	46	43	4	8	2	0	0	1	0	0	3	7	.186	.239	.233
1968	21	OAK	AL	68	197	181	10	32	5	1	1	12	1	1	12	32	.177	.236	.232
1969	22	OAK	AL	35	129	122	10	23	3	1	2	6	1	1	5	16	.189	.220	.279
1970	23	OAK	AL	106	375	350	40	108	23	2	11	42	3	1	16	61	.309	.341	.480
1971	24	OAK	AL	127	556	513	62	137	23	4	10	52	3	2	28	62	.267	.304	.386
1972	25	OAK	AL	147	653	593	94	181	32	9	19	75	3	4	37	62	.305	.345	.486
1973	26	OAK	AL	120	483	437	53	118	25	1	12	66	0	0	30	72	.270	.315	.414
1974	27	OAK	AL	158	639	593	73	174	39	4	22	99	2	3	34	92	.293	.334	.484
1975	28	OAK	AL	126	515	468	66	130	26	6	21	75	2	1	40	56	.278	.338	.494
1976	29	OAK	AL	130	557	500	54	135	32	3	13	94	6	1	41	71	.270	.323	.424
1977	30	CAL	AL	64	272	242	48	64	13	2	13	53	1	0	22	48	.264	.333	.496
1978	31	CAL	AL	133	536	497	58	127	27	1	17	79	2	1	28	82	.256	.295	.416
1979	32	CAL	AL	90	361	330	35	80	11	3	11	61	0	0	24	61	.242	.294	.394
1980	33	CAL	AL	104	399	372	42	88	17	1	16	53	1	0	17	84	.237	.277	.417
1981	34	BOS	AL	49	135	122	14	22	3	0	6	24	0	0	8	29	.180	.239	.352
1982	35	OAK	AL	71	223	193	21	41	6	1	5	18	0	0	24	35	.212	.301	.332

16-Year Totals

G	PA	AB	R	H	2B	3B	HR	RBI	SB	CS	BB	SO	BA	OBP	SLG
1547	6076	5556	684	1468	287	39	179	810	25	15	369	870	.264	.311	.427

219

"Did You Know?"

Lou Brock stole 551 bases for the most stolen bases in the majors during the 1970s.

Bob Gibson had the most strikeouts in the 1960s with 2,071.

"When managing, if you don't win you will be fired. If you do win, you are only putting off being fired." — Leo Durocher

"I was such a dangerous hitter I even got intentional walks during batting practice." — Casey Stengel

Ron Laflore of the 1970s is the only player to lead both leagues in steals.

Tito Fuentes was hit with a pitch three times during one game by the same pitcher.

Arturo Santo Domingo
Major League Baseball Scorekeeper

ART SANTO DOMINGO was born 1938 in New York City. Art's parents were of Columbian decent, and they often took young Art to their home in Columbia, South America. The year when Art was eight years old, 1946, was a memorable one for Art as his father passed away that year. It was also the same year that his mother took him to the Polo Grounds to watch the Giants—for his first major league game! He remembers everything as it was when he first walked into the fashionable Polo Grounds, including the grass, the incredible excitement, and seeing Whitey Lockman, his first major league hitter! Art was hooked on base-ball, and he was hooked on the Giants!

After high school, Art left New York for North Carolina to attend Duke University. He was a student from 1956 to 1960 and majored in history and political science, graduating with honors.

In 1956 he managed the men's basketball team at Duke and was involved in other sports as well.

In 1958, a friend at Duke encouraged him to go with him to Philadelphia to visit the New York Giants when they played the Philadelphia Phillies at Connie Mack

Stadium. The friend was acquainted with Orlando Cepeda, Felipe Alou, and Art was introduced to these baseball legends for the first time!

One time in the summer of 1960 while Art was visiting Philadelphia, there was a rainout. Art talked Orlando Cepeda and Felipe Alou into visiting a minor league game in Allentown, Pennsylvania to watch a promising right-hander playing for the Springfield Giants. The right-hander's name was Juan Marichal! During the game, Marichal not only pitched masterfully, but was hit by a screaming line drive that could have ended the Dominican Dandy's career. New friendships were formed, and fifty years later, they are all still very good friends!

After Art graduated from Duke in 1960, he talked his mother into allowing him to visit San Francisco. He wanted to visit his friends Cepeda, Alou, and Marichal playing with the newly formulated San Francisco Giants. While visiting San Francisco for the summer, he also attended Stanford University.

In the spring of 1962 Art decided to visit Phoenix where the Giants held their spring training games. There he became reacquainted with Russ Hodges, the legendary announcer for the Giants. Russ was an acquaintance from back in New York City—the two families had lived in the same neighborhood. Russ mentioned to young Art that the Giants might possibly be hiring a fulltime statistician. That's how Art's professional career began with the San Francisco Giants.

Art has been in a prominent and official position in management with the Giants since 1962. He has been an official major league baseball scorekeeper for the Giants since 1992.

On November 7, 1962, Art met his wife, Fran, and two years later to the date, they were married—November 7, 1964. Forty six years later, they alternate their residences between San Francisco, California, and Las Vegas, Nevada.

Art Santo Domingo is very well respected and highly thought of in major league baseball circles.

Arturo Santo Domingo

In My Own Words

O FFICIALLY, I'VE BEEN A PROFESSIONAL SCOREKEEPER in San Francisco for major league baseball since 1992, however I have been with the Giants organization since I became a 25-year-old rookie with Giants in '62 doing the daily stats for the media.

I remember clearly toward the end of the 1962 season the way the Giants were chasing the Dodgers. It was my first year working with a major league team, so I was excited and optimistic about the chase, recalling the 1951 season when I was 13 years old. But that Sunday in 1962 before the last week of the season, many of the Giants were expecting to finish in second place. Some of them expressed the view that they had their chances but had not taken advantage of the opportunities. Some had even made travel plans to go home immediately after the September 30th game. That was disappointing to me, because I was still optimistic.

On the last day of the 1962 season, the third playoff game in Los Angeles, I was working in the NBC-TV booth with Bob Wolf. I believe that day, when I provided the announcers with some interesting tidbits of information relevant to the game, was the very first of a new era of stat information and trivia for baseball announced over the air waves.

Having been a New York Giants fan in my youth and something of a fanatic, I was able to describe to the announcers the many coincidences that occurred in those two Dodgers and Giants games, first in the 1951 game and now in this one in 1962. On October 3, 1962, I remember telling the media professionals the following: Giants and Dodgers played each other on the same date in 1951—October 3! Similar to that 1951 game with the famous Bobby Thomson home run, in 1962 the Giants were down in the 9th inning. The Dodgers had a 3-run lead in both games! The Giants scored four runs in the 9th inning in both games to take the lead. In both games, the Giants player wearing #23—Bobby Thomson in 1951 and Felipe Alou in 1962—each scored the winning run! These are just a few examples of information I provided to the NBC Broadcasters team. That 1962 season was one the most memorable and rewarding seasons for me personally!

The second contribution I made to the media while reporting games was during the early 1960s. On ballpark scorecards and scoreboards, the pitchers were always listed by numbers, from 1 to 12, for example. I suggested that, instead, they put the numbers for the pitchers by their uniform number, so they would know that Koufax #32, Marichal #27, Gibson #45, and Ferguson Jenkins # 31 were pitching in those games. That was adopted by all of the major league teams!

Also, the wire service ticker would report on line scores from the other games with the pitchers, pitching changes, and the homeruns that were hit during those games. But they never disclosed to the media or announcers the number of home runs player had hit to date for that season. For example, the ticker information would simply state, HR Aaron, Milwaukee, or HR Cepeda, San Francisco. I suggested to the wire services that they should include the number of home runs to date for the player. For instance, Cepeda (28) had hit his 28th home run of the season in the 8th inning! This was a very simple alteration, but it provided valuable assistance to the announcers and benefited their listening audiences. Before these changes, the reporters and announcers in the broadcast booths and media areas constantly asked, "How many home runs does Cepeda have now?" From that point on, announcers and other media professionals knew immediately the specifics regarding pitchers and hitters!

The First Japanese Player

In September 1964 the San Francisco Giants promoted a 20-year-old Japanese pitcher, a phenom named Masanori Murakami. He was fabulous in his major league debut as he absolutely dominated the hitters. In the last four weeks of the season, the left-handed reliever had 15 strikeouts in 15 innings pitched, with only 1 walk! His ERA was a microscopic 1.80! When Murakami received the call for his promotion to join the Giants, he had been playing for Fresno in the minor leagues. The Giants had already left for New York to play the Mets and Murakami had to find transportation from Fresno to San Francisco and then on to New York City! I wonder what this young man must have thought arriving in New York City. And what an exceptional accomplishment it was for him to have traveled, in a foreign country, from Fresno to San Francisco and on to New York City, especially considering the language barriers he must have encountered!

The Giants had appointed me to meet him, help him feel welcomed and to help get him acclimated. He arrived at the Roosevelt Hotel in New York, and Juan Marichal, Matty Alou, Jose Pagan and I took him to lunch at the hotel his first day. He was an instant hit with the entire Giants team, but he especially bonded immediately with the Latin players.

I've always thought if the Giants had promoted Murakami earlier in the season, he might have made the difference, moving us from second place to first place. That season the Giants finished one game behind the Dodgers for the National League pennant.

Murakami also pitched for the Giants in 1965, but that was the extent of his major league service. Family members, friends and authorities in Japan pressured Murakami not to return to the United States to continue his big league career. It's very interesting to ponder how he might have fared over a longer period of time. He was a very good left-handed pitcher!

One thing for absolute certain, Murakami is an exceptional gentleman! From the very moment he arrived until now, we have been friends and have maintained a mutual respect for one another! He still comes to the United States often, and I am proud of the fact that we always make time for one another and continue with our long-lasting friendship.

Welcome to the Big Leagues!

My first professional year with the San Francisco Giants was 1962. The Giants had won six in a row, six of the first seven games to open the season in San Francisco. The 1962 Giants won 103 games in total and failed to win the World Series! There were four regular players on the Giants who hit over .300. That team was amazing!

On my very first road trip as a Giants employee we flew to Chicago, and I was excited! After we took off, one of the engines of the plane caught on fire! Some people were terrified—I was one of them! I remember our catcher, Ed Bailey, going up and down the aisles telling everyone to keep flapping their arms faster! Bailey was always humorous and coming up with something funny, but this time, it seemed crazy! Jose Pagan was praying, as were others. The plane was directed to make an emergency landing at Salt Lake City. The runway was covered with foam and the fire engines were standing by. This particular plane was chartered from United, and, after we landed safely, we waited forever for our next plane, another charter, to take us to our destination. We arrived in Chicago at 6 a.m. in time for the day game at Wrigley Field between the Giants and the Cubs. Believe it or not, the Giants won! My first experience traveling with the big club was very memorable and exciting. Our future flight did not have the same level of excitement. But it has been great being a part of my favorite major league team.

The Best of the Best

Best Fastball
Nolan Ryan

Best Curveball
Bert Blyleven & Sal Maglie

Most Intimidating Pitcher
Bob Gibson

Best Right-Handed Pitcher
Juan Marichal

Best Left-Handed Pitcher
Warren Spahn

Best Left-Handed Reliever
Luis Arroyo

Best Right-Handed Reliever
Mike Marshall

**Overall Most
Challenging Pitcher**
Juan Marichal

Best Right-Handed Hitter
Dick Allen

Best Left-Handed Hitter
Willie McCovey

Overall Best Clutch Hitter
Willie McCovey

Best Catcher
Johnny Bench

Best First Baseman
Willie McCovey

Best Second Baseman
Red Schoendienst

Best Shortstop
Luis Aparicio

Best Third Baseman
Brooks Robinson (defensive)
Mike Schmidt (offensive)

Best Left Fielder
Billy Williams

Best Center Fielder
Willie Mays

Best Right Fielder
Roberto Clemente

Fastest Base Runner
Maury Wills

Best Base Runner
Willie Mays

Best Overall Player
Hank Aaron

Most Gifted Athlete
Bobby Bonds

Strongest Outfield Arm
Roberto Clemente

Best Team Rival
Brooklyn & Los Angeles Dodgers
vs. Giants

Best Opposing Manager
Walter Alston

Arturo Santo Domingo

Most Trusted Friend
Manny Mota

Most Heart
Pete Rose

Best Work Ethics
Dick Groat

Most Flamboyant
Tito Fuentes

Most Congenial
Ernie Banks

My Favorite Team
San Francisco Giants

Player I Most Admired
Alvin Dark

My Favorite Stadium
Crosley Field

My Favorite City
Chicago

Best Baseball Announcer
Vin Scully

**My Favorite
Baseball Announcer**
Vin Scully

The Best Umpire
Doug Harvey

**Umpire with The Best
Attitude**
Doug Harvey

**Most Respected Baseball
Personality**
Felipe Alou

"Did You Know?"

Masanori Marakami was the first Japanese player in the major leagues. He played for the San Francisco Giants in 1964 & 1965.

Matty Alou, Felipe Alou, & Jesus Alou are the only trio of brothers to play in the same game simultaneously. They. played the three outfield positions in the same game for the San Francisco Giants in 1962.

Willie Mays was the first rookie of the year winner to be elected into Cooperstown's Hall of Fame.

Gaylord Perry won the Cy Young award in both the National and American League.

Dave Kingman hit the most homeruns of anyone in his last season with thirty five homers.

Lon Simmons
Hall-of-fame Broadcaster

L ON SIMMONS, the voice of the San Francisco Giants, was the first baseball announcer ever retained by a major league baseball club from the West Coast. When the Giants made their move west in 1958 from New York, they brought their established broadcasting legend, Russ Hodges.

Lon Simmons was a native Californian who flourished once baseball presented the opportunity! Lon mentioned that if he had personally selected his first broadcast partner, he never could have chosen a better broadcaster—or person—as a partner than his friend Russ Hodges. Russ provided numerous opportunities for Lon to develop, evolving into a legendary baseball announcer. Russ Hodges was a fabulous person and broadcaster with a great sense of humor! It is with great fondness and respect that Lon Simmons speaks of his memories of the gentleman from Dayton, Tennessee, and fellow Ford Frick Award winner, Russ Hodges!

In 2004 Lon Simmons received the Ford C. Frick Award given by the Baseball Hall of Fame for broadcasters. In addition, Lon was elected and inducted in the inaugural year of 2006 to the Bay Area Radio Hall of Fame in the Golden State of California.

Simmons broadcast games for the San Francisco Giants with Hodges from the time the team moved west in 1958 until 1973. After tragedy struck Lon with the loss of his dear wife in 1973, he decided to leave the broadcast booth temporarily. He returned in 1976 for three more years before moving across the bay to call games for the Oakland Athletics from 1981 through 1995. From 1996 to 2002, he returned to San Francisco and called the Giants games part-time.

Lon's initial sixteen years with the San Francisco Giants never offered an opportunity to call a World Series game. After the Giants' new owners decided to replace Lon with their own broadcaster—much to the chagrin of the loyal bay area fan base—Lon finally had an opportunity as a member of the Oakland Athletics to call his first and only World Series game against the Giants in 1989. The Bay Area World Series of 1989 was disrupted for approximately ten days by the tragic earthquake that cost lives and created severe havoc in the entire region. Lon did finally conduct the broadcast as the Athletics won the series against the Giants. Lon's broadcast partner with the Oakland Athletics was Bill King. Bill had a severe throat condition, and Lon with his rich and smooth baritone voice called the majority of the two games.

Lon, with his natural wit, commented that it dawned on him one day crossing the Bay Bridge that the only reason that both the San Francisco Giants and Oakland Athletics terminated him was because each team wanted to be the last to terminate him! One of the enduring character qualities and trademarks of Lon Simmons is his great sense of humor.

When I asked Lon how he would like to be remembered, he said, "I've never given it much thought. But, I suppose when I die, I would hope they would say, 'My, doesn't he look unnatural!' " This was a typical Simmons response!

Simmons' trademark call for home runs was the San Francisco fan favorite: "Tell it goodbye!" Lon does not remember exactly when he first broadcast his famous home run call, but remembers that he used it at Seals Stadium before the Giants moved into Candlestick Park in 1960. The San Francisco Giants Hall of Fame pair, Willie Mays and Willie McCovey, certainly provided hundreds of opportunities for the faithful bay area radio audience to listen to the golden voice of Lon Simmons make their favorite home run call, as you can "Tell it goodbye!" Later in Lon's career he had several opportunities to call the majestic home runs of Barry Bonds, just as he had for Barry's legendary father, Bobby! Here Lon shares his fondest memories and favorite stories in his own unique, entertaining, and humorous style.

Lon Simmons

In My Own Words

B ROADCASTING BASEBALL GAMES was not work because I enjoyed it so much! People use to ask me if I was working. I would reply, "No, I'm broadcasting." Being thankful for the opportunities that were presented to perform an occupation that I truly loved for a lifetime made that perception a reality in my mind.

Candlestick Park

There are so many stories that I can tell about Candlestick Park. I suppose I need to start with when Candlestick first opened in 1960. For those who never visited the park in San Francisco, it was built within a few hundred yards of the San Francisco Bay, right on the water. The wind would blow constantly, and at times furiously! Candlestick was as famous for the wind as it was for baseball. Frequently, fans brought blankets to day games in addition to their heavy coats and hats in the middle of July. Candlestick, to say the very least, was a very unique park to experience the nation's favorite pastime!

The Giants officials set several small flags around numerous locations within the confines of Candlestick to gauge the direction of the wind. The study revealed that the wind would blow within the park from different directions simultaneously. However, the players already knew that!

During the construction of Candlestick, the Vice President of the Giants, Chub Fenney, asked a construction official if the wind always blew with this much force. The official said that the wind usually started around one o'clock in the afternoon. Of course, in the 1960s and 1970s, the Giants played the vast majority of their games in the day and the starting time was 1 p.m.!

Someone said they figured the best way to negate the wind at Candlestick Park would be to face both Russ Hodges and me against the wind. With both of us facing the wind; it would be neutralized! I wasn't offended by their humor as I always felt as though I had a lot in common with Candlestick Park. We were both big and ugly, we were both very windy, and no one could figure out how to get rid us!

During the last month of the 1959 baseball season, all of the Giants fans, officials, and dignitaries were excited as the San Francisco Giants were right in the middle of the National League pennant race into the very last week of the season. Plus the Giants were electrified by their budding stars like Orlando Cepeda and Willie McCovey, both of whom later became Hall-of-Fame players.

The Giants were a very special team in the early 1960s. They were the only team in the history of major league baseball that has had five future Hall-of-Famers on the same team. For several seasons they had Willie Mays, Willie McCovey, Juan

Marichal, Orlando Cepeda, and Gaylord Perry. What a lineup!

On opening day in 1960, Giants pitcher Sam Jones pitched a three-hitter against the St. Louis Cardinals for the first win in the new home park. There were many famous in attendance that day, including our future thirty-seventh president of the United States, Richard M. Nixon.

The Giants officials thought they had provided every luxury while placing state-of-the-art radiant heat beneath the seats for the fans in Candlestick. However, the heat went down instead of up and did not reduce the chill. San Francisco attorney Melvin Belli filed a lawsuit against the Giants over the heat failure and won the court case!

The Dodgers and Giants

One of the most unusual games ever played in Candlestick was the game against the Los Angeles Dodgers during the inaugural year of Candlestick Park. Willie McCovey was the Giants hitter. The Dodgers had their Hall-of-Fame center fielder Duke Snider, and rifle-armed Carl Furillo in right field. Willie McCovey of the Giants hit a towering fly ball between the two Dodger outfielders, and the fog was so thick that the ball completely disappeared. Snider and Furillo ran around looking frantically for the ball. Naturally, the ball dropped, which ordinarily would have been a routine out. McCovey, who could run well, made it to third base easily. The umpires called a fog delay! To my knowledge, it is the only time a major league game has been delayed because of fog. The game later continued, and, unfortunately, the Dodgers won.

Speaking of the Dodgers, they would always complain to the umpires and accuse the Giants management team of wetting the playing surface at Candlestick around first base just before the game for the purpose of slowing the running game of their stolen-base-king, Maury Wills. The Dodgers would insist on drying the field by having the Giants groundskeepers spread sand around the first base area. The Giants were aware that spreading the sand would definitely slow Maury down a step.

When the Dodgers management took their argument to the Giants Vice President, Chub Fenney, one time, Chub mentioned how the Dodgers also manipulated their field for their advantage. The playing field at Dodger Stadium was as hard as a rock so that Maury Wills could chop down at the ball to bounce the ball over the opponent's head. The Dodgers brass told Chub that the playing surface at Dodger Stadium had been completely remedied! Chub asked the Dodger official, "What did you do—pave it?"

One more Dodger story with the Giants: Maury Wills lived a charmed life—so it seemed! Ray Sadecki was pitching for the Giants, and Maury Wills was on first base. Ray threw over to first base twelve times to drive Maury back. On the thirteenth time Ray picked off Maury. The Giants got Maury in a rundown, and just at the last moment with Giants second baseman Tito Fuentes' throwback to first base, Tito's shoulder went out. So Maury made it safely back to first, and the charmed life of Maury Wills lived on!

Dick Allen and Subliminal Messages

Dick Allen, the power-hitting first baseman, was not only a great hitter, but a real character of the game. Dick was the first player I witnessed writing notes with his spikes in the dirt around the first base area when he was playing on the field on defense. The fans could read the messages from Dick's baseball spikes and were amused. Major league baseball was not amused!

In 1965 the Giants were, as usual, in a fight for the playoff position with the Dodgers. The Giants and Dodgers had brought both of their seasons to the very last regular game of the season. The Giants were playing the Pirates in a double header in Pittsburgh. The Dodgers were playing the Phillies in a double header in Philadelphia. The Giants needed to win both games of the double header against the Pirates. After the Giants won the first game, Willie McCovey hit the hardest ball that I have ever seen over the center field wall at Forbes Field for the game winner in the second game.

Now the Phillies had to beat Sandy Koufax and the Dodgers in their second game for Giants' survival The Giants waited at the Pittsburgh Airport. A Phillies win would send the Giants to Cincinnati for a makeup game that could have put them in a playoff game with Los Angeles. A Dodger win would send the Giants back to San Francisco, and the season would be over!

The Giants received the report: bottom of the ninth with Phillies batting with two out, two on base, Dodgers leading by two, and the Phillies slugger Dick Allen was at bat.

The story goes that Allen stepped into the batter's box as he told the Dodgers catcher Johnny Roseboro, "The Giants are going to Cincinnati because no one can throw three fastballs past me." Oh, yeah? Three fastballs later, the Giants were on a season-ending flight to San Francisco. There turned out to be one pitcher who could throw three fastballs past Dick Allen, Mr. Sandy Koufax!

Willie Mays

Let me share some memorable Willie May's stories. When my second wife died, I was living in Palm Springs, and I received a phone call from Willie who wanted to come over to play a round of golf with me. What I did not know was that Willie had to fly to New York from San Francisco on business.

Willie flew into Los Angeles, rented a car, and drove to Palm Springs. We played golf, and I asked Willie if we were going to have dinner together. Willie said no, that he had to fly to New York. Also, Willie said he was going to leave his brand new golf clubs with me. That was typical of Willie! He knew I was hurting and he wanted to help.

In the 1960s the Giants had a pitcher by the name of Ron Herbel. Ron was not a very good hitter. As matter of fact, there was a gentleman's bet whether or not Ron would get a base hit during the entire season. Willie Mays was the only player who bet that Ron would get at least one hit in that entire season. In Chicago, Ron came to bat and drove a line drive to right field in front of Cubs legend Billy Williams. Willie got so excited he jumped up and hit his head on the top of the dugout and knocked himself out cold. While Willie was out, Billy Williams, the Cubs right fielder, charged the ball and threw out Ron at first base. However, later that year Ron did get a base hit and Willie did win his gentleman's bet. This time he stayed enthusiastically seated on the dugout bench.

One time while the Giants were visiting Chicago, Leo Durocher was managing the Cubbies. Even though Willie Mays and Leo Durocher were great friends—almost like father and son—Leo would call for his pitchers to consistently knock Willie down. Willie was sitting in the Giants dugout with the Giants pitcher Juan Marichal. Willie asked Marichal why he didn't knock down the Cubbies great future Hall of Famer, Ernie Banks. Juan replied to Willie, "I can't knock Ernie down. He's a great guy!" Willie looked at Juan and said, "I'm a great guy too, but everybody knocks me down!"

Great Memories

In 1961 the Giants were playing the Cincinnati Reds at Crosley Field. Felipe Alou did not start the game because he should not swing the bat due to a wrist injury. In the eighth inning the Giants introduced Felipe into right field for defensive purposes. The Giants were leading one to nothing in the ninth inning when the Giants came to bat and hit five home runs! The players who connected for the long balls were Jimmy Davenport, John Orsino, Orlando Cepeda, Willie Mays, and—you guessed it—the defensive replacement with the bad wrist, Felipe Alou!

On April 30, 1961, Willie Mays hit four home runs against the Braves in Milwaukee. Willie was sick the night before from eating some bad ribs and wasn't even supposed to play. He could have easily hit his fifth home run. Willie, on one of his trips to the plate, broke his bat but drove the ball deep to the top of the outfield wall where Henry Aaron leaped up and caught it. The fans in Milwaukee were rooting for Willie at this point in the game! In the Giants' ninth inning, Jimmy Davenport made the third out with Willie in the on-deck circle, and the Milwaukee fans booed Jimmy. They wanted to see Willie have another chance at number five.

The San Francisco Giants are the only team in the history of baseball to play three brothers at the same time. The three brothers were all outfielders and, of course, are the Giants' legendary Alou brothers. Matty Alou went on to be an exceptionally fine hitter. Felipe Alou was an excellent right fielder with a great outfield arm who could hit with power. Jesus Alou was a fine outfielder in his own right, and was recognized as a funny and very happy-go-lucky guy.

One time when the Giants were boarding our plane to fly back east, Jesus and I were sitting next to each other. Jesus told me he had an interesting dream the night before. He said that he dreamed our plane would crash. Feeling better about a great takeoff, I looked at Jesus and asked confidently if his dream was about the takeoff? Jesus looked at me seriously shaking his head, "No. His dream of crashing was on landing!" We all had a very relaxed flight!

"Did You Know?"

Bert Campaneris played all nine positions on the baseball field during the same game. In addition, when pitching, Camparneris pitched right handed to right habded batters, and left handed to left handed batters. The idea was the brain child of eccentric Oakland A's owner, Charlie O. Finley.

Harmon Killebrew hit the most home runs (393) during the 1960s.

Los Angeles Dodgers legend Maury Wills swiped the most stolen bases (535) during the 1960s.

1968 was the first year an all star game was played inside a dome stadium, at Houston's Astrodome

Luis "El Tiante" Tiant

Born November 23, 1940, Marianao, Cuba

Height 5' 11" **Weight** 190 lbs.

Bats Right **Throws** Right

Debut July 19, 1964 **Final game** Sept. 4, 1982

Luis Tiant was born on November 23, 1940 in Marianao, Cuba as an only child to Isabel and Luis Tiant Sr. His father, Luis Tiant Sr., was a great left-handed pitcher in Cuba from 1926-1948. He pitched in the Negro leagues for the New York Cubans in the summer and the Cienfuegos team in winter ball in Cuba. Once Tiant Sr. even faced Babe Ruth in a game!

Louis Tiant Jr.'s abilities were recognized by former Cleveland Indians All-Star Bobby Avila, who was in Cuba scouting for professional-level talent, leading to Tiant's his first professional contract.

Tiant progressed through the Cleveland Indians' farm system and got the call to the big club after a 15-1 record at Triple-A Portland. On July 19, 1964, Tiant made his debut at Yankee Stadium: 11 strikeouts and a 3-0 shutout victory against the New York Yankees, the defending World Champs. Luis had out-dueled Hall-of-Famer Whitey Ford. Rookie Tiant finished the year for the Indians with a 10-4 record, 105 strikeouts, and an amazing 2.83 ERA in his first full season.

He played for the Cleveland Indians from 1964-1969, the Minnesota Twins in 1970, the Boston Red Sox from 1971-1978, the New York Yankees from 1979 to 1980, the Pittsburgh Pirates in 1981, and finished his career with the California Angels in 1982.

In 1966, Tiant tied a major league record when he pitched four straight shutouts on his way to 12 wins and a 2.79 ERA. In 1968, Luis developed a unique style: he would turn his back to the hitter and look directly towards centerfield and then look up to God in the sky before delivering his pitch to home plate. This style in effect created a hesitation pitch, causing a disruption for the hitters. According to Tiant, the new motion was a response to a drop in his velocity from an arm injury, and to the fact that baseball lowered the pitcher's mound. Twisting and turning his body into unthinkable positions, Tiant spent more time looking towards the outfield than towards the plate as he propelled his pitch. Tiant had reinvented himself, altering his delivery, and creating a deception for hitters, making him even more effective with his elusive style. As a result, in 1968 he had a breakthrough year! Fans adored him for his charismatic charm, quirkiness, bubbling personality, and his animated pitching delivery!

In that 1968 season, he led the league in ERA (1.60), shutouts (9), and hits per nine innings while finishing with a 21-9 mark. In addition, opposing hitters batted just .168 off Tiant, a major league record. On July 3 he struck out 19 Minnesota Twins in a ten-inning game, setting an American League record for games of that length. His 1.60 ERA was the lowest in the American League since Walter Johnson's 1.49 mark during the Dead Ball Era in 1919, and second lowest in 1968 to Bob Gibson's 1.12—the lowest ever during the Live Ball Era.

In 1971 the Boston Red Sox retained the services of their new idol, Luis Tiant. He quickly won over the Boston fans with his charm and immediately grew to be one of the most beloved and revered players in Red Sox history.

It was in 1972 that the Red Sox fans at Fenway adoringly referred to Luis as "El Tiante," and El Tiante, the legend, grew to national proportions. He regained his old dominant form with 16 wins and an unbelievable 1.91 ERA. He went on to win 20 games in 1973 and 22 wins in 1974.

The Red Sox of 1975 became American League Champions and received 18 wins from their lovable ace even though he had developed a back disorder. He opened the World Series for the Red Sox against the Big Red Machine of Cincinnati. With special arrangements for their visas, Luis's mother and father were able to visit the United States to witness their son's domination over one of the most powerful offensive teams in the history of the game. Luis threw a masterpiece as the Reds tallied a total of five hits. The proud El Tiante pitched brilliantly in front of his parents with a 6-0 shutout against Cincinnati!

Tiant won game 4 as well and ended up with a no-decision in arguably the greatest game ever played, game 6! Carlton Fisk's dramatic game-winning walk-off home run in the 12th inning won the game after Luis had been replaced on the Red Sox mound. The Reds defeated the Red Sox in game 7 to capture the championship.

Tiant went on to a 21-12 record in 1976, 12-8 in 1977, and 13-8 in 1978.

After the end of the 1978 season, Tiant signed as a free agent with the Yankees. breaking the hearts of his New England fans. Tiant compiled a 21-17 record in New York during the 1979 and 1980 seasons. Luis finished his illustrious career after two brief stints with the Pittsburgh Pirates and California Angels.

In his 19-season career, Tiant compiled a 229-172 record with 2416 strikeouts, a 3.30 ERA, 187 complete games, and 49 shutouts in 3,486 innings. He was selected to participate in three All-Star Games. In 1997 Luis Tiant was inducted into the Boston Red Sox Hall of Fame.

Tiant has unfortunately fallen short the past few years of being selected to Baseball's Hall of Fame in Cooperstown. However, He is a genuine Hall-of-Famer in the minds of knowledgeable fans across the country. Fortunately he was recognized for his greatness by the Hispanic Heritage Baseball Museum Hall of Fame on July 23, 2002, and inducted in a pre-game on-field ceremony at Fenway Park.

Luis Tiant is certainly a Hall-of-Fame person, who derives great pleasure from extending his gracious hospitality to his adoring fans worldwide! A first class person all the away!

Former Red Sox Manager Darrel Johnson said, "If a man put a gun to my head and said I'm going to pull this trigger if you lose this game, I'd want Luis Tiant to pitch that game!"

In My Own Words

This is a good opportunity for me as I have a lot of things I would like to express especially to the fans! When I first started looking up towards the sky when I was pitching, it was with the intent of having God on my mind. Then I did it so easily that it really became second nature to me through the years. But that was how it started. I was so thankful to God for allowing me to leave Cuba and providing me with the opportunities I had here in the states to fulfill my dreams. I still feel that way today!

Pudge Messin' With Me?

Carlton "Pudge" Fisk was a great teammate along with all of the Red Sox players. But my first year in Boston was something else at times with Pudge behind the plate. Sometimes if I made a mistake with a bad pitch or gave up a home run and he thought I missed my spot or location, that son-of-a-gun would fire the ball back to me on the mound like it was a missile. One day my glove hand started swelling up from his repeatedly firing the ball back at me like crazy. I called Pudge out to the mound. Pudge said, "What's up?" I replied, "What's up? Look at my hand! Who's pitching—you or me? I'll tell you what's up! You fire that ball back to me like missile again, and I'll let it go out into center field. That's what's up!" He looked at me again and said, "You do that, and I'll kick your behind!" I said "You are not going to kick anything! Get back behind the plate and don't give me any more baloney or I'll cross you up on the next pitches, and you will end up with broken fingers!" Pudge said, "Shut up!" I looked at him in the eyes and I said, "You shut up!" He shook his head and went back behind the plate. Pudge and I became very good friends after that, but to me that exchange was funny! Not only is he a good guy, but Pudge was the best catcher I ever saw!

Funny Aggravation

The Red Sox were playing in New York against the Yankees, and I was pitching. Mickey Rivers was batting and I got two quick strikes on him. Then he fouled off fourteen consecutive pitches. Foul here! Foul there! Constantly fouling off pitches. Rivers was driving me nuts! On the fifteenth pitch, he hit the ball into the right field bleachers for a home run! As Rivers approached third base, I was along the third base line waiting for him, and I told him the next time I'm going to hit you right in your neck. Rivers said, "Hey, brother! What did I do?" I ran a little with him and said, "I have no brothers or sisters. I want you to be aware that I am going to hit you right in the neck! Because that is what you are—a pain the neck!" Of course I never did. Mickey Rivers was a good guy and funny to be around. That particular time, though, he was an aggravating pain in the neck to me!

Clubhouse Full Of Comedians!

The Red Sox had an absolutely great group of guys in our clubhouse. So many guys were pranksters, there was always something going on! Yastrzemski was no different! Everybody knew how I loved my cigars. When I wanted to relax, I lit up one of my special stogies. I would smoke them in the shower or anywhere, really. One time I decided to light up my cigar while soaking in the whirlpool. I was perfectly content and relaxed, puffing on my cigar when Yaz came up behind me where I couldn't see him. All of a sudden, there is Yaz slowly pouring a bucket of ice water on top of my head! Of course, I just sat there with my Cubano in my mouth as he drenched me with ice water. Everyone was laughing uncontrollably! I looked up at Yaz and said, "Just wait! It is coming!" He knew I would get him back for his innocent moment of pleasure. What a group of guys we had—second to none! But you had better be looking around the corners because someone was always up to something for a laugh. Great memories!

Sometimes a guy would be sitting on his stool by the locker reading the newspaper. While everyone in the clubhouse was watching, one of us would sneak around undetected. Then we would take a lighter out and go from underneath his stool and light the guy's newspaper on fire! It was funny to watch the guy jump up, all startled, fanning the newspaper trying to put it out. We had some crazy times!

Yaz & Columbo!

Yastrzemski had an overcoat that was his favorite. We use to call him Columbo after the Peter Falk character on television. We were getting tired of looking at Yaz wearing the ugly coat that he adored. When the Red Sox were scheduled to go to Milwaukee to play the Brewers, I told a bunch of the guys we had to get rid of this old coat. We were going down the highway and Yaz put his coat—his pride and joy—on an empty seat. Doug Griffin was a buddy of Yaz's, and I talked him into throwing the coat out the window of the bus onto the road. Yaz could not believe his eyes! We said to Yaz, "You go buy a new coat—we are sick and tired of this one!" Yaz looked at us and said, "Now don't forget! I will pay each one you back!" Eventually "Yaz" did. He nailed us, one at a time.

Rocky & Me!

Rocky Calavito is one of my very best friends. We played together with the Cleveland Indians, and we had a lot of fun, and we continue to talk often to this day. Rocky had a cannon for an arm, and he was very accurate. Really, he was the best! A lot of people may have forgotten, but Rocky had 374 career home runs, and seven times he walked more than he struck out! He was quite a player, and the fans in Cleveland loved him. Anyway, he was an avid hunter, hunting deer, elk, bear, and a lot more! He was always trying to get me to go hunting with him. I have always told him, "I don't want to go hunting with you because you may mistake me for a black bear!" One time, he sent me a picture of a bear that he had killed. He said, "You could have been there with me and the bear! I didn't know if he meant in place of the bear or with him when he shot the bear. I didn't care to find out either!

Bobby Bonds

Bobby was a good human being who always showed me respect. I liked him a lot, both as a person and as a player. When my team visited the cities where he was playing, he and I would make time for each other. He would ask me for dinner or cocktails, and we always had good times with our visits. I have a lot of fond memories of Bobby. As an opponent, he was tough. On the field, he was something else! He hit me pretty good, as he was a very good fastball hitter. But I experienced success against him too! The thing I remember a lot about him was his great arm. He hit with power and had exceptional speed on the bases. Bobby Bonds was an incredible player and was ahead of his time with his combination of power and speed! Bobby was truly special!

Step Up & Speak Out!

I do not like the designated hitter rule. Of course, it helped some of my friends like Orlando Cepeda and Tony Oliva. This DH rule eliminates a lot of strategy. Besides, as a pitcher, I was one who always enjoyed hitting. One important aspect I don't like is that if a pitcher hits an opposing player, the pitcher never has to take the bat to face his opponent. When Drysdale, Gibson, and Marichal plunked someone, they had to face the opposing pitcher. That is the way it is supposed to be! The DH has changed that! They need to get rid of the DH!

Agents have too much influence over their clients, the players. Today's pitchers place way too much emphasis on pitch counts. Today if a starter goes five innings, they think that is some kind of great accomplishment. We would pitch way over two hundred innings each year. Our arms were strong because they were conditioned. Why can't these kids today pitch past the fifth or sixth innings? Because they don't have the arm strength—they lack the commitment in their minds and the proper conditioning to develop their arms. It is ridiculous that the athletes today do not develop stamina the way we did.

Regarding the Hall of Fame, I don't understand their standards. Some players with fewer credentials are in the Hall of Fame, and then there are others who are definitely deserving who are not in the Hall of Fame. They need to have specific standards for induction. Some players who are deserving who have not made it to the Hall of Fame are Tony Oliva, Dick Allen, Lee Smith, Maury Wills, Bert

Blyleven, Dave Conception, and, of course, Luis Tiant! They need to forget their numbers or quotas for selections-per-year, and get it right, once and for all! If they elect me after I die, I'll come back from my tomb and haunt them all! Just kidding! It would be a great honor, but I really believe I have earned it! However, it is something I want to enjoy while I'm alive.

The Best of the Best

Best Fastball
Sam McDowell
(Threw harder than Nolan Ryan!
This boy could throw a baseball like
no one else!)

Best Curveball
Camilo Pascual & Sandy Koufax

Most Intimidating Pitcher
Juan Marichal, Bob Gibson, Don
Drysdale & Stan Williams

Best Right-Handed Pitcher
Juan Marichal & Bob Gibson

Best Left-Handed Pitcher
Sandy Koufax, Mike Cuellar,
Sam "Sudden" McDowell
(Sam was the best pitcher I saw! He
should have won 25 games every
year!)

Best Left-Handed Reliever
Jack Kralick (He didn't throw
hard but he knew how to pitch)

Best Right-Handed Reliever
Dick Radatz
(Forget it about it! He would go right
after the hitters with lots of mustard
on the pitch!)

Overall Most Challenging Pitcher
Bob Gibson & Juan Marichal
(Marichal and Gibson were fear-
less!)

Best Right-Handed Hitter
Frank Robinson
(It was better to let him sleep, not
make him mad and wake him up.
If we were to knock him down, we
would be fined $100. Frank was a
dangerous hitter!)

Best Left Handed Hitter
Tony Oliva & Carl Yastrzemski
(I played with both of them, and
they were complete hitters!)

Overall Best Clutch Hitter
Orlando Cepeda & Tony Perez
(Cepeda was nasty as a hitter. He
would hit the pitch right back up the
middle –maybe on purpose
sometimes.)

Best Catcher
Carlton Fisk

Luis Tiant

Best First Baseman
Orlando Cepeda
(Orlando was like a cat, and he
could field his position efficiently

Best Shortstop
Luis Aparicio
(Dave Conception belongs in the
Hall of Fame! He was great!)

Best Left Fielder
Carl Yastrzemski

Best Right Fielder
Al Kaline & Dwight Evans
(Kaline was complete! Dwight
could do everything also!)

Best Base Runner
Willie Mays & Maury Wills
(Jose Cardenal was very cagey and
smart as a base runner!)

Most Gifted Player
Willie Mays
(Bo Jackson was incredible with just
pure natural ability!)

Best Team Rival
Boston Red Sox & New York
Yankees

Best Manager I Played For
Eddie Kasco & Billy Martin
(Billy was crazy, but he was very
good to me & I liked him!)

Best Second Baseman
Joe Morgan

Best Third Baseman
Brooks Robinson

Best Center Fielder
Paul Blair & Fred Lynn
(Fred Lynn was a great
centerfielder! For everything, I
take Fred!)

Fastest Base Runner
Lou Brock, Willie Wilson, Maury
Wills

Best Overall Player
Carl Yastrzemski
(He always found a way to beat
you!)

Strongest Outfield Arm
Reggie Smith & Rocky Colavito
(Both were incredible for strength
and they were very accurate!)

Best Opposing Manager
Billy Martin

Most Trusted Friend
Rocky Colavito, Orlando Cepeda,
Juan Marichal, Tommy Harper,
Diego Segui, & Carl Yastrzemski.
(Cepeda, Marichal & Segui and I
are brothers!)

My Favorite Team Mate

Rocky Colavito, Carlton Fisk, & Carl Yastrzemski (It is hard for me to select just a couple! Because I really liked several! But, these three standout!)

Most Heart

Rick Burleson (Rooster was tough!)

Best Work Ethics

Carl Yastrzemski

Most Congenial

Chris Chambliss, Roy White, & Bob Watson

My Favorite Team

1972 & 1975 Boston Red Sox & 1968 Cleveland Indians (Great guys!) But, really I love everybody!

Player I Would Have Liked as a Team Mate

Juan Marichal
(I played with him for six weeks, but I would have liked to have played my career with him! With both of us in our prime, we would have been something else!)

My Favorite City

Anaheim & Chicago
(Comiskey Park)
(I loved to pitch in both of those parks!)

Funniest Player

El Tiante!
Bill "Spaceman" Lee
(He lived in his own universe!)

Most Courageous

Diego Segui, Willie Horton, Juan Marichal, &, of course, the Baby Bull, Orlando Cepeda

Most Flamboyant

Tito Fuentes (This boy is #1 with his style!)

Most Zany

Bill "Spaceman" Lee, Bernie Carbo, & Mark "The Bird" Fidrych (Fidrych was great for baseball at the right time)

Player I Most Admired

Juan Marichal, Carl Yastrzemski, & Carlton Fisk

My Favorite Stadium

1, Fenway Park;
#2, Angels Stadium

Best Baseball Announcer

Curt Gowdy & Nick Martin

Luis Tiant

My Favorite Baseball Announcer
Joe Garagiola

The Best Umpire
Nester Chylak & Paul Runge

Umpire with The Best Attitude
Ron Luciano
(A showman! He was so funny!
I really enjoyed Ron)

Most Respected Baseball Personality
Tom Yawkey
(Mr. Yawkey was a player's
owner, he backed us! He was
awesome!)

Luis Tiant
Lifetime Statistics

Year	Age	Tm	Lg	W	L	W-L%	ERA	G	GS	GF	CG	SHO	SV	IP	H	R	ER	HR	BB	SO
1964	23	CLE	AL	10	4	.714	2.83	19	16	3	9	3	1	127.0	94	41	40	13	47	105
1965	24	CLE	AL	11	11	.500	3.53	41	30	4	10	2	1	196.1	166	88	77	20	66	152
1966	25	CLE	AL	12	11	.522	2.79	46	16	22	7	5	8	155.0	121	50	48	16	50	145
1967	26	CLE	AL	12	9	.571	2.74	33	29	4	9	1	2	213.2	177	76	65	24	67	219
1968	27	CLE	AL	21	9	.700	1.60	34	32	0	19	9	0	258.1	152	53	46	16	73	264
1969	28	CLE	AL	9	20	.310	3.71	38	37	0	9	1	0	249.2	229	123	103	37	129	156
1970	29	MIN	AL	7	3	.700	3.40	18	17	1	2	1	0	92.2	84	36	35	12	41	50
1971	30	BOS	AL	1	7	.125	4.85	21	10	4	1	0	0	72.1	73	42	39	8	32	59
1972	31	BOS	AL	15	6	.714	1.91	43	19	12	12	6	3	179.0	128	45	38	7	65	123
1973	32	BOS	AL	20	13	.606	3.34	35	35	0	23	0	0	272.0	217	105	101	32	78	206
1974	33	BOS	AL	22	13	.629	2.92	38	38	0	25	7	0	311.1	281	106	101	21	82	176
1975	34	BOS	AL	18	14	.563	4.02	35	35	0	18	2	0	260.0	262	126	116	25	72	142
1976	35	BOS	AL	21	12	.636	3.06	38	38	0	19	3	0	279.0	274	107	95	25	64	131
1977	36	BOS	AL	12	8	.600	4.53	32	32	0	3	3	0	188.2	210	98	95	26	51	124
1978	37	BOS	AL	13	8	.619	3.31	32	31	1	12	5	0	212.1	185	80	78	26	57	114
1979	38	NYY	AL	13	8	.619	3.91	30	30	0	5	1	0	195.2	190	94	85	22	53	104
1980	39	NYY	AL	8	9	.471	4.89	25	25	0	3	0	0	136.1	139	79	74	10	50	84
1981	40	PIT	NL	2	5	.286	3.92	9	9	0	1	0	0	57.1	54	31	25	3	19	32
1982	41	CAL	AL	2	2	.500	5.76	6	5	0	0	0	0	29.2	39	20	19	3	8	30

19-Year Totals

W	L	W-L%	ERA	G	GS	GF	CG	SHO	SV	IP	H	R	ER	HR	BB	SO
229	172	0.571	3.3	573	484	51	187	49	15	3486	3075	1400	1280	346	1104	2416

"Did You Know?"

Steve Carlton holds the major league record for highest percentage of his teams wins in a season with 27 wins out of the teams 59 wins for 45.8%.

Gaylord Perry won the Cy Young award in both the National and American League.

The only player in history to lead his league in stolen bases for nine consecutive seasons was Luis Aparicio.

Nellie Fox was the only player ever to lead his league in singles eight times.

Dick Williams

Born May 7, 1929, St. Louis, Missouri

Height 6'0"   **Weight** 190 lbs.

Bats Right   **Throws** Right

Debut June 10, 1951   **Final game** Oct. 1, 1964

RICHARD "DICK" WILLIAMS was born May 7, 1929, in St. Louis, Missouri. He soon moved to California and he attended high school in Pasadena. He was signed as an amateur free agent by the Brooklyn Dodgers as an outfielder in 1947, and played his first major league game in 1951. His playing career consisted of 13 seasons with the Brooklyn Dodgers, Baltimore Orioles, Cleveland Indians, Kansas City Athletics, and Boston Red Sox. Dick retired as a player in 1964 as a utility player who played the outfield, first base, and third base. His career playing numbers included a .260 batting average, 70 home runs, and 331 RBIs.

In 1964, Dick Williams was named as a player coach with the Seattle Rainiers. The next year, 1965, he was promoted to manage the newly formed Toronto Maple

Leafs of the International League, which was the AAA Team of the Boston Red Sox. After winning consecutive Governor's Cup championships, Dick once again was promoted, this time to manage his first major league team, the Boston Red Sox!

The previous Red Sox teams were known for their lackadaisical style, and they sometimes even appeared lazy. Dick as the new sheriff in town was a strict disciplinarian who refused to accept mediocrity. At the beginning of the 1967 season, he boldly stated that the Red Sox would win more games than they lost. At the time, this statement appeared to be funny. In the previous season, 1966, the Red Sox had finished one game from the cellar with a record of 72 wins and 90 losses!

Dick's 1967 Boston Red Sox soon adopted his character of playing fundamentally sound baseball with the purpose of winning. He was hard-nosed, but his new followers became hard-nosed as well. They simply went on to win the American League Championship to contend for the World Championship with the St. Louis Cardinals.

The Red Sox played admirably against the heavily favored St. Louis Cardinals. However, the Cardinals, with their great ace Bob Gibson, defeated the Red Sox in seven games. Dick was named American League Manager of the Year for his efforts. He departed Boston at the end of the 1969 season.

Dick was hired for a brief stint as the third base coach with the Montreal Expos. The next season he was hired by the Oakland Athletics owner, Charles O. Finley, to manage that young and talented team. Charles. O. Finley had ten managerial changes from 1961–1970 and there appeared to be no safety net beneath the tightrope Dick had chosen to walk.

In 1971, the very first year at the helm of the Oakland Athletics, he captured the American League division with his new enigmatic star, the incredible Vida Blue! The Athletics did lose a tough series to the eventual World Champion Baltimore Orioles. But under the brilliant guidance of their new no-nonsense leader, Dick Williams, the A's learned how to prepare and win from their experiences in post-season play!

Together, Williams and Finley were building a genuine dynasty! In 1972, Dick once again led his talented but motley crew to another American League Division Championship, only this time the Oakland Athletics defeated the American League Champion Detroit Tigers in a bitterly fought battle!

The Oakland Athletics earned the right to face the powerful Big Red Machine led by Sparky Anderson's war team of Pete Rose, Johnny Bench, Tony Perez, Joe Morgan and George Foster! Oakland defeated the heavily favored Cincinnati Reds for their first World Championship. This was the first for the A's since 1930 when they were The Athletics of Philadelphia! Now Dick Williams was the toast of baseball, even for Charles O. Finley.

However, Finley was the consummate meddler. He would make calls from across the country while sitting in his Chicago office to direct his team, manager, and players, all the while publicly criticizing specific players.

Again, in 1973, the campaign was historic as the Athletics won their division, beat the Baltimore Orioles to capture the American League flag.

That same year they defeated the New York Mets in America's showcase. The Oakland A's under the tutelage of Dick was the first team to win back-to-back championships since the mighty Yankees had done so in the 1961 and 1962 seasons! This time, however, Dick had a message for his charismatic owner. He had had enough of the constant meddling of Charles. O. Finley and, at the end of the 1973 season, Dick simply walked out the door and left his championship team!

The 1974 baseball season began without Dick Williams as the leader of a team. However, Gene Autry, owner of the California Angels, made a managerial change in midseason and brought Dick into the fold. The Angels did not finish well, but the Oakland Athletics team that was formulated under Dick's guidance won their third World Championship in consecutive years.

Dick Williams had an unconventional leadership style, such as the time he held a batting practice session with the Angels in their hotel lobby. The point was to demonstrate that his team's hitters were so weak that they could not damage the inside of a hotel lobby. Dick's tenure with the Angels ended in the middle of the 1976 season.

He next managed the hapless Montreal Expos from 1977–1981.

At the beginning of the 1982 season the chronic losers of the National League West, the San Diego Padres, hired Dick as manager. After two years of strategic planning and development, Dick Williams once again had a team to go to the World Series. His San Diego Padres defeated the Chicago Cubs for the National League title.

In 1984 Dick took the field to face his old nemesis, Sparky Anderson, who led the Tigers of Detroit to an unbelievable 104 wins during the regular season! Although Sparky's Tigers defeated the Padres, both Dick Williams and Sparky Anderson accomplished a rare feat. They were among a minuscule group of managers who won pennants in both leagues! 1985 proved to be the last season for Dick at the helm of the San Diego Padres.

In 1986, this time it was the Seattle Mariners of the American League West who called Dick to come to the Pacific Northwest and hopefully display his proven recipe for success. However, baseball was changing rapidly, and players were becoming a new breed, no longer willing to follow the autocratic styles of managers like Dick. His last year of managing was the 1988 season for the Seattle Mariners.

In over twenty-one seasons as the master at the helm, Dick accomplished a great deal with his authoritative style of leadership. He proved he could take perennial losers and guide them to become championship caliber teams! He won three American League pennants, one National League pennant, and two World Championships! He was the second manager in the history of baseball to lead three different teams to the World Series. And he was the only manager to lead four different teams with 90 victories or more! The ultimate compliment was delivered when, in December 2007, Dick received the call from the Veterans Committee telling him that he had been selected to be enshrined in Baseball's Hall of Fame. Dick Williams was inducted into the Cooperstown's Baseball Hall of Fame on July 27, 2008.

Dick Williams

In My Own Words

Oh Yeah! I Goofed!

ONE OF MY MOST EMBARRASSING MOMENTS came when I was managing the California Angels. We had a bad ball club, and the only two bright spots on the club were Nolan Ryan and Frank Tanana.

Ryan had just won his last start, and the next day we went to Chicago to play the White Sox. The Chicago press came into my office to talk to me about Ryan while I was in the process of making out the starting lineup. Because I was talking about Ryan, I mistakenly put him down on my lineup as my starting pitcher for that game. To make things worse, I did not have my coach check it out before I gave it to the home plate umpire. I knew Paul Richards, the manager for the White Sox, and I had played for him four different times. When I went to Richards to help me correct my mistake, he just smiled at me! Ryan had to face one batter so he proceeded to change his shoes and put on his equipment. Ryan threw two pitches which both were lobs, and he got the batter to hit into ground out to shortstop. I fined myself $500 for my mistake, and we went on to win the game when my regular starter came on in relief to pitch 8 2/3 innings for the win!

Earl Kickin' Again

Hall-of-Fame manager Earl Weaver had a run-in with the law (DWI) the day before the Oakland A's came to Baltimore to play the Orioles in a three-game series. According to press reports, Weaver and his wife had dinner at a restaurant. While traveling home, they were stopped by the police. Weaver told the officer he had had a Manhattan or two with some oysters for dinner. Weaver then proceeded to kick the door of the police car—and it fell off!

On game day, we took the lineup cards to the home plate umpire for the opener of the three-game series, and I was asked if there were any questions. The only thing I said was, "Where can I get some of those oysters?" Weaver left the home plate area in a hurry and appeared upset. The umpires and I had a pretty good laugh!

Earl Weaver Too

Earl Weaver and I managed against each other in the International League before either one of us reached the major leagues. I managed Toronto (Boston Red Sox) and Earl managed Rochester (Baltimore Orioles). One particular game, Earl presented his lineup card to home plate. This time he had made a lineup card mistake! He had two players in the lineup batting out of order. We played the entire nine innings, and Earl's team beat us 2-0! I never had a chance to use his mistake to my

255

advantage, because neither player helped his club get the two runs that ultimately beat us! What a frustrating night!

Dick Williams

The Best of the Best

Best Fastball
Nolan Ryan

Best Curveball
Bert Blyleven

Most Intimidating Pitcher
Bob Gibson

Best Right-Handed Pitcher
Bob Gibson

Best Left-Handed Pitcher
Sandy Koufax & Steve Carlton

Best Right-Handed Reliever
Rollie Fingers

**Overall Most
Challenging Pitcher**
Bob Gibson

Best Right-Handed Hitter
Pete Rose & Al Kaline

Best Left-Handed Hitter
Carl Yastrzemski & Pete Rose

Overall Best Clutch Hitter
Tony Perez

Best Catcher
Johnny Bench

Best First Baseman
Tony Perez

Best Second Baseman
Joe Morgan

Best Shortstop
Luis Aparicio

Best Third Baseman
Mike Schmidt & Brooks Robinson

Best Left Fielder
Carl Yastrzemski

Best Center Fielder
Willie Mays & Mickey Mantle

Best Right Fielder
Roberto Clemente

Fastest Base Runner
Lou Brock

Best Base Runner
Lou Brock

Best Overall Player
Rod Carew, Willie Mays,
& Hank Aaron

**Player Who Didn't Reach
Maximum Potential**
If you made it to the major leagues,
you did well!

Strongest Outfield Arm
Roberto Clemente & Reggie Smith

Best Team Rival
New York Yankees

Best Opposing Manager
Gene Mauch

Best Manager I Coached For
Gene Mauch

Most Trusted Friend
Russ Nixon

My Favorite Team Mate
Russ Nixon

Funniest Player
George Thomas

Most Heart
Mike Andrews

Most Courageous
Tony Oliva

Best Work Ethics
Steve Carlton & Carl Yastrzemski

Most Flamboyant
Reggie Jackson

Most Congenial
Al Kaline & Harmon Killebrew

Most Zany
Jim Piersall

My Favorite Team
Oakland

Player I Most Admired
Roger Maris

**Player I Would Have
Liked as a Team Mate**
Pete Rose & Mickey Mantle

My Favorite Stadium
Old Yankee Stadium
& Fenway Park

My Favorite City
New York

Best Baseball Announcer
Vin Scully

**My Favorite
Baseball Announcer**
Vin Scully

The Best Umpire
Al Barlick & Nester Chylak

**Umpire with The Best
Attitude**
Nester Chylak

Most Respected Baseball Personality
Harmon Killebrew

"Did You Know?"

In addition to seven no-hitters, Nolan Ryan threw twelve one-hitters.

That the average number of baseballs a major league team uses per year is approximately 30,000!

"About the only problem with success is that it does not teach you how to deal with failure." — Tommy Lasorda

"Baseball is like church, several attend, but few understand." — Leo Durocher

In one game Lou Pinella played while a member of the New York Yankees, he accomplished the reverse of a cycle by being thrown out at each base, first, second, third, and home plate.

Maury Morningstar Wills

Born Oct. 2, 1932 Washington, D.C.

Height 5'11"   **Weight** 170 lbs.

Bats Both   **Throws** Right

Debut June 6, 1959   **Final game** October 4, 1972

MAURICE WILLS, later nicknamed Maury, was born in Washington, D.C., on October 2, 1932. As a kid, Maury always loved playing baseball and had dreams of escaping the projects of Washington through his baseball skills. He played for Cordozo High School as an all-city pitcher. Maury was a legitimate three-sport prep star as a teenager. Maury often dreamed of playing along side of his hero, Jackie Robinson of the Brooklyn Dodgers.

Maury, in fact, was signed by the Dodgers' organization and he toiled in the organization's minor leagues for 8 1/2 years. Then, in 1960, he was promoted to the major league club. In his first full season with the Dodgers, he accomplished a very impressive .295 batting average and actually led the National League with 50 stolen bases. Maury made his presence known immediately and he quickly altered the game. He became the first National League player to steal more than fifty bases since 1923. In addition, Maury actually stole more bases in 1962 than all of the other National League teams combined! Maury truly was a pioneer with the stolen base, especially in the National League. Catchers were alerted that the fleet-footed Dodger rookie had arrived and would create havoc in their lives. Baseball would never be the same! More than anything, Maury Wills brought a new winning strategy to the major leagues!

In 1962 Maury had his breakout year while becoming the first player in major league history to steal 100 bases, at the time an inconceivable feat. Maury stole 104 bases in 1962 while batting .299 with ten triples! He created absolute pandemonium on the base paths with all of the Dodgers' opponents.

Maury won the National League's Most Valuable Player Award for the 1962 season beating out Willie Mays. In addition, he won his second Gold Glove and was selected to his second All-Star game in as many years where he also won its Most Valuable Player Award also!

Maury brought exuberance, creating a new level of entertainment and unbelievable excitement to Los Angeles! The fans chanting at Dodger stadium were deafening at times. Every time he got on base, they yelled, "Go, Maury Go!" Soon the beloved Maury Wills, along with his gifted and fabulous teammates, provided fans at Dodger stadium perennial championship baseball—they were a truly a dynamic team!

Maury lead the league in steals for six consecutive years while stealing 585 lifetime steals. He revolutionized baseball! Maury truly belongs in Baseball's Hall of Fame in Cooperstown, New York.

Maury Wills

In My Own Words

I'M VERY THANKFUL I played baseball during the time I did—it was a great era! What made the 1960s and 1970s so special was that players played for the love of the game! The players also were more fan-friendly, which I appreciated. After spending 8 1/2 years in the minor leagues, I learned to work hard and appreciate my accomplishments—and I enjoyed the fans!

It was challenging during those times because we did not make close to the type of money today's players make. In the off-season, we had to work to provide more income. I won Most Valuable Player Award in 1962, but the next year there I was selling season tickets for the Spokane Indians. The guy I was hawking the tickets for was hammering me to be on time as it was a 9-to-5 job. That same year, I was voted the number one athlete in the world beating Arnold Palmer by one vote. Other times in the off-seasons I worked in a sporting goods store. I even hammered nails as a carpenter in the off-season. In 1962 I went into the Dodgers executive offices hoping to receive a small raise for winning the Most Valuable Player Award and changing the game with the emphasis on stealing bases. Ten minutes later, as I left the Dodgers executive offices, not only had I not received a raise, I felt lucky to still be on the team!

Today's players are great people. Some of the kids—today's players—that I would purchase a ticket to watch play are Jose Reyes, Maicer Izturis, Juan Pierre, and Carl Crawford! These guys are exciting to me! Albert Pujols is one of a kind! I sincerely believe that you can't practice enough to be that great; he just fell out of the sky with unbelievable God-given talent! But we are all products of our times. In our day I believe we more frequently played while hurt than today's players do.

The Dodgers' Legacy

I've always been proud of the Dodgers with their legacy of once a Dodger, always a Dodger—an attitude which started in Brooklyn and was carried to Los Angeles. That simply has been its tradition forever. It doesn't matter if you are a star or the twenty-fifth player, a defensive specialist or pinch hitter. We always had that respect for one another. That is one of the great things about the Dodgers that make the organization so special.

Sandy Koufax exemplified that Dodger attitude of the team first! Today, players leave the dugout and go into the clubhouse and perhaps watch the game on television screens. Not Sandy! When Sandy wasn't pitching, he was in the dugout. The Dodgers had, and still have, a sense of pride for the name on the front of their jerseys.

The Enforcer

The Dodgers had an enforcer in big Don Drysdale. Don stood 6'6" and weighed 220 pounds—and he was absolutely fearless! The Dodgers' opponents sometimes would pick on me because of my base stealing. Infielders and catchers tried to lean on me or beat me up a little as I was running the base paths. Once I'd get into our dugout, big Don would ask me if I thought a certain play that was rough on me, if it was intentional. If I answered yes, Don would simply say, "Don't worry buddy. I'll get them the next time for you!" And he would! A lot of times I said to him, "Let's let them slide this time because we only have a one run lead." Sometimes he would just nail them for picking on me and other times he would agree, saying, "Okay, buddy. I owe you one." At any time I could have two or three that Don owed me, and I would approach him. Then he would simply balance the books. I was sad that Don retired a couple of years before I did. I missed Don!

Frank Robinson

Several years ago an interviewer asked me who I thought was the best ballplayer and I answered Frank Robinson. Frank had incredible talent and literally could do it all. Most all of the superstars had nicknames or monikers such as, Willie "The Say Hey Kid" Mays, Stan "The Man" Musial, and "Teddy Ballgame" Williams. However, Frank didn't appear to care about a lot of things, including nicknames. I do praise Frank every chance I get even though I don't think he likes me much, but that's okay too! I still have respect for Frank. I also have enough memories as scars on my legs from Frank Robinson barreling into me at second base. Maybe he still has some dirt in his ears from me forcing him to hit the dirt low and hard. That's the way the game was played—hard—real hard!

Don Drysdale vs. Frank Robinson

When answering the question about the most courageous player, I listed both Don Drysdale and Frank Robinson. Here is a typical example of the altercations between these two legends. Drysdale was pitching to Robinson one time when our manager Walter Alston gave Drysdale the signal to walk Frank intentionally. The Dodgers catcher Johnny Roseboro also signaled to Drysdale to deliver four wide ones. The first pitch Drysdale threw was high and tight with a lot of giddyup on it right under Robinson's chin. Robinson went down in a cloud of dust right on his backside. Anyone else would have gotten back to his feet after receiving the loud and clear message and appealed to the umpire. Not Robinson! Robinson just looked back at Drysdale, got back into the batter's box and inched himself closer to the plate. The next pitch Drysdale threw was just a little bit lower with a little more on it, making it even harder to get out of the way. Again, Robinson went down hard, right square on the numbers on the back of his jersey. This time Robinson's feet went up in the air. When your feet are in the air over your head, it is certain you just received an obvious knockdown pitch. This game happened in the second season of my big league career, and I remember thinking to myself at shortstop, "Oh, my gosh! This is really serious!"

Robinson glared at Drysdale and he glared back! Robinson leaned closer over the plate and spit towards Drysdale, all the while glaring directly in Drysdales' eyes. Drysdale unleashed the next pitch with even more fire on the pitch under the chin of Robinson and again he hit the dirt flat on his back! Robinson bounced to his feet and charged the mound; Drysdale was charging headfirst towards Robinson. Both benches emptied and, after about 15 minutes, Drysdale and Robinson were separated by umpire Shag Crawford and the other players. Both teams went back to their benches. And what happened next? The fourth pitch was unleashed by the 6'6" Drysdale towards Robinson's chin for ball four! Robinson ran down the first base line like Ferdinand the Bull as he was snorting, huffing and spitting. It was obvious to everyone in the ballpark that Robinson was fuming!

There was now only one out, and the Dodger second baseman was Jim Gilliam. I was at short. Both Gilliam and I knew exactly what was on Robinson's mind. If there was a groundball in the infield, he had every intention of taking out one of us hard, killing the unlucky player who happens to cover the bag at second—if he got the opportunity. I looked over at Gilliam and told him "If he hits it to you, don't bother! I will not be there!" Gilliam looked back at me and said, "If the ball is hit to you at short, don't bother looking for me because I won't be there either!"

The batter hit the ball to second, and we didn't even consider throwing the ball to second for the force out or a double play. We simply threw the ball to first for the second out. Frank Robinson hit that big pillow bag we use to use at second, pulled that thing completely out of the ground, and sent that bag flying halfway to left field! Robinson ran past me on his way back to the dugout, and I swear I could still hear him snorting and growling! After that, I always had the greatest respect for those two guys because of their unbelievable courage!

Deceiving Cepeda

One time when the Dodgers were playing the Giants, I was leaning too far towards second base and got picked off. Orlando Cepeda was the Giants first baseman and he started to run towards me with the ball. Instead of trying to get out of a rundown, I ran just fast enough to stay away from Cepeda's tag, still encouraging him to chase me. When I knew he was ready to throw the ball to Tito Fuentes, the Giants second baseman, I turned quickly and intentionally ran into Cepeda. Orlando attempted to dodge me, but I hooked him with my elbow. The umpires called obstruction on Orlando and therefore I was awarded second base. Cepeda was furious!

265

That was another way to steal a base.

Later that year in San Francisco at Candlestick Park, I got caught leaning the wrong way and got picked off again. This time I bolted like lightening for second base. Once again Orlando Cepeda was the first baseman. This time Orlando threw the ball that whizzed past my neck. I'm not convinced Orlando was throwing to second base. Perhaps he threw at my back. His throw just missed my neck and came nowhere near Tito, the Giants second baseman. The errant throw sailed deep into left field. I do believe, however, that also is part of the game. Orlando Cepeda was another fierce competitor.

My Hometown

Early in my career I was selected to play in my first All-Star game in my hometown, Washington, D.C. I was really excited about playing in the mid-summer classic in front of my entire family. I stayed at my parents' house and when I arrived at the ballpark to go in National League clubhouse, I was stopped abruptly by the guard. He asked where I thought I was going. I explained to him that I played for the Los Angeles Dodgers. He said, "Sure you do." I guess because of my small stature he thought it wasn't possible. Anyway, I was very polite and I said, "Sir, if you will open the clubhouse door, the fellas will see me and verify that I am, in fact, a big league player. Well, players have a sick sense of humor. When the guard opened the door and inquired, "Do any of you fellas know this guy?" They all looked at me in the hallway and said, "No. We have never seen him before!" The guard was chasing me away when a gentleman with a white shirt, tie, and credentials around his neck helped me enter the clubhouse.

The really neat part was that after the All-Star classic had ended, I walked out of the clubhouse with the Most Valuable Player Award I had just won. When I walked past the same doubting guard, he just looked at me in disbelief as if I were carrying the award for someone else. It was a great day for me and my family, even though I was embarrassed by being denied access to what I had earned. And in my hometown, no less!

Breaking Cobb's Record

At the end of the 1962 season, the season when I broke Ty Cobb's 47-year stolen base record, I was in the clubhouse when newspaper reports told me that Ford Frick, baseball's Commissioner, said baseball would not recognize the record if I broke it in more games than Cobb. Ford Frick did not want me to break Cobb's record! The reporters said that Cobb had 96 stolen bases in 156 games, Cobb played for the Tigers and they had two extra games that year over the normal 154 games.

Many times throughout the year, the reporters asked me who was the easiest and most difficult for me to steal bases off of and I simply refused to answer the question. If I named who was the most difficult, I would build his confidence and give him even more of a psychological edge. If I named who was the easiest, I would make another enemy! The truth was that both answers played with the St. Louis Cardinals. The easiest was Curt Simmons, the very good left-hander. But I could read his moves!

The Dodgers were in St. Louis and, on Friday, September 21, we played our 154th game. And I stole my 95th base. The next night I was ready and well rested. It just so happened that Simmons was scheduled to pitch in our 154th game. I was excited! In Saturday's game, the 155th game for the Dodgers, I did not steal a base. On Sunday, my toughest opponent, Larry Jackson, was pitching. Not only did I have difficulty with Jackson's move and did not like to steal off of him, but he was also tough on me as a hitter! In the top of the third inning, I got a single to right field and stole my 96th base. In the top of the seventh inning the Dodgers were losing and we needed runs badly. I dribbled a single between first base and second base. Larry Jackson then threw over to first base 16 consecutive times to hold me there on first base. The St. Louis fans were booing, as they were rooting for me to break the record. Bill White, the big Cardinal first baseman, was slapping me hard with each throw as I was sliding back head first into the first base bag. White was hitting me in the face, on the shoulder, and on my arms, all hard tags. Finally when I got up one time to dust myself off, I said, "Come on! Give a brother a break!" White said, "Don't give me that brother crap! You aren't wearing a Cardinal uniform!"

Both dugouts were standing to get a better view. On the 17th throw from Jackson, he went home with it and I was off to second base like a bolt of lightening. Fortunately for me I did have one advantage. Carl Sawatski was the Cardinal catcher and he couldn't throw me out if he were standing on the pitchers' mound! I did it! I stole my 97th base in game 156, and my teammates were happy for me. Our great manager, Walter Alston, before the game had said to me, "Kid, we are pulling for you. Go out there get Cobb's record!" The fans in St. Louis were great, as they stood cheering, enjoying the opportunity to see a great record broken.

St. Louis, My Favorite

St. Louis was my favorite town to visit, not only because of their great fans, but because they had the best banjo club that I knew. The "Father's Mustache Club" would always have a banjo waiting for me, and I had a blast jamming with those guys. Great memories! Playing my banjo was always exciting to me and I looked for those moments to relax.

The Best of the Best

Best Fastball
Chris Short, Jim Maloney

Best Curveball
Juan Marichal

Most Intimidating Pitcher
Bob Gibson

Best Right-Handed Pitcher
Juan Marichal

Best Left-Handed Pitcher
Whitey Ford
(Sandy Koufax was the best I ever witnessed!)

Best Left-and Reliever
Ron Perranoski

Best Right-Hand Reliever
Mike Marshal

Overall Most Challenging Pitcher
Nolan Ryan

Best Right-Handed Hitter
Frank Robinson

Best Left-Handed Hitter
Vada Pinson

Overall Best Clutch Hitter
Frank Robinson, Tommy Davis

Best Catcher
Johnny Bench, Steve Yeager

Best First Baseman
Wes Parker

Best Second Baseman
Joe Morgan, Charlie Neal
(Joe Morgan was the best player in the game for about 4 years.)

Best Shortstop
Luis Aparicio

Best Third Baseman
Brooks Robinson, Clete Boyer

Best Left Fielder
Dusty Baker

Best Center Fielder
Willie Mays

Best Right Fielder
Frank Robinson

Fastest Base Runner
Vada Pinson

Best Base Runner
Willie Mays

Best Overall Player
Frank Robinson & Willie Mays
(Frank Robinson was not very well liked, so he is over looked!)

Player Who Didn't Reach Maximum Potential

Willie Davis, Tommy Davis,
& Charley Neal
(Willie Davis reached only 80% of
his talent!)

Strongest Outfield Arm

Frank Howard, Reggie Smith,
Roberto Clemente,

Best Team Rival

San Francisco Giants, absolutely!
(Even today I can still taste it, and
smell it!)

Best Opposing Manager

Bobby Bragan
(Most Astute)

Best Manager I Played For

Walter Alston
(Great gentleman, but don't mess
with him!)

Most Trusted Friend

Sandy Koufax

My Favorite Team Mate

Sandy Koufax

Funniest Player

I was a no-nonsense guy! I enjoyed
the game. To me there was no place
for nonsense!

Most Heart

Claude Osteen (Gomer had a burning
desire!)

Most Courageous

Don Drysdale & Frank Robinson

Best Work Ethics

Sandy Koufax
(Always stayed after he left the
games and sat on the bench with us
until the game was over. Even the
days he didn't pitch, he was on the
bench with us.)

Most Flamboyant

Leo Durocher
(Great dresser, also!)

Most Congenial

Sandy Koufax

Most Zany

Jay Johnstone

My Favorite Team

Los Angeles Dodgers
(All of the Dodgers' teams, however
the 1965 team was very special!)

Player I Most Admired

Sandy Koufax
(Great courage, and I
never heard him ever say anything
negative about anyone.)

Player I Would Have Liked as a Team Mate
Willie Mays
(I learned a lot from Willie)

My Favorite City
St. Louis (Great Banjo Club where I would play my banjo at the Father's Mustache! San Francisco was great also with their Red Garter Banjo Club!)

My Favorite Baseball Announcer
Bob Prince, Jack Buck, Jack Brickhouse, & Harry Carey!

Umpire with The Best Attitude
Doug Harvey
(No nonsense!)

My Favorite Stadium
Dodger Stadium &
Connie Mack in Philadelphia
(I had a great deal of success playing at Connie Mack.)

Best Baseball Announcer
Vin Scully

The Best Umpire
Doug Harvey, Shag Crawford

Most Respected Baseball Personality
Sandy Koufax

Maury Wills
Lifetime Statistics

Year	Age	Tm	Lg	G	PA	AB	R	H	2B	3B	HR	RBI	SB	CS	BB	SO	BA	OBP	SLG
1959	26	LAD	NL	83	258	242	27	63	5	2	0	7	7	3	13	27	.260	.298	.298
1960	27	LAD	NL	148	559	516	75	152	15	2	0	27	50	12	35	47	.295	.342	.331
1961	28	LAD	NL	148	687	613	105	173	12	10	1	31	35	15	59	50	.282	.346	.339
1962	29	LAD	NL	165	759	695	130	208	13	10	6	48	104	13	51	57	.299	.347	.373
1963	30	LAD	NL	134	580	527	83	159	19	3	0	34	40	19	44	48	.302	.355	.349
1964	31	LAD	NL	158	685	630	81	173	15	5	2	34	53	17	41	73	.275	.318	.324
1965	32	LAD	NL	158	710	650	92	186	14	7	0	33	94	31	40	64	.286	.330	.329
1966	33	LAD	NL	143	643	594	60	162	14	2	1	39	38	24	34	60	.273	.314	.308
1967	34	PIT	NL	149	664	616	92	186	12	9	3	45	29	10	31	44	.302	.334	.365
1968	35	PIT	NL	153	685	627	76	174	12	6	0	31	52	21	45	57	.278	.326	.316
1969	36	TOT	NL	151	690	623	80	171	10	8	4	47	40	21	59	61	.274	.337	.335
1969	36	MON	NL	47	211	189	23	42	3	0	0	8	15	6	20	21	.222	.295	.238
1969	36	LAD	NL	104	479	434	57	129	7	8	4	39	25	15	39	40	.297	.356	.378
1970	37	LAD	NL	132	578	522	77	141	19	3	0	34	28	13	50	34	.270	.333	.318
1971	38	LAD	NL	149	654	601	73	169	14	3	3	44	15	8	40	44	.281	.323	.329
1972	39	LAD	NL	71	152	132	16	17	3	1	0	4	1	1	10	18	.129	.190	.167

14-Year Totals

G	PA	AB	R	H	2B	3B	HR	RBI	SB	CS	BB	SO	BA	OBP	SLG
1942	8304	7588	1067	2134	177	71	20	458	586	208	552	684	.281	.330	.331

The Bottom of the Ninth!

The bottom of the ninth represents, in this particular case, the last portions of our lives. Thank you to the legends and celebrities who were so gracious in trusting me with their stories and legacies. It is an honor that they have allowed me to share some of their stories, opinions and experiences during the fabulous sixties and seventies era.

One individual that I would like very much to thank is Julian Javier of the St. Louis Cardinals. He was my first friend in the majors. Julian looked out for my best interest and welfare; therefore, he mentored me and was a great example of grace and hospitality. In addition, I believe Julian knew that deep within my soul there was a great deal of pain when I was twelve and thirteen years of age. He unselfishly provided an escape for me within the majestic walls of baseball, and provided momentary relief and offered a glimpse of life in the big leagues.

Which brings me to today's players and today's game. Baseball appears to be far more serious and less personal today because of the business aspects that have evolved within the parameters of major league baseball. But, I would like to encourage today's players and major league teams to emulate these great legends with their deeds of hospitality for the benefit of the game. We never know whose lives we are impacting by simply offering a few moments of our attention, generosity and kindness. Baseball is more than a game to many, and should be for everyone including the players!

One player who clearly represents the legends of the past with his attitude and approach is the gregarious Pablo Sandoval of the San Francisco Giants. This young man is a great player, but, more importantly he plays the game with enthusiasm. Today's players would do well if they were to emulate the Panda's example; Pablo enjoys the game and plays it with jubilation and joy!

Thank you to my readers!